PREPARING FOR A HOME ECONOMICS CAREER

G. Polly Jacoby *Gertrude*
Mansfield State College
Mansfield, Pennsylvania

Ruth P. Hughes
Contributing Editor
Iowa State University
Ames, Iowa

Elizabeth Simpson
Consulting Editor
University of Wisconsin
Madison, Wisconsin

Gregg Division
McGraw-Hill Book Company

New York   St. Louis   Dallas   San Francisco   Auckland   Bogotá   Düsseldorf
Johannesburg   London   Madrid   Mexico   Montreal   New Delhi   Panama
Paris   São Paulo   Singapore   Sidney   Tokyo   Toronto

CAREERS IN HOME ECONOMICS

Preparing for a Home Economics Career
Jacoby
Child Care Aide Skills
Conger · Rose
Children: Their Growth and Development
Terry · Sorrentino · Flatter
Child Nutrition and Health
Hutchins
Safety and Sanitation
Border

Library of Congress Cataloging in Publication Data

Jacoby, Gertrude Polly, (date)
   Preparing for a home economics career.

   Inclues index.
   1. Home economics—Vocational guidance. 2. Home
economics. I. Hughes, Ruth P. II. Simpson, Elizabeth
Jane, III. Title.
TX164.J3   640'.23   78-13190
ISBN 0-07-032240-6

Preparing for a Home Economics Career

1 2 3 4 5 6 7 8 9 0 VHVH 7 8 5 4 3 2 1 0 9 8

The editors for this book were Gail Smith and Claire Hardiman, the designer was
Eileen Thaxton, the art supervisor was George T. Resch, the photo editor was
Gina Jackson, the cartoonist was Jared D. Lee, and the production supervisor was
Regina R. Malone. It was set in Times Roman by Waldman Graphics, Inc. Cover
illustration: Jared Lee; photograph on page 1, Bruce Roberts/Photo Researchers:
page 111, Kenneth Karp; page 169, Kenneth Karp; page 233, Hugh Rogers,
Monkmeyer Press.
Printed and bound by Von Hoffman Press, Inc.

CONTENTS

iii

PREFACE

Changing roles for men and women in today's society have brought new challenges for America's teachers and students. Roles and responsibilities overlap as increased numbers of women work outside the home and as men begin to assume more homemaking responsibilities. More demands are made upon individuals and families, as each person seeks to meet his or her potential and upgrade the quality of life. To meet these new needs and new challenges, career education, promotion of nutritional knowledge, and parenthood education have become national goals. Greater emphasis has been placed on consumer responsibilities and participation in community and government.

Preparing for a Home Economics Career is designed to help young men and women assume their multiple roles as homemaker, family member, wage earner, consumer, and citizen. The text accents homemaking as a career, as well as the six clusters of paid occupations in home economics: food service, child care and development, clothing and textile services, institutional maintenance, family and community services, and interior design and furnishings. Basic home economics competencies are related to the world of paid jobs and to success in other real-life roles.

The text is made up of four parts. Part One alerts the reader to the kinds of occupations available, gives job descriptions and requirements, and promotes self-analysis and general sophistication regarding the world of work. In Part Two the reader leans how to look for a job, prepare for and follow up job interviews, and weigh possible job offers. Part Three provides opportunities to develop and enhance skills basic to employability and success in home economics and most other occupations. These include image, relationships, productivity, communication, computation, safety, and satisfaction with one's work. Part Four relates work success to home. This section accents consumer and family member responsibilities, management of time, money, and other resources; and takes a last look at changing roles and values.

Enabling objectives introduce each chapter in the text. These objectives let the students know exactly what is expected of them, in accordance with the principles of mastery learning. The chapter summaries are written largely as generalizations, to assist the learner with retention of knowledge. Teachers may wish to check their students' ability to verbally state a simple generalization at the completion of each lesson, a technique which provides immediate feedback regarding student achievement and enhances the possibilities for retention and transfer of learning. End-of chapter activities are designed to clarify and reinforce chapter concepts. They put to immediate use the information presented in the text, so that both student and teacher can test comprehension at once. Vocabulary exercises at the end of each chapter aid development of reading skills.

Preparing for a Home Economics Career contains a multitude of basic home economics concepts. The text may be used to provide a solid background for students who have had little or no prior training in home economics, for example, in child guidance or in nutrition. Or, the text may serve as a quick review for those who do have a strong background in home economics. Teachers are encouraged to contract or expand these basic concepts according to the time available and to the needs and interests of individual classes and students.

G. Polly Jacoby

ABOUT THE AUTHOR

G. Polly Jacoby has recently served as associate professor of home economics education at Mansfield State College in Pennsylvania, where she supervised student teachers and taught undergraduate and graduate home economics courses in curriculum development and evaluation. Dr. Jacoby has earned both her bachelor of science degree and Ph.D. in education from Cornell University. As research associate at Cornell she has also participated in studies concerned with occupational home economics, and as full-time consultant with the New York State Education Department helped to develop and supervise innovative programs in home economics education for school-aged children, youth, and low-income adults.

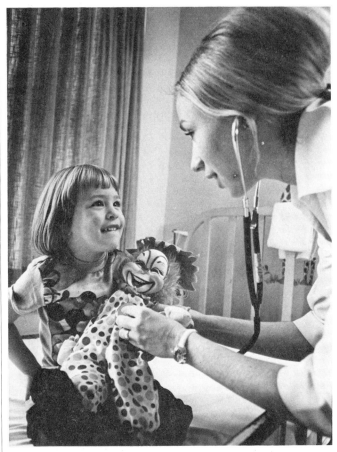

PART ONE

CHOOSING AN OCCUPATION

One of the most important decisions you will make in your life is to decide on an occupation. This decision will shape your personal lifestyle. To a large degree, it will decide the quality of your life.

At one time the choice was fairly easy to make. Women were expected to devote full time to their families. Men were expected to provide money income. Most men worked as farmers. There weren't many other job choices.

Today, work has changed. Family life has changed, also. There are many more choices. They are difficult to make, and the results of your decisions are long lasting.

Through the choices they make, young people, and older ones too, can control the direction of their lives. In a sense, you can "invent yourself." By making the right choices you can become the person you want to be.

Home economics is a field of study which seeks to help people make choices which improve the quality of their lives. It concerns your private life at home and can also prepare you for a number of paid occupations.

In Part One we will look at ways both work and family life are changing. We'll look at you: your abilities, interests, and values. Later, we'll learn how to look for and decide on a job, and how to develop some skills that will help you in a variety of home economics occupations. Finally, we'll look at the family and ways we can improve our quality of life at home as well as on the job.

1 WHY WORK?

After studying Chapter 1 you will be able to:

1. Explain ways in which work helps people satisfy basic human needs.
2. Give examples of major occupational groups.
3. Describe ways to have more choice in your life's work.
4. Explain why home economics occupations are growing.
5. Define the occupational terms *entry level, job cluster, career ladder, career lattice, task analysis, competency*.

In this chapter we'll look at reasons for working and ways to have more job choices. We'll learn some working words, terms that will help you read and talk about work. We'll find out what kinds of occupations there are and why job opportunities in home economics are growing.

Since the beginning of time, most people have had to work in order to survive. The energies of whole families were required to provide for the basics: food, clothing, and shelter. Even today, in some countries around the world, life *is* work and there is little, if any, leisure.

Until the last hundred years or so most people in the United States lived on farms. They produced their own food, built their own shelters, and made their own clothing. There was always plenty of work for the whole family, including the children. Where you lived was where you worked.

This lifestyle persisted on the frontier even after the Industrial Revolution and the invention of machines that could do the work of many families. With the development of industry people began to move off the land and into villages and cities. Families became mostly consumers rather than producers of goods.

Home and work became separate and people left home to *go* to work. Before long, families had another basic need. Transportation to work was added to food, shelter, and clothing as basic for survival.

With the development of labor-saving technology work became easier at home as well as on the job. Workers began to have some leisure time. Women were able to care for their families and, also, to enter the work force. Today most women, as well as men, work outside the home for much of their lives.

Figure 1-1. Why work?

INCOME

When families produced their own needs for basic survival at home, little money was required. Once families became consumers of goods, money income was important in order to *purchase* food, clothing, housing, and transportation. Money income is also needed for education, leisure activities, savings, insurance, and the many other things that make up the standard of living for most Americans.

Even today, however, not all of a family's income is money income. The unpaid homemaker is a home producer who adds to the family's standard of living by providing goods and services such as food, child care, laundry, repair and maintenance, clothing, and health care.

The homemaker—man or woman—adds to the family income by producing goods and services which would otherwise have to be purchased. This combination of money income and home production is called *real* income.

Whatever the source, all human beings need the sense of security that an adequate standard of living can give. We must all feel sure that our survival needs will be met before we can look beyond ourselves and care about the rest of the world.

EMOTIONAL NEEDS

People work for other reasons than to earn money. They work because human beings have basic emotional needs, just as we have basic physical needs for survival. One's personal and family life, which will be discussed later, plays a big part in meeting emotional needs. But working can also help satisfy these needs.

Need for Challenge. Everyone needs variety, something to think about and something to do. Our abilities must be challenged. Work challenges people to solve problems and develop new skills, whether in a paid occupation or in unpaid homemaking or volunteer activities.

Need to be with Others. For many people an important value of their work is the friendships they have with other workers on the same job. They have a group to which they belong and in which they share experiences and interests. Even when their work does not bring them into contact with others, they can feel a common bond with other people who have similar jobs.

Need to Excel. People need to believe that they can achieve something and do something well. All of us can excel at something, and often it is our work. Also, we all need recognition for our achievements. At the least, work brings a paycheck as recognition of a job well done. Advancing on the job is another specific proof of excellence.

Need for Belief and Commitment. A basic emotional need is to believe in something beyond ourselves. Some people find it in their religion or philosophy of life. Many people find it in their work. It may come from the importance of the work they are doing. For example, a parent or paid child care worker knows how important it is for children to have stimulating experiences in a safe and sanitary environment. Or the commitment can come from the satisfaction of being a team member that fellow workers can rely on. Some examples are a food server or cook or other member of a food service team, or a dietary aide or other member of a health team.

Another kind of commitment many workers have is called the Puritan work ethic. The idea goes back to the first Puritan settlers. According to the ethic, all work is useful and all citizens have a right to work and a duty to do so. In this way they build the nation.

Some of the work that people do in building the nation is measured by the Gross National Product (GNP). The GNP is the country's *total output* of *goods*, for example, production of new clothing, and *services*, such as food service or child care or care of the elderly. Total output is computed by adding up the value of every hour of work in a paid occupation. Another kind of work, the unpaid occupation of homemaking, is not counted in the GNP, but is vital in the quality of life of all Americans.

Figure 1-2. Some young people are not aware of the many different kinds of jobs that are available to them. (Left, Bruce A. Dart; right, Michael Ramey; bottom, Bruce A. Dart)

Today, at least in theory, we are all free to choose our occupations, limited only by our natural abilities and training. In *fact*, many young people drift into, you might say "stumble into," their life work, rather than making a free choice. This is true not only for students in high school but for those in college, as well. Young people say they do not know what different jobs are like or what jobs are available to them. This feeling is so common among young people that career education has been adopted as a national policy.

There is plenty of help around, once you know about it. Free education in high schools and vocational-technical schools, college scholarships and loans, free counseling available for the asking, and free information about job openings all exist to help you toward a free choice of work.

The Bureau of Labor Statistics (BLS) of the United States Department of Labor continually collects and analyzes information about work and workers. This information appears in BLS publications and in many newspapers and magazines. It helps government planners, employers, counselors, and people seeking jobs to understand the exact nature of jobs and workers. This information is usually organized into occupational groups.

KINDS OF OCCUPATIONS

Table 1-1 shows nine major occupational groups and some examples of each.

Table 1-1 KINDS OF OCCUPATIONS

Major Occupational Group	Examples
Professional and technical workers	Lawyers, teachers, nurses
Managers and administrators, except farm	Buyers, shop owners, department heads
Clerical workers	Cashiers, typists, ticket agents
Farm workers	Owners and managers of farms, farm laborers
Laborers, except farm	Unskilled construction laborers
Operators	Machine workers in factories and mills, truckdrivers
Service workers	Police officers, food servers, launderers
Craft workers	Carpenters, bakers, tailors
Sales workers	Retail and wholesale salespersons

Most beginning jobs in home economics, called *entry-level occupations*, are found in the service, craft, and sales groups. There are also operators, such as sewing machine operators in clothing factories. Many higher-level jobs in home economics fall in the professional and managerial occupational groups.

Of the nine occupational groups, service workers are among the groups expected to grow the fastest during the 1980s. Job outlook does not depend on growth alone, however. More jobs are always opening in every field as people retire or leave their job for other reasons.

One way to keep up to date on employment trends is to read the *Occupational Outlook Handbook*, especially prepared by the BLS for counselors and students. There should be a copy in your guidance office and public library. The handbook is updated every few months with a magazine, the *Occupational Outlook Quarterly*. These publications give information on training and education requirements, chances for advancement, earnings, and working conditions in hundreds of occupations.

MORE TRAINING, MORE CHOICES

Beginning workers have several ways to increase their choices of jobs. One way is to get as much training and education as you can. With more training, you are qualified for more jobs and are more likely to get one. Also, the more education you have, the more income you can expect to earn over a lifetime.

Another way to increase your job choices is to train for a *cluster* of jobs. A job cluster is a group of jobs which are similar. They all require the same basic training or make use of the same knowledge and skills. Sometimes the term is used to describe all the jobs in a major industry; food service is an example. Or the term might be used to refer to just one level of jobs, such as those shown in Figure 1-3.

Jobs in this cluster are divided into levels, according to the amount of training needed at each level. Notice that secondary (high school) training prepares you for one level of jobs, two years of college for another, and so on. Thus, high school training in food service offers you a choice of jobs such as short order cook, dietary aide, or counterworker. Adult education programs prepare for similar jobs, but also for jobs requiring more training and experience.

In addition to preparing you for a number of jobs requiring similar knowledge and skills, the cluster idea allows you to try out different kinds of jobs in order to find the ones you like best.

HOME ECONOMICS OCCUPATIONS

Home economics prepares people for unpaid work at home as a family member and also for paid occupations. For example, in home economics classes you learn about human development and the family, nutrition and food management, clothing and textiles, housing and living environment, and consumer education and management.

Knowledge and skills in *all* these areas are used at home, so that the homemaker—male or female—is a *generalist*. Workers in some paid home economics occupations are generalists also. On the job they use their knowl-

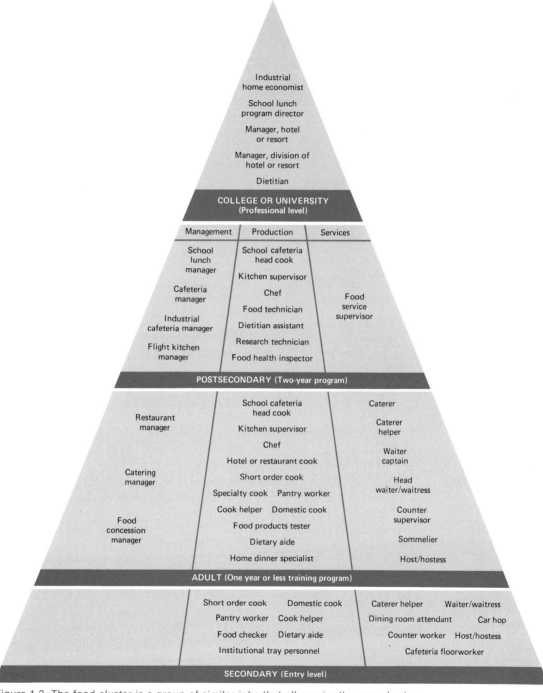

Figure 1-3. The food cluster is a group of similar jobs that all require the same basic training and skills. (Adapted from Arizona State University: *Home Economics Related Occupations Handbook*, 1975.)

edge and skills in child care and human relationships. They also provide clothing, nutritious food, and a comfortable living environment for others. They use buying and management skills, too.

Other workers in home economics occupations are *specialists*. They specialize in recreation for children, *or* food preparation, *or* clothing alteration. They may lay carpet, or counsel troubled families, or work in another special home economics occupation.

JOB CLUSTERS IN HOME ECONOMICS

There are seven major occupations in home economics. The first is the unpaid occupation of homemaking. In addition, there are six clusters of paid jobs:[1]

· Child care and development
· Food service
· Clothing and textile services
· Interior design and furnishings
· Institution and household maintenance
· Family and community services

Each cluster of paid occupations will be looked at more closely in later chapters in this part. The unpaid occupation of homemaking is the subject of Part IV.

TASK ANALYSIS

Occupations in home economics have been closely studied in order to identify the tasks that workers in different jobs are expected to perform. The procedure is called *task analysis*.

Task analysis tells students and teachers the exact requirements of a job. All the tasks performed in a particular job are listed.

In addition, task analysis points out which tasks are performed most often in a job and which are rarely done. Workers can know what a job will be like and what will be expected of them.

Task analysis also shows which tasks are common to a variety of occupations. When a student is able to perform these common tasks well, a big step has been taken toward *competency* in a cluster of occupations.

COMPETENCIES

Competencies can be defined as knowledge, skills, or attitudes which the student or worker can demonstrate at a specific level of performance. That

[1]*Identification of Tasks in Home Economics-Related Occupations*, Iowa State University and University of Northern Iowa, in cooperation with the Iowa Department of Public Instruction, 1974.

is, on the job you can demonstrate that you are as skillful as the employer requires you to be. You know as much as is expected, and you have the proper attitude.

Some tasks require all three kinds of competencies. Loading a tray of hot foods and beverages, for example, requires knowing how to load the tray, actually loading it quickly and carefully, and following correct safety procedures in order to avoid burns or spills and breakage.

Table 1-2 CAREER LADDERS AND LATTICES IN FOOD SERVICE

Professional/ Managerial	Food and Beverage	Manager	Dietitian	Owner/ Manager	Food Service Supervisor	Owner/ Manager
Supervisory	Host/ hostess	Chef	Dietary assistant	Caterer	Cook	Baker
	Captain	Cook				
Assistant	Waiter/ waitress	Assistant cook	Dietary aide	Assistant caterer	Assistant cook	Assistant baker
Entry-Level	Busser	Kitchen helper	Food service worker	Caterer's helper	Kitchen helper	Baker's helper

CAREER LADDERS AND LATTICES

Career ladders (see Table 1-2) are just what they seem, steps which lead up a ladder of success. They are paths of advancement to higher positions.

At the lower end of a career ladder are entry-level workers who are often called *aides* or *helpers*. Typical entry-level jobs are kitchen helpers, child care aides, and nutrition aides.

Further on are "assistants," such as recreation assistants and assistant cooks. At the next step are supervisors. At the top are managers and professionals.

A *career lattice* (also shown in Table 1-2) is a branch going sideways between one career ladder and another. When workers cannot or do not want to advance on the same career ladder, job cluster training may allow them to move sideways, across a lattice, onto another ladder.

For example, suppose you have a job busing trays in a restaurant, but prefer working in a hospital. You move sideways on the lattice to a job as food service worker. The next step would be dietary aide. And, now you are on the career ladder leading to dietitian. You must have a college degree, however, to climb the final step to the top job.

The story of Bill follows the course of one person's move up and across career ladders on a food service lattice.

Figure 1-4. There are often several paths to the same career goal.

WHY HOME ECONOMICS OCCUPATIONS ARE GROWING

We have seen that paid jobs in home economics fall into occupational groups that are growing, especially the service worker group. There are major trends that are causing this rapid growth. One is our increasing population. The nation continues to grow in size as new Americans are born and others enter the country from other lands.

Since there are more people, there is more demand for services such as education and health care. There are more buildings to work and live in, and they must be repaired and maintained. There are more people with problems and workers are needed to help them cope. There are more shopping centers to be staffed with sales people. Also, incomes are rising and living standards are rising along with them. People have more leisure and more time as well as money to spend on recreation, education, and dining out.

BILL

Bill started work at 16 as a caterer's helper. He and several other young people worked summers helping a caterer who specialized in class reunions at a nearby university and other special events. The helpers barbecued chicken, steamed clams, and served a variety of foods prepared by other cooks.

Bill found he liked food service as a career and decided to climb the career ladder leading to a chef's position. He worked summers, first as short-order cook at a small restaurant and later as assistant cook at a large resort hotel in Florida. Meantime, he earned an associate degree at a college offering professional training for chefs.

Bill enjoyed his work at the resort and climbed the ladder to cook, but he decided to complete a four-year degree in hotel administration at a university.

By the time he was 24 years old Bill was assistant food and beverage manager of the resort. He helps supervise the hotel dining room and steak house, and works closely with groups using the resort's convention center.

The company which owns the resort plans to expand the convention center, the steak house, and the marina, and to build another large restaurant on the grounds. They have also purchased another resort on a nearby island.

Bill expects his job opportunities to expand along with his company.

Changes in home life produce a demand for paid services outside the home that once were provided by family members. Some major changes occurring in family life are:

· *More* singles are establishing their own homes. Young people leave home earlier and marry later. There are *more* aged persons in the population and *more* of them live alone.
· *More* women of all ages are working outside the home, including *more* mothers of young children.
· *More* families are small and living apart from other relatives. When an emergency arises, there is no family member close by to help.
· *More* children live in single-parent families. There is *more* divorce and separation of parents. *More* fathers are rearing their children alone. *More* singles are adopting children.

Many of these new kinds of families buy services once performed by family members at home: child care, housekeeping services, care of the sick and elderly, laundry, meals eaten away from home or purchased at fast-food carryouts.

With rising levels of income and education, there is:
More concern for

· Population control and human ecology (the way humans relate to their surroundings)
· Child neglect and abuse
· Saving energy
· Healthful and safe food, water, and air
· Poor nutrition and drug abuse
· People with special needs

Since many of these problems are family-centered, there are home economics occupations which try to deal with them.
    Other trends are:

· *More* casual lifestyle, especially in the way people dress
· *More* interest in handicrafts and other forms of self-expression and development
· *More* appliances, easy care fabrics, and available services which simplify housekeeping.

These trends also result in home economics jobs, or they free homemakers to enter the work force part- or full-time.
    We can see that many occupations in home economics provide products or services for busy family workers. Others help people from troubled homes or those with special needs which their families cannot fill. Because of this concern for people and families, home economics occupations are often called *people occupations*.

CHAPTER SUMMARY

1. At one time in America, families built their own shelters and produced their food and clothing at home. *Where you lived was where you worked.*

2. After the Industrial Revolution and the invention of machines that could do the work of many families, home and work became separate, and people left home to *go to work* in new factories and businesses. Household work became easier, so that today *most women—as well as men— work outside the home* for much of their lives.

3. *Money income* is needed to pay for transportation to work, food, clothing, shelter, education, and leisure activities. Money income is not a family's total income, however. Goods and services produced at home add to money earned to make up a family's *real income*.

4. People work for other reasons than to earn money. Work, for many, helps satisfy emotional needs for *challenge, recognition, achievement, sense of belonging,* and *commitment*.

5. There are nine major *occupational groups*: professional and technical workers, managers and administrators, clerical workers, farm workers,

laborers, operators, service workers, craft workers, and salesworkers. Beginning jobs in home economics are found in the service, craft, sales, and operative groups.

6. With more training, a worker has more job choices and chances to earn more money income over a lifetime. When students are trained for a *cluster* of jobs, they can try out different kinds of occupations and find out which they like best.

7. There are seven occupations in home economics: the unpaid occupation of homemaking and six clusters of paid jobs. The paid jobs include child care and development, food service, clothing and textile services, interior design and furnishings, institution and household maintenance, and family and community services.

8. Analysis of these jobs shows which tasks are common to a cluster of occupations. When a student is able to perform these tasks well, a big step has been taken toward competency in a job cluster. *Competencies* can be defined as knowledge, skills, or attitudes which the student or worker can demonstrate at a specific level of performance.

9. *Career ladders* are steps which lead up a ladder of success on the job. Beginners are called *entry-level workers*. A *career lattice* is a branch going sideways between one career ladder and another. When workers cannot or do not want to advance on the same career ladder, job cluster training may allow them to move sideways, across a lattice, onto another ladder.

10. Home economics occupations are growing as the population grows and lifestyles change. Many occupations in home economics provide products or services for busy family workers. Others help people from troubled homes or those with special needs which their families or friends cannot fill. Because of this concern for people and families, home economics occupations are often called *people occupations*.

• FOLLOW-UP PROJECTS

1. Interview another class member about what work means to her or him. Write down what the person whom you interview says, but do not put down the person's name. Be sure to find out whether the person is working or has ever worked. (The person you interview should not interview you or you may influence one another's answers.)

   Meet in small groups and compare the responses obtained by your group with what others have said. Do the opinions of those in your class who have held jobs agree with the opinions of those who have not?

2. Interview persons outside of class about why they do or do not work outside the home and what work means to them. Try to interview a variety of people, for example:
   a. A male head of household

b. A female head of household

c. A married man who works outside the home and one who does not

d. Friends who are working

e. Friends who are not working

f. A young mother who works and one who does not

g. A retired person and a person eligible to retire who continues to work

Analyze their responses. What do they like about working? What do they dislike? What emotional needs were mentioned in regard to work? Do some seem to work only for money? How long have they worked? How many years do they expect to work?

3. Invite a guidance counselor to class to explain the general employment picture in your area. What is the labor market for youth? Do most young people who want jobs have them? How does youth employment in your community compare with the national scene? What service jobs are available? Jobs for operatives? Craftsworkers? Unskilled laborers?

   What percentage of students in your high school go on for further training? Where do they go?

   Ask about education programs in your area for out-of-school young people and adults who did not complete high school. Where and when do high school equivalency classes meet? Basic education classes for adults who cannot read and write? Classes for people who cannot speak English?

4. Look at the Table of Contents in the *Occupational Outlook Handbook* and select an occupation to read about. Take notes on your reading and report to the class. Can you identify the occupational group to which your selected occupation belongs?

5. Most occupational reports in the *Occupational Outlook Handbook* suggest organizations you can write to for additional career information. Select an organization and write for this information. (Help each other with your letters, and check with your teacher before mailing them to be sure you have used the proper form.)

6. Discuss reasons why home economics occupations are growing. Are the trends mentioned in the chapter also evident in your community? Give examples.

   Debate the pros and cons of the trends. What is good about each? What is not so good?

2 YOU–YOUR PAST AND FUTURE

After studying Chapter 2 you will be able to:

1. Compare how heredity and environment influence the person you become.
2. Draw some conclusions about your abilities and interests.
3. Explain how aptitude testing can help you decide on an occupation.
4. Explain what values are, where you get your values, and how they help you find your directions.
5. List steps to follow in making choices.
6. Find pleasure in self-discovery and in clarifying your personal values.

Finding out about the changing world of occupations is one step in getting a job. Just as important is knowing what you want to do and what you can do well. By analyzing your own interests and abilities you can, with the help of your teachers and counselors, solve the puzzle of where you might fit in the adult working world.

In this chapter we'll suggest ways to better understand yourself, recognize your strong points, and find the directions that are good and right for you. All these are steps toward inventing yourself, toward becoming the person you want to be.

Who are you? Is there anyone else in the world who looks like you? Thinks like you? Acts like you? How are you like everyone else and how are you different?

WHO ARE YOU?

You know that all human beings are enough alike so you can tell the people from the flora (plants) and fauna (animals). You have also seen that everyone has basic needs for security, challenge, recognition, and sense of belonging. But we are all different in appearance, behavior, attitudes, abilities, and experiences.

HEREDITY AND ENVIRONMENT

Heredity is responsible for some of people's characteristics. Certain features are passed from parent to child by the genes of the mother and father. At

Figure 2-1. Take a
moment and ask
yourself, "Who am I?"

the moment of conception your sex is decided, as well as the color of your
hair, eyes, and skin. The genes of the parents also seem to play a part in
intelligence and certain personality traits. Some examples are how sociable
you are and whether you prefer excitement to a more quiet life.[1]

No two people are ever exactly the same, not even identical twins. And
even if two people had the same heredity, they would never have the same
experiences. These experiences and the surroundings you live in make up
your *environment*.

Thousands of things are part of a person's environment. People are affected by the house they live in, their neighbors, their friends, the weather,
what they see on television, and so on.

Some of the most important environmental influences are nutrition, the
size and composition of the family a person is born into, and the care, love,
and attention a person receives as a baby and child.

Nutrition. Nutrition means eating the right kind of food to make you grow
and keep you healthy. Nutrition plays a vital role in a person's life from the
moment of conception. Babies who do not receive proper nutrition before

[1] E. M. Hetherington and R. D. Parke, *Child Psychology: A Contemporary Viewpoint*,
McGraw-Hill, New York, 1975.

birth are more likely to be premature and underweight. Their brains may not develop properly and they may have difficulty learning, in their later life.[2]

Nutrition continues to be important throughout life, but is most crucial to the growing child. Children who do not receive essential nutrients cannot reach their potential in health, energy, and appearance.

Sometimes children are poorly fed because of poverty. More often, children do not have adequate diets because their families do not know the nutritive value of foods. They do not know what foods to buy or prepare for their children's good nutrition. Older children and teenagers, who make their own choices, may know food values but follow food fads instead.

People of all ages are interested in weight control and its effect on health and appearance and self-concept. Nutrition has, in fact, become the *in* thing. For many men and women employed in home economics occupations a knowledge of nutrition is essential on the job.

Your Place in the Family. How many children there are in your family, and whether you are the first, second, third, or last child, also affect the person you become. The first child in a family has a different growing-up experience from the second, the second from the third, and so on.

Are you the oldest in the family? Your parents had more time to spend with you, and may expect more of you. As a result, oldest children tend to be more independent and responsible, and to achieve more.

Are you a middle child? If so, you probably had to compete for attention as a child. You may be more stubborn and aggressive, because you had to try harder to be seen and heard. But you may also be more sociable, as you looked to others outside your family for attention.

Are you the youngest? You may try to achieve like firstborns do. You may also feel more self-confident and secure because of the extra care and attention you had while growing up.

Only children tend to have characteristics of the firstborns and also the sense of security and self-esteem of youngest children. They are assured of the undivided attention of their parents.

Care, Love, and Attention. How close together children are, the *denseness* of the family, also affects behavior. When there are four or more years between children, the second or later children are much like the oldest. They are dependable and take pleasure in achievement. Children from very dense families tend to seek attention outside the family. Their parents have only limited time for each child when there are several small children requiring a lot of care.

Do you see yourself in any of these descriptions? They do not hold true for everyone, but they do suggest how important it is for each child to

[2]*Birth Defects: The Tragedy and the Hope,* The National Foundation/March of Dimes, White Plains, N.Y., 1975.

receive care, encouragement, and love. Our emotional needs are as important in our development as our physical needs. Children may be well-fed and physically cared for, but unless they are also given affection and attention their full potential will not be realized.

So we see that heredity and environment combine to have very strong effects on the kinds of people we become. We can summarize the relationship between heredity and environment this way: heredity provides the basic raw material, and environment shapes that material. The more you can learn and understand about your own heredity and environment, the more you can understand about the person you are.

YOUR ABILITIES AND INTERESTS

Part of inventing yourself is recognizing your abilities and interests and making the most of them. Your attitudes, skills, interests, training, and work experience are all *assets* (strong points) which make you employable and successful at work and at home. They include willingness to learn, ability to get along with others, attractive appearance, and many other qualities.

You can discover some of your abilities and assets from *aptitude tests* given by trained counselors. Others can be discovered by simply considering experiences you have had and what they've meant to you.

Work Experience. Perhaps you have already had some experience in a job for which you were paid. If not, you almost certainly have done some work—perhaps at home, perhaps as a volunteer—which can tell you a lot about yourself.

What jobs have you had? What did you like about each? What did you dislike? Look back on any work you have done and ask yourself such questions as these:

1. Do you like working with *people*, or with *things*, or with *ideas* most? Or do you seem to like them all equally well?
2. Do you prefer working on a team or alone?
3. Do you like a job with a lot of unexpected variety or are you happier when you know what's going to happen next?
4. Do you prefer a quiet atmosphere or a lively one?
5. Do you like a change of scenery in your work or do you prefer to settle in one spot and stay there?
6. Do you like a job where you help other people? Where you sell something? Where you make something?

Ask yourself the same kind of questions about your courses in school. The answers you get will help you take stock of your strong points and interests.

Special Talents. What special abilities or talents do you have? Are you good

Figure 2-2. What special skills do you have that
might lead to a job you'd enjoy? (Bruce A. Dart)

at operating machines and using tools? Can you operate a commercial dishwashing machine? A cash register? Use a French knife? Can you meet
people easily and feel comfortable talking to them? Can you style hair, make
bread, play the guitar, sing, make up jokes, add and subtract very quickly?
These questions are only a beginning to help you get started on finding out
what you already know how to do.

Perhaps your special abilities lie not so much in what you can do, but
what you *are*. Are you unusually serene and calm? Very energetic? Quick
to look ahead and good at making plans? Seldom sick? Good at organizing
your time so that you almost always get done the many things you need to
do? Always neat and well groomed? More than likely you can find several
qualities that are excellent assets for which other people admire you.

How you spend your spare time may indicate some talents you have
overlooked. Do you like to cook? Sew? Fix things? How about macramé
and woodworking? Sports? Gardening and care of plants? Many people
expand a hobby into a job. Can your hobbies lead to a job you will enjoy?

Attitudes toward Work. Your greatest assets may be your attitudes toward work. Positive work attitudes and basic skills in home economics make you employable in a number of entry-level jobs. The positive attitudes are familiar:

· Accepting supervision with grace
· Tolerance and understanding of coworkers
· Willingness to cooperate with others
· Caring about your responsibilities as a worker, as well as your rights
· Being flexible rather than stubborn
· A calm, patient outlook, rather than looking for trouble
· Pride in oneself and one's work
· Ambition

What are your attitudes toward work? Are you generally positive?

If you have negative feelings about work, you did not become that way overnight. Attitudes are hard to change, but realizing that poor attitudes hurt you in the work world is a step in the right direction. And a little success at school and at work can do wonders in making you feel better both about yourself and the work world.

School Experiences. The record you make as a student in school is very important in giving you clues about the kind of person you are. Naturally,

Figure 2-3. Your school record provides clues to the kind of person you are and to what you'd like to do. (Kenneth Karp)

the subjects that you like and do well in are important clues to your interests and abilities. So are activities out of class, like sports, music, drama, Future Homemakers of America (FHA), and Home Economics Related Occupations (HERO). But just as important are such things as regular attendance, being on time, and having a good behavior record. It is also important that your teacher thinks you are responsible and willing to learn. If you are doing all these things, you are building good work habits of reliability and cooperation. These also give an employer some evidence about what kind of a worker you will probably be.

Because of the Privacy Act, school records contain less information about you than they used to. Your grades and record of attendance are still in your file. There may be little other information on hand. You will probably have to ask teachers and counselors or club advisors about their opinions of your work habits and personality.

YOUR PRODUCTIVITY CURVE

What is your productivity, or work, curve? When are you most efficient? Are you a morning person or an evening person? A "lark" or an "owl"? How long does it take you to reach your top efficiency on a job? Individuals have typical patterns of alertness during a day. You probably already know if you are more alert and efficient and productive in the early morning or later in the day. People seem to be divided between those who do their best early in the morning and those who say they can't even get started until after noon.

People also seem to have warming up periods of different lengths, the time it takes them to reach their top efficiency. For example, a morning person may take 5, 10, or 20 minutes to get into the job at hand. Typically, the work curve of this person soon reaches the highest level and then falls off before lunch. After lunch, morning people often start at a higher level of productivity, but the afternoon curve may never get as high as the morning curve. It may fall again toward the end of the workday. The curve may be reversed for an evening person, or it may follow some other form.

APTITUDE TESTING

Aptitude tests help you find out what you can learn to do best. Different people are good at learning different kinds of tasks or jobs. Aptitude tests help show you some of the things you could learn to do if you had the interest and the chance.

Aptitude tests, by themselves, will not tell you what you should do. But when aptitude tests are used along with what you know about yourself already, they can help point you in the direction of success.

Very often people have aptitudes they don't know they have. Also, many young people (and older ones, too) have a fairly clear idea of what they like and what they can do. They do not, however, see how these qualities can add up to particular aptitudes that will make some jobs especially suitable and desirable for them.

Most schools give their students various kinds of tests, including aptitude tests, at some point during their schooling. Probably you have already had one or more aptitude tests. You may have talked over the results with your guidance counselor. If testing is needed, counselors in your guidance office or in community agencies (especially the state employment or job service) can help you get it. Then, by studying the results, they can guide you toward occupations for which you show yourself to be particularly well suited.

One of the tools counselors will use to tell you about jobs is the *Dictionary of Occupational Titles (D.O.T.)*. Occupations in the *D.O.T.* are coded according to special aptitudes needed for the job.

To be successful in some jobs, people must like to work with *information*, such as facts and figures. People who like to work with their *hands* do best in other jobs. Still other jobs require men and women who like working with *people*.

Which do you prefer? Once you know, counselors can suggest occupations which require your special aptitudes.

By looking at your background, you have tried to learn more about what kind of person you are. You have considered your heredity and environment and how they have affected you. You have reviewed your experiences and thought about your attitudes toward work and school. You have identified some assets and abilities. Once you have looked back and tried to learn what kind of special person you are, it is time to look ahead and see what kind of special person you can become.

FINDING YOUR DIRECTIONS

Your heredity and your surroundings have played a very large part in making you what you are now. Your experiences and your reactions to them have also had a large effect on you. None of us has any control whatever over our heredity, and while we are young we have little control over our surroundings. Nor can we change the experiences we have had in the past.

But where you are now is not where you have to stay. You have some choice over what happens to you in the future.

Find out what you want and then take steps toward getting where you want to go. What directions do you want to take?

YOUR VALUES

The directions you want to take are determined mostly by your values.

What are values? Values are personal guides which have been developed over time. These values or guides are considered "good" by society. Consider human dignity. It is a value of our society, and of many other societies. Our laws are designed to protect it. But it is not a value of all persons who live in our society. It may or may not be one of yours.

Figure 2-4. An important first step to choosing an occupation is to decide what your values are. For example, do you want: lots of leisure time; lots of money; to help others; to work outdoors?

Consider work. At one time in our society nearly everyone valued work. It was "good" for people to work. There is less agreement now. Most people believe that we should work for a living—but not everyone! You are in a course which was planned because certain persons believe there should be opportunity to learn a skill. That belief indicates a value.

Values direct your behavior. Some people's values show clearly that they know how they relate to society. These people have a proud, positive outlook. Other people are confused and uncertain about how they fit into their surroundings. Their values are not clearly defined. In other words, the positive people have clarified their values; the uncertain ones have not.

You may know what your own values are or you may wonder about some of them. There are ways to find out what your values are, to help you clarify them. The exercises are called *value clarification*. They help you to recognize the values, or guides, which you are following.

But suppose finding out what your values are comes as a surprise to you? Where did they come from? Can they be changed?

Values come from part or all of our environment: family, friends, religion, home, school, TV, neighbors, community. We may be able to recognize some values from our own attitudes, opinions, or goals. But not necessarily. A goal of wanting a job may be a step on the way to valuing work. It is not a real value until it is recognized by us and admitted to others—that is, until we are working, are comfortable working, and are proud to discuss our job with others.

If everyone in your family works and if most of your friends have a job (or are learning one), then you are more likely to value work. But it could become a value of yours without that background.

Some beliefs or attitudes appear to be contradictory. Before they can become your values, they have to be settled, or made to agree. Take money and leisure time. For some people a well-paying job they want—in food service, for example—may require that they work when others have time off. The money from the job may be more important to them than free time. By clarifying values the persons who have such conflicts are able to work them out.

Values can be changed, but not easily. Simply recognizing your values may cause you to change quickly. Usually it takes time, or it takes an event which really makes an impression. For example, only after legislators were presented with evidence that women were paid less than men for the same work did they support equal-pay laws.

You may have had some experience with changing values. Can you think of any? Looking at your values is another way of understanding behavior.

MAKING CHOICES AND DECISIONS

Once you know where you want to go, you can begin to make some choices that will help you move in the right direction. When you understand your values, you have one set of clues as to what your choices should be. To help you decide, think through each choice to where it might lead. Then you can make a list of the advantages and disadvantages of each choice.

Making lists such as these is one way to make a choice. Another way is to use the steps in decision-making. The steps are simple:

1. Clarify your goal. What is it you want?
2. Check your resources. Do you need money, time, or energy in order to reach your goal. How much of each do you have?
3. Find out what alternatives (choices) there are.
4. Be informed about each choice and where it might lead.
5. Make your decision, based on your values.

Suppose you are still in high school, but your *goal* is to have your own apartment. So, you check your *resources*. You have little money, lots of energy, and some time. (Much of your time is spent in school.) What are your *choices*?

1. You might drop out of school and get a full-time job.
2. You might get a part-time job and start saving for an apartment.
3. You might share expenses of an apartment with friends.
4. You might get a part-time job, save for college, and live in an apartment then.
5. You might ask your parents to make an apartment in an attic or garage.

Where might each choice lead?

1. If you drop out of school, you may not be able to get a job, or your job may not pay enough to support an apartment. You may not be able to move up on the career ladder of your choice.
2. May be a good choice, but what about your savings for college? Can you afford both?
3. May be a good choice, but are their values the same as yours? Will you get along well? How will the expenses and work of keeping up an apartment be divided?
4. Who will cook and clean? Would you be happier in a dormitory?
5. Will you have the privacy you desire? What about the energy shortage? Will the apartment cost your family more to heat or cool?

These are just a few examples of some of the choices and where they might lead. They illustrate steps in decision-making.

Making decisions is hard enough for a young, single person. For families, decision-making can be very difficult. In Part Four we'll look more closely at the decision-making process.

Part of exploring occupations in home economics depends on understanding yourself—your abilities, interests, and values. The next step is to look at the occupations themselves, what they are like and where they will take you.

CHAPTER SUMMARY

1. Understanding yourself, recognizing your strong points, and finding the directions that are good and right for you are all steps in inventing yourself. They are steps toward becoming the person you want to be.

   Human beings all have the same basic physical and emotional needs. But we are all different in appearance, behavior, attitudes, abilities, and experiences. Some characteristics people have come from their *heredity*. They are passed from parent to child by the genes of the mother and father. Other characteristics come from your *environment*: your surroundings and your experiences in those surroundings.

2. A major factor in environment is *nutrition*, starting from the moment of conception and continuing throughout life. Other environmental influences are *your place in the family* and the *care, love, and attention* you received as a child.

3. You can discover some of your abilities and interests from *aptitude tests* given by trained counselors. Others can be discovered by considering *experiences* you have had and what they have meant to you. Your *school record*, how you spend your *spare time*, your *attitudes toward work*, and your *productivity curve* all tell a lot about you.

4. None of us has any control whatever over our heredity, and while we are young we have little control over our surroundings. Nor can we change the experiences we have had in the past.

5. But where you are now is not where you have to stay. You have some choice over what happens to you in the future. You can chart your own directions by making decisions based on your *values*. Values are personal guides which have been developed over time. *Value clarification* helps you recognize the values, or guides, which you are following.

6. Values come from our environment, our family, friends, religion, school, TV, and community. They can be changed, but not easily.

7. Once you know where you want to go, you can begin to make some choices that will help you move in the right direction. There are different ways to make choices. One way is to follow the steps of *decision-making*: clarify your goal, check your resources, find out what the choices are, consider each choice and where it might lead. Then make your decision, based on your values.

• FOLLOW-UP PROJECTS

1. Prepare a collage entitled ''Who Am I?'' Include pictures, clippings from newspapers, poems, drawings, song titles, and other items which reflect your appearance, interests, abilities, and aptitudes. Do not put your name on your collage or discuss it as your work. Mix up the unnamed collages; students try to guess the name of the designer.

   Does this exercise help you better understand your classmates? Does it give you an idea how others see you?

2. Information about volunteer and paid work experience, school activities, and hobbies is often asked for on job applications. Prepare a list of these kinds of experiences, for example: Work experience:
   a. Dates
   b. Place
   c. Name of employer
   d. Job title
   e. Special work skills (ability to operate a cash register or a dishwasher or power sewing machine; ability to load a tray properly or make change)

3. Write a paragraph about your school record. How will it look to an employer?

4. What is your productivity curve? Are you a lark or an owl? If you don't already know, keep a record of your activities for a few days. When do you feel most energetic and alert? When do you seem to be at your best? Your most tired?

5. What do you think your best points are? Your ability in sports? Music? Crafts? Mechanics? Your good looks? Grooming? Personality? Sense of humor? Manners? Your attitudes toward work?
   Where do you think you could stand for some improvement?

6. How do you think you are just like everybody else? How do you think you are different?

7. Write your answers to the questions on page 19. Do they give you an idea of jobs you might like and do well in?

8. Meditate about the life you hope to have next year, in five years.

9. Each student should check with the guidance office about aptitude tests. What tests have you already had? Are other tests planned? Do you need aptitude testing? If so, how, where, and when can you get it?

10. Discuss with your class the characteristics that students have inherited. What environmental influences affect your behavior? Do you feel peer pressures (pressures from fellow students)? Consider your place in the family and its effect on your development. How about nutrition? Are you making wise food choices now?

11. Rank your values in the order of their importance to you. Where will you put work? Religion? Family? Education? Friendship? Love? Health? Is money a value? Popularity? Patriotism? Honesty?

12. Can you identify the values of your friends? Your family? Your community? Your school? Are they the same as yours? If not, what can you do about the conflict?

13. Discuss the following topics. What are the possible choices for action on each? Where might each choice lead? What values help you decide on the choice which is right for you?
    a. How to earn money
    b. Where to go on a date
    c. How to give a great party
    d. How to get along with your family
    e. How to make friends

3 | OCCUPATIONS IN HOME ECONOMICS

After studying Chapter 3 you will be able to:

1. List and compare the kinds of tasks performed by workers in six home economics job clusters.
2. Discuss the advantages and disadvantages of occupations in each cluster.
3. Describe how and why workers may move from one job cluster to another.

In Chapter 1 we saw that home economics teaches you knowledge and skills for use in many paid occupations as well as in the unpaid occupation of homemaking. We also discussed job clusters in home economics and career ladders and lattices. You were shown that preparing for a cluster—that is, a group of related occupations—rather than just one job gives you more choices of jobs. You will be able to advance *up* career ladders in these occupations, or *across* career lattices to similar jobs.

When you try out more kinds of jobs and see what they are like, you can see which ones best suit you. With this kind of information and experience you can make better decisions about further education and training to help you reach the jobs you want most. Even when you cannot get your first job choice, you can see how other jobs in a cluster might help you gain work experience, skills, and income until you can find an opening in the job you prefer.

In this chapter we'll examine six job clusters in home economics and consider some advantages and disadvantages of jobs in each.

In addition to the unpaid occupation of homemaking there are six major job clusters in home economics. They are:

HOME ECONOMICS OCCUPATIONS

- Child care and development
- Food service
- Interior design and furnishings
- Institution and household maintenance
- Family and community services
- Clothing and textile services

CHILD CARE AND DEVELOPMENT CLUSTER

The child care and development cluster includes a variety of jobs for both men and women. People are needed to care for young children in their homes, in institutions, in nursery schools, and in day care centers. Recreation specialists work with school-age children and youth. Foster parents and houseparents are in demand to care for children of all ages.

There are many opportunities for *paraprofessionals* in child care. Paraprofessionals are aides who work as members of a team with professionals like teachers or social workers. Working under close supervision of the professionals, the aides perform some of the tasks that require less training. For instance, paraprofessionals in a school system may assist the teachers by doing clerical tasks like taking roll. Or they may prepare bulletin boards and other teaching aids, or give special attention to individuals or small groups of children.

Formal career ladders exist in some institutions and school systems where men and women enter as teacher aides. They have the opportunity to become teacher assistants or fully certified teachers. Head Start workers may have similar opportunities.

Handicapped children and others with special needs require help from trained teams of professionals and paraprofessionals. This is especially so in the new field of bilingual education, which means teaching children in their own language while, at the same time, helping them learn English.

Whatever the setting—home or school, institution or playground—child care programs should do more than just keep children safe from harm. They should also provide for the best possible development of the children. Also, they should improve the childrearing skills of the children's parents. A good child care program will help children develop:[1]

· Positive self-image
· Body and hand coordination appropriate for age
· Ability to communicate with and relate to others
· Self-confidence in relationships with others
· Skill and independence in caring for self
· Ability to use imagination and demonstrate creativity
· The highest degree of intellectual development possible for age and ability

A good child care program may assist the whole family in many different ways:

· Understand the needs of children and how they may be met
· Increase parenting skills
· Improve interpersonal relationships

[1]Irene B. Rose and Mary E. White, *Child Care and Development Occupations: Competency Based Teaching Modules*, Department of Health, Education, and Welfare, Washington 20402, 1974.

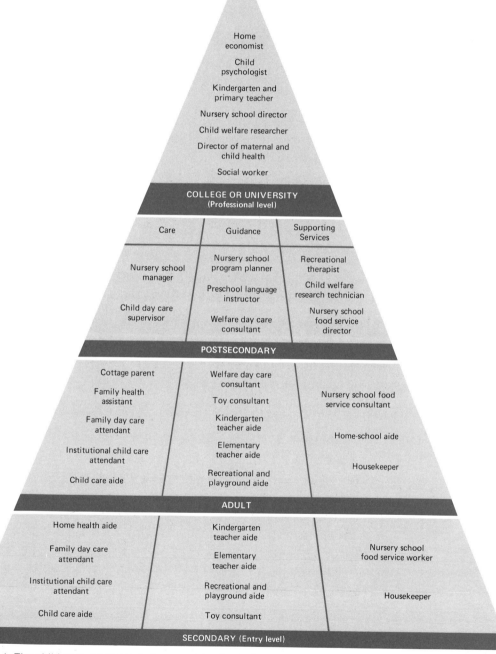

Figure 3-1. The child care cluster includes a variety of jobs in centers, private homes, nursery schools, and institutions. (Adapted from Arizona State University: *Home Economics Related Occupations Handbook,* 1975.)

33

· Increase family stability
· Identify and secure services needed by the whole family and by its individual members
· Prevent or reduce juvenile delinquency and child abuse
· Prevent or reduce drug abuse
· Increase income (adequate child care makes possible more flexible work schedules and, therefore, more opportunities to study and advance on career ladder)

What Do Workers in This Cluster Do? An analysis was made of the tasks performed in five occupations in the child care and development cluster. The occupations were:

· Day care parent
· Foster parent
· Houseparent in an institution
· Nursery school/day care center teacher
· Child care aide

Major tasks in child care were found to be guiding and encouraging the child's social and intellectual development, supervising play and routines, communicating with children and parents, care and maintenance of the center, and food service. Specifically, these tasks could include:[2]

Guiding social and intellectual development
· Talk and listen to children
· Help child learn acceptable behavior patterns
· Assist child in developing positive attitudes toward sharing
· Encourage development of child's curiosity
· Help children develop good table manners

Supervising play and routine activities
· Assist children in developing good housekeeping habits
· Practice safety procedures
· Supervise outdoor play
· Supervise puzzles, woodworking, dramatic play, clay, painting, crafts
· Read or tell stories
· Supervise rest time
· Teach and lead singing and rhythmic activity
· Arrange materials and equipment so they are ready for use

[2]Adapted from *Identification of Tasks in Home Economics Related Occupations: Care/Development of Children*, Iowa State University and University of Northern Iowa, departments of Home Economics Education, in cooperation with Iowa Department of Public Instruction, 1974, pp. 64–76.

Communicating with children, parents, and others
· Welcome children when they arrive
· Help children learn the established routines (meals, rest, etc.)
· Assist children in a sense of ''belonging''
· Report accidents, signs of illness and discomfort in children
· Talk informally with parents
· Take messages

Household care and maintenance
· Dispose of wastes
· Clean and straighten cabinets and shelves
· Dust and vacuum
· Store toys, equipment, and materials

Food service
· Wash off tables
· Serve food
· Prepare snacks

2032247

Advantages and Disadvantages of Jobs in the Cluster. There are several major advantages of jobs in this cluster.

· There is almost always some kind of work in this cluster, either at part-time or full-time jobs, because some amount of child care is a basic need for all families. This is especially so for the 6 million preschool children whose mothers work outside the home. One-sixth of all children and youths under 18 live in one-parent families. Many of these parents work outside the home. One-half of the mothers of school-age children work.
· Many jobs in the cluster provide on-the-job training, whether the worker is employed in a private home, institution, Head Start program, or other child care center.
· If you work for an agency or institution there may be fringe benefits, such as low-cost insurance and retirement plans.
· Working conditions are generally pleasant, cheerful, and healthful whether employment is in private homes, day care centers, schools, or camps.
· Education and training for child care jobs prepare the student for a paid occupation. They also increase the parenting skills of the homemaker. Also, there are some chances for qualified child care workers to care for other children in their own homes, along with their own children.
· Understanding human development—physical, social, emotional, intellec-tual—helps people understand themselves better. The result for the stu-dent can be improved relationships with people at home, at school, and on the job.
· Probably the biggest advantage of working in this cluster is that caring for

Figure 3-2. Training in child care can provide you with skills for a paid occupation as caregiver as well as for the role of parent.

children and watching them grow and develop can be a cause for personal pride and satisfaction. Where children have special needs because they are mentally or physically limited, in trouble with the authorities, or do not speak English, the satisfactions can be even greater.

There are certain disadvantages of jobs in this cluster.

· Most entry-level jobs, and even some of the middle-level jobs, have not always been well paid. However, our society is beginning to appreciate more the importance of jobs in this cluster. There is a better understanding of the effects of early childhood experiences on the developing child. Also, the number of working mothers is increasing. The result is that many of the jobs are being upgraded in both pay and status.

· Workers may be on duty at night, weekends, and holidays, which is a disadvantage for some workers. (Students may take advantage of this opportunity to work.)

· Foster parents and workers in private homes may feel isolated and lonely. They may wish for more contacts with adults.

· The places where children live and play are apt to be noisy and full of activity. Some workers may find this atmosphere hectic and tiring.

But, if you are the kind of person who likes helping others and enjoys children, likes activity and variety, welcomes responsibility, and responds with sensitivity to the needs of others, *you will find that the rewards in* keeping children safe and comfortable and guiding their development are great indeed.

THE FOOD SERVICE JOB CLUSTER

Food service is one of the largest industries in America. About 4 million people work in entry-level, middle-level, and professional-level jobs. These people provide food and services in a wide variety of businesses such as hotel dining rooms, fast-food and other kinds of restaurants, snack bars, camps, department stores, airlines, cruise ships, parks, and sport centers. Food service workers are also employed in industrial cafeterias and in institutions such as schools, colleges, hospitals, and prisons.

So much demand for food service means that you can find many different kinds of jobs at entry level. The industry also provides chances to advance on the job to higher-level positions or to establish a business of one's own.

What Do Workers in the Cluster Do? Major tasks performed in most food service establishments are production of food, sales and service, sanitation and safety, planning meals, buying food and equipment, supervision, and management. Here is a list of sample tasks performed by workers in entry- and middle-level jobs:[3]

Service
· Set tables
· Greet patrons and seat them
· Take orders and relay them to kitchen
· Serve food and beverages
· Present bill
· Portion foods

Production
· Follow recipes
· Prepare food for cook's use: wash and slice fruits and vegetables, slice meat, cheese
· Weigh and measure foods for special diets
· Prepare leftovers for storage
· Operate equipment such as food mixer, slicer, grill, coffeemaker
· Prepare for meal service such foods as fruits, salads, sandwiches

[3]*Identification of Tasks in Home Economics Related Occupations: Clothing, Apparel, and Textile Services,* Iowa State University and University of Northern Iowa, departments of Home Economics Education, in cooperation with the Iowa Department of Public Instruction, 1974, pp. 109-133.

Sanitation and safety
· Return soiled dishes to dishwashing area
· Receive dishes bussed
· Dispose of waste materials
· Operate garbage disposal, dishwasher
· Follow health rules and regulations
· Wash cooking and serving utensils by hand
· Clean counters, refrigerators, hot tables, work tables, urns
· Clean windows and woodwork, storage areas
· Maintain safe working conditions
· Check cleanliness and suitability of dress for self

Menu planning and buying
· Check menu for color, flavor, and texture
· Inspect quality and quantity of delivered items
· Place received items in storage

Supervision
· Make arrangements for special events
· Decide number of portions needed and served
· Check holding temperatures of food and beverages
· Calculate food waste by checking plate returns
· Discuss and plan work schedules
· Decide on portion sizes
· Write work instructions

Advantages and Disadvantages of Jobs in the Cluster. Food service has many advantages.

· This large industry continues to grow as the average American eats one out of every three meals away from home. The ratio is quickly becoming one in every two meals.
· There is great variety in the kinds of jobs and places to work.
· On-the-job training and chances for advancement are common.
· Advanced training in food service is available at many technical schools and community colleges, and through the Armed Forces.
· Working conditions are improving, with a trend toward shorter hours and more benefits, such as paid vacations, low-cost insurance, meals, and uniforms.

   Some characteristics of the industry are disadvantages for some, but not for others. For example:

· Many jobs have split-shift hours, which means working over a meal period, having several hours off, and then returning to complete the shift.
· Working at night, on weekends, and over holidays is common in many food service jobs.
· Work at resorts, and other tourist businesses, may be seasonal.

These conditions, which can be disadvantages for the full-time worker, provide opportunities for students and others seeking part-time jobs.
In addition,

· Much of the work requires physical strength and stamina.
· Food service workers may have to work with difficult customers, students, or patients.

Figure 3-3. Advancement is very possible in the food service occupations.

· Work may be performed under pressure, such as mealtime rushes.

· Work areas may be hot and crowded, and there is danger of burns, cuts, and falls.

But, if you are the kind of person who finds satisfaction in providing nutritious and healthy meals, helping people enjoy their leisure time, and working as a reliable team member, food service *may be the career* for you.

CLOTHING AND TEXTILES SERVICES CLUSTER

In this job cluster you will find people with very different interests and skills. For example, many jobs, such as those in textile mills and clothing factories, are technical and mechanical. On the other hand, many craftworkers are found in jobs such as tailoring and alteration of garments. People with artistic abilities hold jobs as designers, merchandise displayers, and models. Also, a growing number of workers produce homespun yarn, handwoven fabrics and shawls, knitted or crocheted baby clothes, and other apparel.

Advertising and sales of clothing and textiles provide other job opportunities. Once clothing has been advertised, sold, and altered, another group of workers takes over. Experts launder, clean, mend, and provide other clothing care.

There are entry-level jobs, highly skilled jobs, and managerial and professional positions in each part of the industry. Production, alteration, clothing care, and sales are involved. Therefore, there are a number of career ladders possible.

What Do People in This Cluster Do? Clothing and textiles are either mass produced in factories and mills, or produced by hand. Handwork is also called *custom production*.

The major operations in mass production of clothing are designing the garments, cutting the fabrics, sewing the pieces together, pressing and finishing. Each operation is performed by a different set of workers.

In custom production, tailors and dressmakers construct a garment from start to finish. They work with individual customers, producing garments designed and fit exactly as the customer wishes.

Textiles and clothing which are handwoven, knitted, or crocheted may also be produced to the customer's order. Or they may be made by craftworkers and offered for sale through small shops, craft fairs, or other retail outlets.

Many workers in the industry alter and repair clothing. To *alter* a garment means to change it in order to make it fit better. Mass produced clothing often needs to be shortened or lengthened, taken in, or let out. Some alterations are fairly simple, but others require the skill of a tailor or dressmaker.

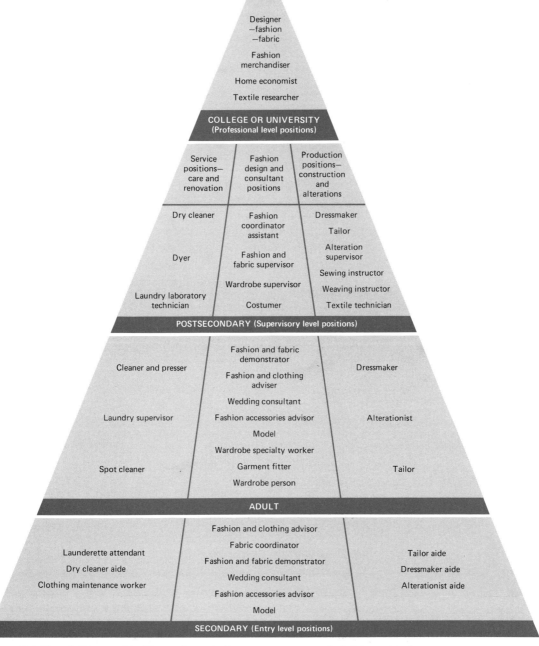

Figure 3-4. The clothing and textile services cluster covers an array of clothing-related jobs: designers, tailors, models, launderers, pressers, dyers, salespeople. (Adapted from Arizona State University: *Home Economics Related Occupations Handbook,* 1975.)

Sample tasks performed by tailors and dressmakers are listed below.[4]

· Use information and knowledge of fabrics and fiber types
· Do routine office work
· Keep financial records
· Order and stock supplies
· Maintain equipment
· Use of construction techniques
· Give advice to customer
· Do housekeeping duties
· Use hand equipment
· Handle customer complaints
· Observe standard safety practices

Most home economics occupations have a sales element. It is particularly strong in the clothing and textile job cluster. Sales jobs provide many entry-level openings with excellent possibilities for advancement and careers. Salespersons in stores work directly with customers, advising them on fabrics and styles. Salespersons also sell and distribute clothing and textiles from manufacturers to retail stores. In advertising and merchandising there are many different kinds of jobs available to display and advertise the clothing and textile products to be sold. Workers in this cluster are also found in commercial drycleaning and laundry plants, and in laundries in large institutions.

Advantages and Disadvantages of Jobs in the Cluster. Some advantages of jobs in the clothing and textile services cluster are:

· There are many chances for part-time and full-time work because employment in the cluster is growing.
· Entry-level jobs can be found in almost every community, although high-level jobs tend to be concentrated in large urban areas.
· This cluster offers chances for establishing a small business of your own, possibly in your own home. Examples are tailor, dressmaker, or alteration specialist. Or you might open your own yarn shop or drycleaning business.
· There is a wide variety of occupations, ranging from artistic to technical jobs.
· There are many benefits for factory, institution, and retail store employees,

[4]*Identification of Tasks in Home Economics Related Occupations: Clothing, Apparel, and Textile Services*, Iowa State University and University of Northern Iowa, departments of Home Economics Education, in cooperation with the Iowa Department of Public Instruction, 1974, p. 36.

Figure 3-5. One of the advantages of the clothing service occupations is that you can set up your own business.

including the chance to shop at discount (lower) prices for their own clothing. Many workers in this field also have chances for bonuses, commissions, and extra pay for faster work.

· Retail stores and many factories are well lighted and air-conditioned.
· There are esthetic satisfactions in many of these jobs. *Esthetic* means an appreciation for beauty and order. Garment producers often find satisfaction in changing fabric into useful and attractive clothing. Tailors and alteration specialists enjoy making clothes look and fit better. Cleaners can take pride in turning soiled garments into fresh, clean ones. Designers and advertisers can find satisfaction in seeing their ideas come to life.
· Operator jobs in the clothing industry often pay the beginner better than other entry-level jobs. They can be quickly learned and may be available over vacation periods. These features make them attractive to high school and college students.

Some disadvantages of jobs in this cluster are:

· Opportunities for factory operators to advance are limited. It is possible, however, to advance on the job to supervisor, tailor, or dressmaker. Pay-wise, operators advance from simple sewing tasks to more complicated procedures that are paid at higher rates.
· Factory production can be boring because of the need to repeat the same tasks over and over. Also, there may be seasonal layoffs.
· Working conditions present some disadvantages for jobs in this cluster. Noise and lint can be problems in factories. People employed in laundries and drycleaning plants often work around steam and heat.
· Salespeople and managers often work long hours. There is much competition in all parts of the industry, especially among designers and advertisers.

But if you are the kind of person who can work creatively with your hands, likes a fast work pace, and likes to depend on your own skills and ability, *you may like* working in this cluster, which helps over 215 million Americans meet their clothing needs.

THE INTERIOR DESIGN AND FURNISHINGS CLUSTER

Interior design refers to the planning of inside spaces of buildings, including homes, places of business, and institutions. Colors, lighting, floor surfaces, and furnishings are all part of interior design. *Furnishings* includes the furniture, appliances, lamps and decorative objects, and window coverings.

In this field, much as in the clothing and textiles cluster, workers with a variety of skills and abilities are needed. Some of the skills are the same. For example, household textiles and textiles used for clothing are produced by the same processes. Sewing skills used by operators and tailors are much the same as those needed by curtain and drapery makers.

Just as in the textile and clothing services cluster, there are jobs which require technical skills and ability to work with one's hands. Examples are furniture upholsterers and floor-covering mechanics.

Also needed in this job cluster are salespersons, advertisers, and merchandise displayers. They help customers learn about what new products are available and how to choose the right materials. Some jobs in this cluster call for artistic, technical, *and* sales skills.

What Do Workers in This Cluster Do? An analysis was made of tasks performed in four occupations in this cluster:

· Assistant interior designers
· Floor mechanics
· Upholsterers
· Drapery makers

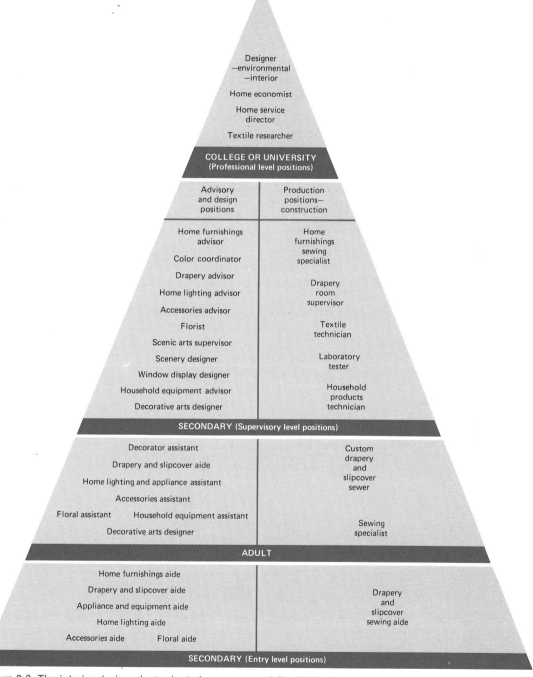

Figure 3-6. The interior design cluster includes many specialized jobs: interior designers, furniture upholsterer's, floor mechanics, drapery makers. (Adapted from Arizona State University: *Home Economics Related Occupations Handbook,* 1975.)

Common tasks in interior design and furnishings occupations are clerical, sales, maintenance of displays and workroom, and use of industrial sewing machines in construction. Some examples of tasks are listed below.[5]

Clerical
· Inspect merchandise for damage, both when received and when shipped
· Keep records of sales and service
· Order supplies and equipment; type purchase orders
· Answer telephone, take messages, answer questions
· Pack and unpack merchandise
· Do filing and routine office work

General maintenance
· Store supplies and equipment in appropriate places
· Keep workroom clean and orderly
· Keep display room clean and orderly

Sales
· Estimate amount of material needed for the work to be done
· Load, unload, and move merchandise or material to and/or from client's home
· Straighten drapery, upholstery, or other samples
· Take measurements at client's home

Construction
· Use power sewing machine to do stitching
· Select and coordinate fabric, thread, and/or linings, facings
· Repair and alter items

Design
· Choose coordinating fabric, paint, and other samples
· Take on-site measurements

Installation
· Sharpen and keep tools in good condition
· Drive pick-up truck to and from jobs
· Install wall-to-wall carpet
· Prepare floor before installation of floor coverings

Recovering
· Strip old coverings from furniture
· Attach upholstery fabric to furniture

Woodworking

[5]*Identification of Tasks in Home Economics Related Occupations: Interior Design and Furnishings*, Iowa State University and University of Northern Iowa, departments of Home Economics Education, in cooperation with the Iowa Department of Public Instruction, 1974, pp. 42–50.

Figure 3-7. One of the satisfactions of interior design work is making nondescript places beautiful.

Advantages and Disadvantages of Jobs in This Cluster. Some advantages of jobs in this cluster are:

· There is a wide variety of jobs, from artistic to technical, and many offer opportunity to advance on the job.
· There are many part-time jobs available.
· Some occupations can be performed in your own home and can lead to establishing your own business. Examples are upholstery, handcrafts, and drapery making.
· Self-employed workers are able to set their own hours and work pace.
· Workers employed in private businesses or institutions often have paid vacations, low-cost insurance, sick leave, discount privileges, and other benefits.
· Entry-level sales jobs can be found in most communities, and operator occupations in many.

Perhaps the biggest advantage of this job cluster is that it offers many esthetic satisfactions. People who work in interior design and furnishings have many different ways of changing dingy or useless interiors into pleasant, comfortable, and useful places for people to live and work.

There are some disadvantages to these jobs:

· One feature of the job cluster which may be a disadvantage for some people is the need for more technical knowledge and training than in some other clusters. This training is available in many communities, however. There may be vocational courses offered, or apprentice programs sponsored by unions. Since craftworkers need helpers, informal on-the-job training may be available also, especially in small businesses.

· Some work, such as carpet laying for a place of business, must be done at night when workers are out of the building. Interior designers and self-employed workers may need to work evenings and weekends, when their clients are free to meet with them.

· Much of the work is carried out at the customer's home or place of business. This means travel, loading and unloading samples or materials, and skill in getting along with the family or business staff involved.

· Removing old floor coverings or upholstery causes dust and lint. For factory operators, work may be monotonous and surroundings noisy.

· Top-level jobs in sales, advertising, and decorating are mostly available in urban centers. Institutional jobs are not as plentiful as in the food service cluster.

But, if you are the kind of person who likes to work with color and fabrics, or wants to learn a craft, enjoys moving about on the job, likes selling, and finds pleasure in helping to improve the appearance and comfort of the interiors of homes and public buildings, *this may be the job cluster for you.*

THE INSTITUTION AND HOUSEHOLD MAINTENANCE CLUSTER

To *maintain* means to take care of something, to keep it in good working condition. Workers in the maintenance cluster clean and keep in good repair schools, universities, office buildings, apartment houses, department stores, churches, museums, theaters, restaurants, and even ships and planes. Hotels, motels, camps, hospitals, and nursing homes also have housekeeping and maintenance staffs to care for buildings, furnishings, and, often, the grounds around them.

We have seen, from the tasks most performed in the four clusters discussed so far, that maintenance is a large part of almost every occupation. In addition, specialists in maintenance are needed in most businesses and institutions.

Private homes need constant housekeeping and maintenance, as everyone knows. Family members often take care of these responsibilities, but in cases of illness or age, they may not be able to do so. Men and women working away from home in paid or volunteer occupations often need help with household management.

Household employment can be a good entry-level job where people can improve their job skills, establish a work record, and explore their interests in other home economics occupations. In a joint project the American Home

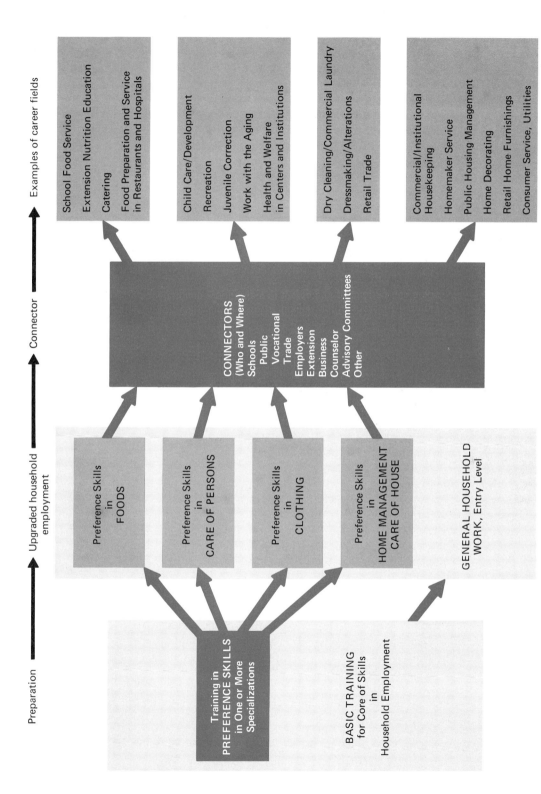

Figure 3-8. With basic training in home economics, people can decide which field they prefer to specialize in, look for a job or go to school for additional training, and enter a career field. (American Home Economics Association: *Career Ladders and Lattices in Home Economics and Related Areas*, 1971.)

49

Economics Association (AHEA) and the Women's Bureau of the U. S. Department of Labor (USDOL) joined forces both to acquaint young people with the opportunities in household employment and to upgrade these opportunities.

Basic home economics training can lead to household employment where people can find their *preference skills*. They can decide if they like and are qualified for jobs in foods, clothing, home management, care of persons. With the help of teachers, employers, and counselors—called *connectors*—they can move to the whole spectrum of career ladders in home economics occupations.

Not everyone wishes to leave household employment, and, indeed, the advantages of the occupation are many. But many people who begin their work career in household employment—and that is just about all of us—do use their earnings and work records as stepping-stones to other jobs or further education.

What Do Workers in the Cluster Do? Major tasks have been identified for supervising housekeepers, institution maintenance managers, household managers, and housekeeping aides. Listed below are some of the tasks performed across the range of job titles.[6]

Housekeeping procedures
· Note, report, or perform necessary repairs
· Organize supplies
· Maintain stocks of supplies

Planning
· Plan work schedules
· Decide standards for work to be done
· Develop ways to improve efficiency

Selection, use, and care of equipment and appliances
Providing for safety and sanitation
· Inspect premises, report or correct hazards
· Perform or supervise tasks related to sanitizing
· Control pests

Supervise or perform
· General cleaning, laundry, and routine maintenance

Maintaining pleasant relationships with clients
In addition, outside maintenance is a factor in some occupations. Meal preparation and personal care are tasks in others.

[6]*Identification of Tasks in Home Economics Related Occupations, Institutional and Household Maintenance*, from Iowa State University and University of Northern Iowa, departments of Home Economics Education in cooperation with Iowa Department of Public Instruction, 1974, pp. 77–97.

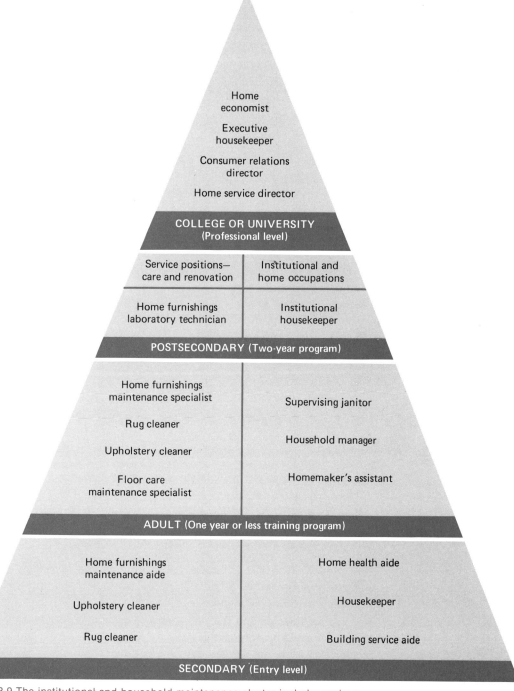

Figure 3-9 The institutional and household maintenance cluster includes various
housekeeping jobs. Adapted from Arizona State University: *Home Economics Related
Occupations Handbook*, 1975.

Figure 3-10. Many of the skills that you may have learned while maintaining your own home can be utilized in a career in institutional maintenance.

Advantages and Disadvantages of Jobs in the Cluster. The chief advantages of jobs in this cluster are:

· Entry-level jobs are readily available. Many people have their first jobs in some sort of household maintenance: for example, lawn mowing, window washing, dusting, vacuuming.

· Because of the demand for both entry-level and skilled workers, jobs in this cluster are being upgraded in pay and status. New occupations and businesses are being developed. The visiting homemaker, also called the *home health aide*, is one example. New businesses specialize in providing maintenance services for families and businesses. A trained team may offer weekly cleaning service, or window washing, floor waxing, upholstery and carpet cleaning, and other special work.

· Working costs are low. Workers are usually supplied with uniforms or can wear casual and inexpensive clothing on the job. One or more meals a day may be provided. Some workers have live-in jobs, so they are provided with a home and have no transportation-to-work costs.
· Working conditions for institution maintenance workers are generally good. Most of the work is done in heated and well-lighted, often air-conditioned, buildings. Some outside work may be required.
· Jobs in this cluster call upon many of a worker's abilities and skill, and therefore can be varied and satisfying.

Unfortunately, advancement to top jobs is somewhat limited, both for building maintenance managers and executive housekeepers, since there is just one top person for the building or building complex. One executive housekeeper may supervise 100 workers. There are assistant supervisory positions, however, in such large operations.

Disadvantages of jobs in the cluster may include:

· The *on call* nature of the jobs, requiring that one be ready to work 24 hours a day, or to work evenings and holidays.
· There may be low pay, few benefits, and little on-the-job training.
· Most jobs require a lot of bending; there may be heavy lifting.

Many workers, however, are members of unions which help to negotiate for improved pay and working conditions. Paid holidays and vacations and health insurance are usually among the fringe benefits. Household managers may work through agencies which set pay scales and working conditions. In some jobs, tips from customers and guests can add to wages.

But if you are the kind of person who likes to plan and can organize well, likes to be active on the job, and likes using human relationship skills, *you may be interested in jobs* in this cluster. They provide for the health, comfort, safety, and well-being of workers, children, travelers, the aged, and the ill.

THE FAMILY AND COMMUNITY SERVICES CLUSTER

New opportunities for jobs are developing in occupations which work directly with families and communities with social, economic, and health problems. Legislation is written in Congress to provide the necessary help for people with special needs. Often these programs are a federal/state partnership. There may also be state and local programs. People for whom the programs are designed do not always know about or use them.

Professional workers—nurses, social workers, teachers—carry major responsibility for *delivering* health, education, and counseling services to those who need them. These professionals need helpers, called *paraprofessionals* or *aides*.

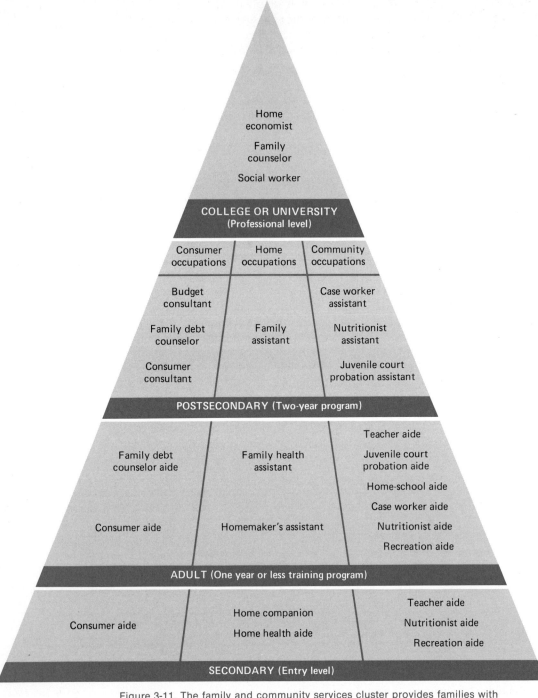

Home
economist

Family
counselor

Social worker

COLLEGE OR UNIVERSITY
(Professional level)

Consumer occupations	Home occupations	Community occupations
Budget consultant		Case worker assistant
Family debt counselor	Family assistant	Nutritionist assistant
Consumer consultant		Juvenile court probation assistant

POSTSECONDARY (Two-year program)

		Teacher aide
Family debt counselor aide	Family health assistant	Juvenile court probation aide
		Home-school aide
		Case worker aide
Consumer aide	Homemaker's assistant	Nutritionist aide
		Recreation aide

ADULT (One year or less training program)

Consumer aide	Home companion	Teacher aide
	Home health aide	Nutritionist aide
		Recreation aide

SECONDARY (Entry level)

Figure 3-11. The family and community services cluster provides families with counseling in many areas: alcoholism, budgeting, nutrition, consumerism, health. (Adapted from Arizona State University: *Home Economics Related Occupations Handbook*, 1975.)

Paraprofessionals who understand the people, the neighborhood, and the problems and the ways to solve them can make a major contribution to the quality of life of people in need. Since the problems tend to be related to nutrition, child care, consumer education, housing, family relationships, and employability, workers with a home economics background can be especially helpful.

Most teams of professionals and paraprofessionals work through agencies which are supported by government funds. Some are supported by private agencies such as the church or Salvation Army.

Those aides who are called *outreach* workers contact people in their neighborhoods to explain and discuss agency services and encourage people to use them. In the process, the aides learn about the needs of individuals, families, and neighborhoods and can report these needs to the agency. The paraprofessional is a link between people in need of services and those agencies which are prepared to help.

The aides may work out of neighborhood centers or mobile units. The typical outreach aide goes from home to home, knocking on doors to contact people.

Some paraprofessionals provide services themselves, perhaps in the homes of the needy. Nutrition aides and visiting homemakers are examples. Other aides work in agencies, hospitals, schools, or other institutions. They perform most of their duties there, but always serve as a link between the agency and the people.

What Do Workers in the Cluster Do? A task analysis was made of six jobs in the cluster: visiting homemaker, alcoholism counselor, family planning health aide, housing management aide, deputy juvenile probation officer aide, and family management counselor. Tasks likely to be performed are listed below.[7]

· Refer clients to agencies which can help them with special problems
· Counsel clients
· Write reports
· Provide education and training for others
· Present talks
· Develop budgets
· Keep records
· File and do office work
· Conduct interviews
· Be a friend and good listener

[7]Adapted from *Identification of Tasks in Home Economics Related Occupations*: Iowa State University and University of Northern Iowa, departments of Home Economics Education, in cooperation with Iowa Department of Public Instruction, *Family and Community Services*, 1974, p. 35.

· Provide transportation
· Write letters
· Answer telephone
· Follow-up cases to be sure clients get the help they need

Advantages and Disadvantages of Jobs in the Cluster. A major advantage of jobs in this cluster is that they directly help people and the community. Therefore, if you are a worker in this job cluster, you will have many causes for pride and satisfaction. Other advantages are:

· Jobs tend to call for a broad background of skills, many of which the worker may have acquired through experience rather than formal training.
· Many of the employers in this job cluster are state government agencies with employee retirement plans, health insurance, paid vacations and holidays, and other benefits.
· There is a chance to work closely with professionals. There may be planned career ladders to encourage and assist the entry-level worker to study and advance to higher-level positions.

Figure 3-12. The greatest reward of working in family services is the chance to help people directly.

· Jobs in this cluster are rapidly increasing, including many opportunities for part-time work.

A disadvantage of jobs in this cluster is that many of them are funded on a year-to-year basis. As economic conditions in the country improve or grow worse, the level of economic support may increase or decrease. Some of the jobs are experimental or *pilot* programs which may not last beyond a few months. Other disadvantages are:

· Some people find it depressing to be in constant contact with sick, old, disturbed, or very poor persons. Poverty and its related problems are not pleasant.
· You may be expected to visit homes and neighborhoods in the evenings and on weekends when family members are home from work or school. This may not appeal to some people, and may occasionally be dangerous. But workers often go out in pairs, and are trained to protect themselves.
· Working as part of a team which includes professionals usually means that the professional—whether a social worker, teacher, or home economist— makes the final decisions. This may sometimes be frustrating to the non-professional members of the team. They may feel they are closer to the people and the actual problems than the professionals.

But if you are the kind of person who likes solving problems, working with people, working on a job with varied tasks, and working as a member of a highly trained team, *you may find* your career in this cluster.

MOVING FROM ONE JOB CLUSTER TO ANOTHER

We have looked at six job clusters in home economics, and we have seen that it is fairly easy to move sideways from one job to another in the cluster. Often, workers can move easily from one cluster of jobs to another cluster. For example, counterworkers who are interested in food production may move across the food service lattice to positions on the career ladder for cooks and chefs. Or, if they find they are more interested in repair and maintenance tasks, they may wish to move to the institution and household maintenance cluster. If they work in a hospital, school, or industrial cafeteria they can easily investigate opportunities in both clusters.

Job skills in clothing and textiles allow easy movement across the cluster. Examples are pressers, tailors, and dressmakers, who may work in a dry-cleaning business, in custom production, or in a factory making coats and suits. Or these workers may transfer to the interior design and furnishings cluster, where they can use their basic skills in other sewing and pressing occupations.

An aide in the child care and development cluster may decide to change to the clothing and textile services cluster. He or she finds a job as a stock clerk in the children's department, and moves up the merchandising career ladder. Figure 3-13 illustrates the move.

How easily a worker moves from one cluster to another depends, of

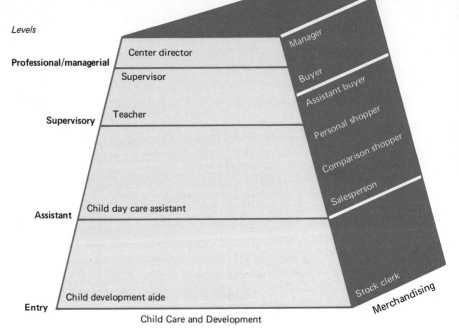

Figure 3-13. Workers in the child care and development cluster may decide to change to the clothing and textile services cluster. (American Home Economics Association: *Career Ladders and Lattices in Home Economics and Related Areas*, 1971.)

course, on how much training the worker has and how similar the jobs are. Some job titles seem to fall in more than one cluster. For example, some family and community services workers are chiefly concerned with housing, and could be considered a part of the institution and household maintenance cluster. Some jobs emphasize nutrition education and can be a part of the food service cluster. Those aides working with troubled youth could about as well be included in the child care and development cluster. Task analysis of home economics occupations, however, has placed job titles in the clusters used in this book.

All home economics occupations have a common base of knowledge and training. Some knowledges, attitudes, and skills (competencies) are more useful in one cluster than another. Specific competencies which are useful or even essential to a specific job cluster will be discussed in the next chapter.

CHAPTER SUMMARY

1. In addition to the unpaid occupation of homemaking there are six major job clusters in home economics. The *child care and development* cluster offers a variety of jobs for both men and women—caring for children and youth in their homes, institutions, day care centers, and playgrounds.

2. There are many opportunities for *paraprofessionals*, aides who work as

members of a team with professionals like teachers, home economists, social workers. There may be built-in career ladders in institutions, public schools, and Head Start programs.

3. *Major tasks* in this cluster are guiding and encouraging children's social and intellectual development, supervising play and routines, communicating with children and parents, and care and maintenance of centers.

4. *Food service* is one of the largest industries in America. It provides food and services in a wide variety of businesses such as hotel dining rooms, fast-food restaurants, camps, cruise ships, airlines, parks, and sports centers. Food service workers are also employed in industrial cafeterias and institutions like schools and hospitals. There are many jobs at entry-level and chances to advance on the job or to establish a business of your own.

5. *Major tasks* are production of food, sales and service, sanitation and safety, planning meals, buying food and equipment, and supervision and management.

6. In the *clothing and textile services* cluster are people with very different interests and skills. Many jobs are technical and mechanical; others require craftworkers like tailors and dressmakers. Artists hold jobs as designers and merchandise displayers. Advertising and sales provide many job opportunities, and the care and repair of clothing still more.

7. In the *interior design and furnishings* cluster workers with a variety of skills and abilities are needed. There are drapery makers, upholsterers, furniture finishers, floor covering mechanics, salespersons, merchandise displayers, and interior designers.

8. *Major tasks* are clerical, sales, maintenance of displays and workrooms, and construction using an industrial power sewing machine.

9. To maintain means to care for something, to keep it in good condition. Workers in *institution and household maintenance* clean and keep in good repair schools, office buildings, department stores, restaurants, and even ships and planes. Hotels, camps, hospitals, and nursing homes also have housekeeping and maintenance staffs to care for their buildings and grounds. Private homes need maintenance, also.

10. Most people begin their work career in household employment, where they can earn money at an early age, build a record of dependability, and get some ideas on what kinds of jobs they would like to prepare for in the future. *Because of the demand* for both entry-level and skilled workers, jobs are being upgraded in pay and status. *New businesses* are being started where trained teams offer weekly cleaning services to homes or businesses.

11. New opportunities for jobs in *family and community services* are developing in those occupations which work directly with families and communities with social, economic, and health problems. Since the problems tend to be related to nutrition, child care, consumer education,

housing, family relationships, and employability, workers with a home economics background can be especially helpful.

12. Most entry-level workers in family and community services work are employed by government or private agencies. Some provide services in people's homes.

13. It is fairly easy to move sideways from one *cluster* of jobs to another cluster of home economics occupations. All home economics occupations have a common base of knowledge and training. Some knowledges, attitudes, and skills (competency) are more useful in one cluster than another.

• FOLLOW-UP PROJECTS

1. Prepare a collage or bulletin board made up of newspaper and magazine pictures, want-ads, and snapshots illustrating job opportunities in home economics occupations. Organize the material around the six clusters of paid jobs.

2. Survey your teachers, clergy, neighbors, and friends about entry-level jobs they have held. How many held jobs in household employment? How do they seem to feel about their first jobs? How many times have they changed jobs in their lifetimes?

3. Interview a worker employed in a home economics occupation about training, experience, working conditions, special requirements of the job, and chances for advancement. These workers can be family members, friends, neighbors, and workers in the school and community.

4. As a class or in small, interested groups, visit the following work places or invite an employer from each cluster to class:
   a. *Food service*: a restaurant or institution such as a prison, college, or hospital to see how food is produced and served
   b. *Clothing/Textiles*: a textile mill, clothing factory, or the stockroom, advertising department, or alteration workroom of a department store
   c. *Interior design*: a department or furniture store, a new home being built, a home or apartment being remodeled, or a modular or mobile home to observe floor and wall coverings and color schemes
   d. *Community services*: extension service offices
   e. *Maintenance*: executive housekeeping department of a hotel/motel or hospital
   f. *Child care*: day care center or nursery school

4 | JOB DESCRIPTIONS AND REQUIREMENTS

After studying Chapter 4 you will be able to:

1. Recognize basic home economics competencies which help people succeed at home and on the job.
2. Give job descriptions for entry-level jobs in home economics.
3. Sketch a career ladder of interest to you.
4. Appreciate what it's like at the top of career ladders in home economics.
5. Describe where to find additional information on occupations in home economics.

In Chapter 3 we examined each of six job clusters in home economics occupations. We looked at the kinds of tasks workers perform on their jobs and saw some of the advantages and disadvantages of jobs in each cluster.

In this chapter we'll discuss job titles in each cluster. That is, the names and descriptions of the most important kinds of jobs and their places on career ladders will be shown.

You'll find answers to such questions as:

· What are the requirements for employment in jobs I might like?

· Am I qualified now?

· If not, what further training or experience must I have?

· What are entry-level jobs in home economics like?

· What is it like at the top of the career ladder?

We'll also look at basic competencies in home economics which are needed on the job as well as in the unpaid occupation of homemaking. In Chapter 1, we saw that home economics competencies are sets of attitudes, knowledge, and skills related to the study of nutrition and food, clothing and textiles, housing, human development, consumer education, and management.

CHILD CARE AND DEVELOPMENT

Several job titles are used for a number of occupations in child care centers, schools, playgrounds, and camps. Titles often used for entry-level workers are *child development aides*, *teacher aides*, and *playground* or *recreation assistants*. The top-level professional jobs are known by such titles as *supervisors*, *directors*, *teachers*, *counselors*, and *social workers*.

Figure 4-1. The teacher aide, an entry-level job in the child care and development field, leads and supervises children's activities. (Menschenfreund)

Some children are cared for in private homes by *foster parents* and *day care parents*. Children who live in residential or institutional settings may have *houseparents*. Many cooks and housekeeping aides are also employed in child care centers and institutions.

CAREER LADDERS

Several career ladders for workers in child care and development have been prepared. If you are interested in working with children in recreational centers, institutions, or child care centers, the ladders shown in Tables 4-1, 4-2, and 4-3 will help you. They will show you at exactly what point you will need further training in order to advance.

Short job descriptions are shown on the career ladders. An example of a *job specification*—a job description or summary of tasks that also includes other information about a job—is shown on page 66.[1]

[1]Adapted from *Specifications*, New York State Department of Labor.

Table 4-1 CHILD CARE DEVELOPMENT CENTERS

Levels	Titles	Work Descriptions	Minimum Qualifications
Professional/ managerial	Director	Full-time director with no teaching responsibilities. Responsible for business and personnel of center.	Bachelor's degree, M.A. preferred, plus experience and certification in child development or early child education.
	Assistant director	Assists director. Plans and directs educational program with teaching responsibilities. Supervises child development supervisor(s).	Bachelor's degree plus experience in child development or early childhood education.
Supervisory	Child development supervisor	Assists teacher in working with children. Plans work schedules and supervises child development assistants and aides.	Bachelor's degree, certification, and experience.
	Teacher, child development or early childhood education	Works directly with children.	Associate degree or technical school diploma in child development.
Assistant	Family day care parent	Licensed to care for up to 5 children, including own, in own home, or 10-12 children with an assistant. (May move to a larger center.)	High school with a secondary or adult program in child care and development, preferably in a cooperative program.
	Child day care assistant	Leads activities of children under supervision of child development supervisor or teacher.	Two years experience plus high school equivalency which may be earned while on the job and which includes an educational program course for child development workers.
Entry	Child development aide	Works under direct supervision with children.	On-the-job experience while enrolled in a cooperative educational program for child development aides. On-the-job secondary or adult education course for child development aides.

Adapted from Irene B. Rose and Mary E. White, *Child Care and Development Occupations: Competency Based Teaching Modules*, Department of Health, Education, and Welfare, Washington 20402, 1974.

Table 4-2 RECREATION CENTERS

Levels	Titles	Work Descriptions	Minimum Qualifications
Professional/ Managerial	Superintendent, recreation	For entire community system.	Master's degree or doctorate in recreation.
	Recreation supervisor	Supervises paid and volunteer personnel. In public recreation assists superintendent in promotion and administration of recreation programs including *music, dance, arts and crafts, games and camping*. In agency setting, such as settlement house, institution for children or aged, hospital, armed services, or prison, works with other departments.	Bachelor's degree in recreation or physical education.
Supervisory	Director, recreation center	Plans, organizes, and directs recreation programs under recreation supervisor.	Two years college to bachelor's degree in recreation or physical education.
	Recreation leader	Conducts recreation activities with assigned group in public department or agency. Cooperates with other staff members in community-wide events.	Two years college in specialty such as art, music, crafts.
	Playground leader	Organizes and leads recreation activities. Supervises and plans work schedule for assistants and aides.	Associate degree.
Assistant	Playground assistant	Leads recreational activities under direction of playground leader.	Two years experience plus high school equivalency which may be earned while on the job and includes an educational course for child development workers.
Entry	Playground aide	Works under direct supervision with children.	On-the-job experience while enrolled in a cooperative program for child development aides. On-the-job secondary or adult educational course for child development aides.

Adapted from *Career Ladders and Lattices in Home Economics and Related Areas: Possibilities for Upgrading Household Employment*, American Home Economics Association, 2010 Massachusetts Avenue N.W., Washington 20036, 1971, pp. 64–65.

Table 4-3 INSTITUTIONS FOR CHILDREN

Levels	Titles	Work Descriptions	Minimum Qualifications
Professional/ managerial	Superintendent/ manager of institution	Administers activities of institutions such as prisons, hospitals, clinics.	Master's or bachelor's degree plus experience.
	Assistant superintendent		Same as above
	Child development specialist	Plans for physical needs: menus, sleeping arrangements, clothing; emotional needs; counsels. Plans recreation and social activities. Supervises child development supervisor.	Bachelor's degree in home economics.
	Vocational counselor	Works with individuals and groups giving guidance on personal problems, educational and vocational objectives.	Standard for vocational counselor.
	Social worker or home economist	Works with children and parents or guardian and works as the connecting link between institution and society. Works closely with child development specialist and vocational counselor.	Bachelor's degree in social work or home economics.
Supervisory	Child development supervisor (houseparent)	Acts as housemanager for children's homes or similar institutions; hires and supervises housekeepers, food service people, attendants, and aides.	Associate degree.
Assistant	Child care attendant	Assists child development supervisor in caring for children; may give special services to handicapped or mentally disturbed.	Two years experience plus high school equivalency which may be earned while on the job and which includes an educational course for child development workers.
Entry	Child development aide	Works under direct supervision with children.	On-the-job experience while enrolled in a cooperative educational program for child development aides. Completed a secondary or adult educational course in child development.

Adapted from *Career Ladders and Lattices in Home Economics and Related Areas: Possibilities for Upgrading Household Employment*, American Home Economics Association, 2010 Massachusetts Avenue N.W., Washington 20036, 1971, pp. 66–67.

Job Specification: TEACHER AIDE

Job Description: Assists teachers or supervisors in day nurseries or classrooms, organizing and leading activities. Aids in increasing verbal abilities by reading to children or listening to children read. Leads discussions with children. Organizes and instructs games, arts and crafts, tours of buildings, and so on. Sets up and operates multi-media presentations to instruct and amuse children. Supervises examinations. Assists in correcting test papers and maintaining files and reports. Maintains discipline in teacher's absence and monitors study halls, lunchrooms, and corridors. Attends meetings with parents, teachers, community leaders. Assists in overcoming children's health, emotional, speech, or other problems under supervision of teacher and consultant.

Estimated Training Time: Varies greatly from several months to one to two years. Depends upon the complexity and extent of the duties and the amount of responsibility.

Worker Traits:

1. Able to speak, read, and write English at eighth grade level or above
2. Able to establish and maintain a warm, accepting relationship with small children
3. Able to handle children and parents with tact, patience, and understanding
4. Able to maintain discipline
5. Able to sit, stand, and move easily with no health problems detrimental to children
6. Able to learn story-telling and interpretation and child development patterns, etc.

REQUIREMENTS FOR EMPLOYMENT

Notice that requirements for employment in this job cluster vary greatly, depending on the job title. Teams of workers may include paraprofessionals with less than a high school education but with some special skill such as knowledge of the neighborhood, ability to speak a second language, or extensive experience in working with children. Such a paraprofessional may serve as a link between the people in the neighborhood and the school faculty trying to help their children.

On-the-job training is common in this job cluster. Together with experience, it can lead to some advancement. However, advancement to middle level often requires some advanced college or special training, and top-level jobs almost always require a four-year college degree.

Here are examples of what entry-level jobs in child care and development are like, and what it is like at the top of the career ladder. They are stories of real jobs and real people.

Mike

Mike is a recreation aide in a state psychiatric center, where he works with teenaged patients hospitalized for a variety of reasons. On a typical day the recreational therapy staff for Mike's unit meet first with their team leader, usually a doctor. They discuss any problems that have arisen and make plans for activities that will best help the patients. Then, depending on the weather, Mike and other recreational therapy aides take groups of five or six patients to the miniature golf course, the driving range, the swimming pool, or maybe even on a camping trip. When the weather is bad Mike will accompany his patients bowling, or maybe to the gym for volleyball or basketball, or to a lounge to play card games.

Bingo is available once a week. There are movies, occasional dances, and intrahospital baseball, tennis, and other sports. Sometimes tickets are ordered and patients bused to professional hockey games or concerts, ice shows, or the circus. There are also sing-a-longs and other musical activities.

Mike enjoys his job. He has gone as far as he can on his career ladder unless he gets more formal education. He worked for several years as a ward attendant before qualifying for his present job. Mike likes the fringe benefits that go with his job: his pension rights and vacation and sick days. Most of all he likes the variety and activity in his job, and he likes being a member of a health team.

Helen L.

Helen is supervisor of a day care center in a large southern city. She has a college degree in home economics and supervises a staff of six teachers, three teacher aides, a cook, and two housekeeping aides.

Helen opens the center at 6:00 a.m. She plans the master schedule for the center and supervises morning activities, lunch, and naptime. The head teacher assumes responsibility for supervision from 2:00 a.m. until the center closes.

Helen works with a group of children for part of each day and gives special attention to children with problems. But her job is mostly administrative, supervising her staff, training new people, talking with parents, keeping records. The larger agency of which the day care center is a part plans menus for snacks and meals, buys the food, and provides on-the-job education for teachers in this center and others like it.

Helen likes her job. She enjoys watching the children grow and learn. She is thoughtful and considerate as a supervisor and is skillful in working with her staff, the children, and the parents. As a result this staff of aides, paraprofessionals, and professionals work together harmoniously for the good of the children.

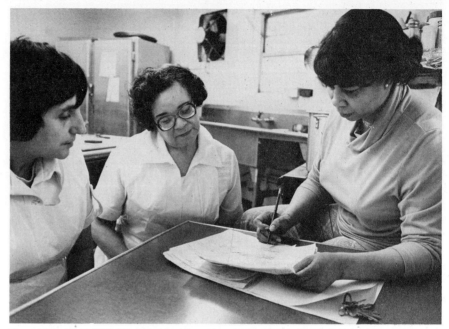

Figure 4-2. The child development supervisor, a top-level position, plans meals and supervises the food service staff for the child care center. (Kenneth Karp)

COMPETENCIES

The basic competencies[2] needed by both parents and workers in paid child care occupations include the abilities to:

· Recognize the stages a child goes through and accept behaviors typical of the stages.

· Accept and encourage children's curiosity and questioning, and do not punish child for being active and explorative.

· Describe the effects of heredity and environment on a child's social, physical, emotional, and intellectual development.

· Appreciate the importance of self-esteem, and describe some ways to provide experiences where a child can feel successful.

· Recognize ways to help children better understand the world around them.

· Use positive guidance techniques with children; avoid making threats and belittling remarks, or making children feel guilty.

[2]Sources of all competencies in Chapter 4 are: a) Kansas City Clinic for Home Economics Educators, sponsored by AHEA and U.S. Office of Education, 1977. A publication is in process. b) H. Nelson and G. Jacoby, *Evaluation of Homemaking and Consumer Education Programs for Low-income Adults*, University of the State of New York, State Education Department, Bureau of Occupational Education Research and Bureau of Home Economics Education, Albany, 1975.

· Recognize common signs of illness and know how to handle health emergencies.
· Appreciate the value of play to child development and demonstrate skill in planning and supervising play activities.
· Willingly follow safe and sanitary practices and child care.
· Appreciate the importance of preventive medicine, such as immunizations, dental care, and eye examinations.

FOOD SERVICE

Jobs in food service are to be found in a great variety of places, ranging from fast-food restaurants to executive dining rooms, and from baseball parks to hospitals. There are also a number of different kinds of jobs in each food service operation. These can be called *production, sales,* and *sanitation* jobs.

PRODUCTION

Food production in food service means the preparation of food to be served or sold. Since this work usually takes place in kitchens and pantries where customers seldom go, they are also known as "back-of-the-house" jobs. In restaurants food production is supervised by a chief *cook* or *chef.* The chef may have several assistants, depending on the size of the operation and the variety of food served. Some examples of chef assistants are: *second cook,*

Figure 4.3 A baker usually works during early morning or late night hours, preparing bread, rolls, and other items for the day's sale. (Sybil Shelton, Monkmeyer)

pastry chef, broiler, vegetable cook, or *baker*. In a large operation the first assistant to the chef is called the *sous chef* (pronounced soo sheff). A job specification for baker is shown below.[3]

Sometimes cooks are titled according to the meals they prepare; for example, *breakfast cook*. Or, in smaller or fast-food operations, cooks may be titled according to the shift, *day cook* or *night cook*.

Entry-level jobs in food production are held by the people who help the chef and the chef's assistants. These jobs have titles such as *kitchen helper, pantry worker,* or *baker's helper*.

Figure 4-4 shows how a typical large restaurant is organized. In smaller restaurants there may be only one cook or chef, and entry-level workers may assist this person with all the food preparation tasks, as well as with clean-up chores.

In the kitchens of institutions like schools and hospitals, the job titles are much the same as in restaurants. However, the food production is supervised by a person called the *food service manager*, who usually has the extra responsibility of training students, inmates, and other workers.

Job Specification: BAKER

Job Description: The baker prepares bread, rolls, muffins, and biscuits according to recipe, measuring and mixing ingredients. Forms, kneads, cuts, and shapes dough and bakes in oven, regulating temperature. Often is required to prepare and bake pies, cakes, cookies, and other pastries. The baker may specialize in one type of product as a feature item.

Job Requirements: High school graduation is preferred. Experience as a baker helper or baking training is required by many employers. Vocational and technical schools often offer such training. The baker must be able to measure ingredients accurately and needs some mathematical ability to adjust recipes. Must be able to work alone without supervision. Usually has a time deadline to complete work but is not subject to mealtime rushes. Manual and finger dexterity is necessary. Prolonged standing and some heavy lifting are involved.

Employment and Advancement Opportunities: Increased demand for restaurant services, combined with replacement of experienced bakers, should create more baker openings. Many restaurants today are specializing in bakery goods and will add to the demand. Advancement to supervisory or management positions is not unusual.

Working Conditions: Most of the work is done during early morning or late at night when other kitchen workers are gone. There may be some heat and chance of burns from baking equipment. The standard work week is from 36 to 48 hours.

[3]*Food Service Careers*, Iowa Employment Security Commission, Des Moines 50319, 1973, p. 7.

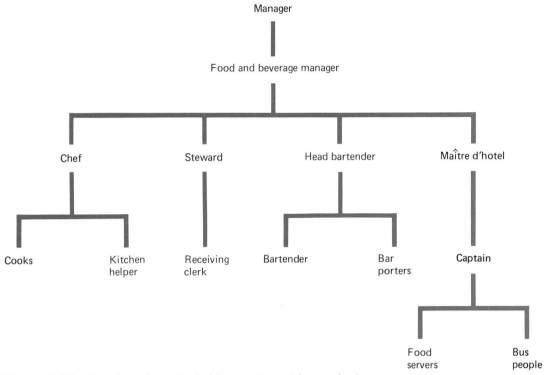

Figure 4-4. This chart shows how a typical large restaurant is organized.

SALES AND SERVICE

Jobs in food sales and service are often called "front-of-the-house" jobs because the servers work directly with the customers, students, or patients. *Food servers* (often called waiters/waitresses) make up the largest number of workers in sales and service. They take orders from the customers and then bring them the food and beverages ordered. In large operations they may be assisted in the setting up and clearing of tables by *bussers* (or *dish carriers*.) Several servers may be supervised by a *captain* responsible for one part of the dining room. The dining room manager usually has such titles as *guest seater* or *host/hostess* or the French terms, *maître d'/maîtresse d'*.

Food servers have various titles, depending on where they work. Some examples are: *tray workers* in hospitals, *room service waiters/waitresses* in hotels and motels, *flight attendants* on passenger airlines, *counterworkers* in cafeterias and fast-food restaurants, *carhops* at drive-in restaurants.

Several kinds of jobs in food service combine some food production with sales and service. Examples are *grill cooks*, who prepare quick and simple foods and serve them to customers; *bartenders*, who prepare and serve beverages; *caterer's helpers*, who help the catering cook prepare the food and who also may deliver and serve the food.

In institutions like hospitals and nursing homes, *dietary aides* help the

Figure 4-5. The food server, an entry-level food-service position, needs to have a good memory for taking orders and to be able to compute checks with accuracy. (Michael Ramey, South Seas Plantation, Captiva, Florida)

dieticians plan menus for people with special diets. They often prepare special foods, and then deliver the meals to patients or residents. Here is the story of Nancy, a dietary aide in a large hospital.

Nancy

Nancy is a dietary aide in a hospital. She works in the diet kitchen, which in her hospital is a section of the main kitchen. She sets up trays for patients who require special diets. She does some cooking herself; for example, she uses the blender to prepare special foods. But the most important part of her job is to follow exactly the instructions she receives from the therapeutic dietician. There can be no mistakes in the amount and kind of food delivered to the patients.

Nancy likes her job because she is an important member of a medical team. She works closely with the dietician who plans the menus for the patients, the assistant cook who prepares foods for the trays, and the workers who deliver the trays. She may go with the aides who deliver trays to the acutely ill to be sure that the trays are distributed properly.

The young woman who formerly held Nancy's job has just graduated from a two-year college that trains assistant dieticians, and has decided to work a while and then go on to become a dietician. Nancy recently graduated from high school and is just beginning to feel sure of herself on her job, but she is already thinking of getting further training also.

SANITATION

Sanitation workers clean and sanitize—that is, keep germ-free—pots, pans, equipment, cooking utensils, and all china, glass, and silver used to serve guests. Others clean, repair, and maintain the building and grounds.

Some typical job titles in sanitation are *dishmachine operators* and *pot washers*. Kitchen helpers and *food service workers* help with sanitation as well as with production and service. Because their job is so important, sanitation workers often work under the direct supervision of the manager.

RELATED OCCUPATIONS

There are a number of entry-level jobs which are related to the food service industry. These jobs are not always considered home economics occupations, but students trained in occupational home economics may be hired for these positions. They include *food checkers* and *cashiers*, *receiving clerks* and *stewards*, *salespersons* (in groceries), and *operators* in food processing plants. Here is the story of Ron, a steward for a large hotel.

Ron

Ron is the steward for a large hotel which has a dining room and coffee shop. His main responsibilities are to keep track of food and other supplies on hand and to place orders when more are needed. In addition to taking inventory and ordering supplies, he checks invoices for completeness when supplies are delivered, and inspects the quality of supplies. The work is sometimes heavy, but only for short periods. When delivery trucks come in, for example, there are supplies to uncrate and some lifting of cases of canned foods and boxes of frozen supplies. Ron seems to be always in the freezer, but he also spends a lot of time making sure other supplies are stored in a sanitary and efficient way and rotated so that older products are used first and top quality maintained.

Ron is supervised by the chef and by the food and beverage manager. He helps out in the kitchen when not busy with his steward duties, acting as kitchen helper or assisting the pantry worker. Overall, Ron does not find his job difficult and likes the fringe benefits of one meal a day and furnished uniforms. He also likes the opportunity to learn on the job and move up to cook or chef.

Food checkers and cashiers work chiefly in restaurants and cafeterias. They note the price of the food served to each guest and take payment.

Receiving clerks and stewards receive supplies and store them. They keep records, and supply food and equipment to other workers in the restaurant.

Operators may work in canneries and industrial bakeries. There are also jobs in plants processing frozen food for supermarkets and fast-food places.

Salespersons in retail stores wait on customers and keep food merchandise in order. Some salespersons also hold higher-level jobs selling supplies from food wholesalers and processors to restaurants and institutions.

Other high-level jobs in the food service industry are purchasers who

Table 4-4 CAREER LADDER: RESTAURANT COOK

Levels	Titles	Work Descriptions	Minimum Qualifications
Professional/ managerial	Owner or manager	Coordinates and supervises cooks, chefs, kitchen helpers, food servers, and others. Hires and trains.	High school graduate. College may be required. Experience as cook or food server helpful. Experience as Assistant Manager.
	Assistant manager	Assists in above.	Same as above.
Supervisory	Head cook or chef	Responsible for all entree preparation and directing the work of others in the kitchen.	Previous cooking experience or vocational training or both. High school graduation or equivalent often required.
Assistant	Second cook	Short-order work (broiler, fryer) and assisting the head cook.	Same as above.
	Third cook or vegetable cook	Responsible for preparation of vegetables.	Vocational training or capacity for on-the-job training. Experience at entry-level desirable. Good health.
Entry	Kitchen helper or counterworker or pantry worker	(See job descriptions on pp. 76-77.)	High school graduate preferred. Good health.

SOURCE: Prepared by author from training manuals, job specifications, from restaurant chains and state employment service.

supervise the buying of food and equipment, controllers and accountants who handle finance, and experts in public health laws and marketing (advertising and public relations).

CAREER LADDERS

Tables 4-4 and 4-5 show the career ladders in food production for a restaurant cook and for a food service manager in a public institution. Food servers are on a career ladder leading to dining room supervisor and then to restaurant manager.

Career ladders for sanitation workers can be the same as those for food servers and cooks. In addition, these ladders can lead to more advanced jobs in the institution and household maintenance cluster.

Sample job descriptions[4] and a job specification[5] are shown on pages 76-7.

[4]SOURCES: Commercial training manuals, State Employment Service, New York State Department of Mental Hygiene.

[5]Adapted from *Food Service Careers*, Iowa Employment Security Commission, Des Moines 50319, 1973, p. 11.

Table 4-5 CAREER LADDER: INSTITUTIONAL COOK

Levels	Titles	Work Descriptions	Minimum Qualifications
Professional/managerial	Institution food administrator, Grade 20	Plans, organizes, and directs food preparation and service program. Plans and supervises personnel training programs; prepares budget.	Bachelor's degree in dietetics, nutrition, hospital administration, institutional management, or home economics, with a major in nutrition or business administration *and* 4 years of experience in a food administrative position.
	Food service manager, Grade 15	Assigns and supervises large force of kitchen employees and others; supervises bakery.	3 years of experience in supervision of large-scale cooking *and* 2-year degree in food preparation, or high school graduation *and* satisfactory completion of cook's training course.
	Food service instructor, Grade 14	Teaches at a school for food service employees of state institutions.	High school graduation, completion of a course of 30 class hours in teaching methods, *and* 3 years of experience in large-scale cooking.
Supervisory	Head cook, Grade 12	Supervises and directs others; trains kitchen personnel; may personally perform cooking duties.	5 years of experience in large-scale cooking, 2 years of which included regular supervision of others.
	Cook, Grade 9	May be in charge of kitchen on a given shift, or responsible for specific type of cooking such as range cooking. Supervises others; personally performs cooking work; may do some baking or canning.	3 years of experience in large-scale cooking, one year of which included regular supervision of others.
Assistant	Assistant cook, Grade 6	Does general cooking: meat, vegetables, desserts; supervises Kitchen Helpers. May do some baking and canning; may dispense food at a counter; substitutes for cooks; may be in charge of small kitchen.	One year of experience in large-scale food preparation or cooking *or* satisfactory completion of the six-month training program sponsored by the Department of Civil Service.
Entry	Kitchen helper, Grade 3	(See job description, p. 76.)	No examination is required. Good health.

SOURCE: *Specifications*, New York State Department of Civil Service.

Job Description: KITCHEN HELPER

Performs routine tasks to keep kitchen work areas, equipment, and utensils in clean and orderly condition. May wash dishes, pots, pans, and silverware either by hand or by machine. Preparation of salads and vegetables and assisting the cook in other general work may be included. Other possible duties are helping to set banquet tables and assisting in maintaining supplies.

Job Description: FOOD SERVICE WORKER

Serves food to patients and staff and maintains high standards of cleanliness and order in a dining room, cafeteria and/or serving area. Cuts margarine; makes toast, coffee, or tea; fixes salads; serves trays; controls portion size; prepares dishmachine for use, operates and thoroughly cleans it after each use; sweeps and mops dining and serving room floors; washes dining room furniture, windows, and woodwork. Cleans all serving room equipment; may take inventories and requisition supplies; stores supplies; keeps records of number of people served each meal. May perform all these duties alone or may supervise others.

Job Specification: FOOD SERVER

Job Description: The food server waits on customers in coffee shops, lunchrooms, and restaurants. Presents menu, answers questions, takes orders, and relays it to kitchen. Serves food and beverages and carries out any other requests for food or drink. Computes meal charges and may collect payment and make change. Often clears and resets tables. May assist in the preparation of some food items and maintenance of supplies in the service area.

Job Requirements: High school education with home economics courses preferred. Minimum age varies with employers. Accuracy with figures and a good memory are essential. Personal appearance and attitude should be pleasant. Should enjoy meeting and serving the public. Courtesy should be shown under all conditions, from mealtime rushes to slack periods. Cleanliness and good health are required. Must be able to stand and walk most of the work period. Some lifting and carrying are involved.

Employment and Advancement Opportunities: Openings are constantly available due to turnover and the increase in the number of people who eat away from home. Advancement to guest seater or manager is possible.

Working Conditions: The food server may work a split shift as well as evenings, weekends, and holidays. Working area is generally clean and pleasant. The standard work week is from 40 to 48 hours. Due to tips, it is difficult to estimate wages. Tips will average from 10 to 15 percent of the customers' checks.

Job Description: COUNTER WORKER

The counterworker serves food and beverages at a restaurant counter or from counters and steamtables in a cafeteria. He or she relays orders to the kitchen but may prepare also sandwiches, salads, and desserts. In many instances, the counterworker will operate a grill for short-order items. A cafeteria worker usually serves only one particular item, such as meat, vegetables, or beverages. Duties may include meat carving and coffee making. Assists in cleaning counters, steamtables, and other equipment. Often computes prices of food order and may collect money and make change. Where a soda fountain is involved, the counterworker may specialize in preparing sodas, sundaes, and shakes.

REQUIREMENTS FOR EMPLOYMENT

For many entry-level jobs in food service, little or no experience is required. Workers can be taught on the job, and on-the-job experience can also prepare them for some advancement. For more specialized and advanced jobs, formal vocational training may be needed. Some vocational programs are provided by restaurant associations, hotel management groups, trade unions, manpower programs, and technical schools. The Armed Forces train cooks and chefs.

Many businesses like to promote from within, a policy which helps them recruit able workers at all levels. Therefore, there may be built-in training programs to help workers reach higher-level positions.

In large restaurants or hotels, the food and beverage manager usually needs college training. Dietary aides also need college training before they can advance to positions as dieticians.

Workers must have physical stamina and must be free from contagious diseases (e.g., tuberculosis). They must like to work with others as a member of a team and be able to work under pressure during rush periods. Additionally, workers in sales and service must have a pleasant appearance, the ability to concentrate and remember details in the midst of noise and confusion, a skill in arithmetic, and the ability to speak clearly and write legibly.

Here is the story of Scott, who holds a higher-level job in food service.

Scott

Scott is the food and beverage manager at an island resort off the coast of Florida. In his late twenties, he has a degree in hotel administration from a 4-year college.

Scott is responsible for hiring and firing all food and beverage workers in the dining room, bar, and snack shop: the chefs, cooks, kitchen helpers, maître d', captains, waiters and waitresses, wine stewards, bartenders, and others. The executive chef supervises kitchen workers and the maître d' supervises dining room personnel, but Scott is responsible for the overall performance of them all. Routine mealtimes require only occasional supervision, but he has to be sure that everything runs smoothly and that the customers are satisfied. Closer supervision is required for specially catered events.

As part of management, Scott has an office and secretarial help. He reports to the general manager and also to the owners of the resort.

Cost control is a big responsibility of Scott's, so he must make sure that food cost figures are good and that the staff he supervises "produces." He does not always train new workers himself, but makes sure they get the help they need to do their jobs quickly and well.

Scott is paid a high salary and his luxurious living accommodations are paid for as well. As a live-in employee he is, of course, on call 24 hours a day as a troubleshooter should the need arise.

COMPETENCIES

Home economics competencies which are helpful to the paid food service worker, as well as the unpaid homemaker, include the abilities to:

· Plan and select a variety of foods to meet nutritional needs throughout the life cycle: prenatal, infant, child, teenager, adult, and aged.
· Relate food intake to health and appearance.
· Demonstrate skill in food preparation.
· Demonstrate procedures to enhance the appearance of food.
· Explain ways to get the most value for your money when planning menus and buying food.
· Demonstrate safe and sanitary practices in producing, handling, and storing food.
· Demonstate skill in offering food in a variety of service styles in home or commercial settings.

CLOTHING AND TEXTILE SERVICES

Jobs in the clothing and textile services, like those in the food service cluster, provide opportunities to work either with the product or with people, depending on what you prefer. There are four major choices of jobs: design and production, alteration and repair, drycleaning and laundry, and sales.

DESIGN AND PRODUCTION

Clothing and textiles are produced both by machine and by hand. The manufacturing process usually begins with *designers*, who create new styles and types of clothing. *Sample makers* sew samples of the designs to show management and sales staffs.

Once a design is approved, *pattern makers* construct master patterns.

Then *pattern graders* change the master patterns to fit different sizes. Or, grading may be done by computer.

In the cutting rooms, *spreaders, markers,* and *cutters* lay out the fabric, trace the patterns on it, and cut out the pieces. Then the pieces go to the sewing room, where *sewing machine operators* assemble them into garments. Usually the machine operators will do just one part of the sewing, like putting on collars or hemming skirts. They use different kinds of machines, depending on the operation they are performing. A job specification for a sewing machine opeator is shown below.[6]

Job Specification: SEWING MACHINE OPERATOR

Overall Duties: Operates single- or multiple-needle sewing machine to join dress parts. Places spool or spools of thread, chosen according to color of material, on spindles. Draws thread through machine guides, tensions, and needle eye. Draws thread through guide and looper eye. Starts, stops, and controls speed of machine with pedal, knee lever, or wheel. Cuts excess material or thread, using scissors. May work on a variety of parts, or on a complete garment, or on specialties such as ruffles and buttons.

Variables: Maintains coupons showing pieces worked on. Sews on labels. May be a "floater" and be placed on special assignments as the need arises.

Overall Selection Factors: Able to distinguish colors. No specific number of years of formal education required. Good eye, hand, and foot coordination. Able to understand and follow instructions. Able to sit on stool throughout shift. Normal (adjusted) vision. Should not be allergic to lint dust. Works close to other workers—must be able to maintain good relationships.

Expensive garments, like coats and suits, are usually completed by *tailors* and *dressmakers* who do the more skilled hand tasks. Many garments, like shirts and jeans, are sewn entirely by machine. *Finish pressers* use various types of steam pressing equipment or hand irons for a final pressing at the end of the sewing operation.

Unskilled workers are needed at all stages of production to perform such tasks as taking the bundles of partly finished garments from one operator to the next, making small repairs, removing lint, and trimming loose threads. Experienced and trained people work in production as *inspectors, supervisors,* and *production managers.* Production workers also include mechanics who maintain the machines.

Many job opportunities exist for tailors and dressmakers in custom production, where they make garments from start to finish. Beginners work as *tailor's aide* or *dressmaker's aide* in custom production as well as in alteration and repair.

[6]SOURCE: *Specifications*, New York State Department of Labor.

Figure 4-6. The presser,
an entry-level job in the
clothing service, presses
clothes after they have
been sewn or altered.
(Paul Conklin,
Monkmeyer)

Alteration and Repair. In large department stores there may be a *fitter* who determines what must be done to a garment, and a *sewer* who actually makes the changes. Or, one person may do both tasks. Tailors and dressmakers may have their own businesses, or work in their homes, doing alterations and repair.

Some alterations workers specialize in the entertainment field. They alter and repair costumes for actors and actresses. They may have job titles like *wardrobe supervisors* and *costumers*.

SALES AND ADVERTISING

In retail stores, *fabric specialists* assist home sewers; *stock clerks* receive new merchandise and prepare it for sale; *personal shoppers* compare the merchandise of their employer with that of the competing merchants; *salespersons* assist customers; and *buyers* decide what clothes or fabrics the store should sell.

When clothing and textile products are mass produced, many salespersons are needed to help distribute them from the factory to retail stores around the country. These include *sales agents* for wholesalers who stock apparel from many factories and sell to retail shops. Another position is *manufacturer's sales representative*; one who is well informed about the products of just one manufacturer.

In advertising you will find *copywriters, commercial artists, photographers*, and *models*. They all work to produce advertisements, the pictures and words that tell the public about items to be sold. They are directed by *advertising managers*, who supervise and help plan advertising campaigns for department stores and other clients.

Another kind of advertiser is the *merchandise displayer*, who arranges products to be sold in store windows and on racks and counters in the store,

Figure 4-7. The merchandise displayer arranges products in store windows and on racks and counters in the store to attract customers. (Kenneth Karp)

all to attract customers and to persuade them to buy. Nearly all these people have helpers and assistants, who can be entry-level workers. Here is the story of the Buffie, who holds an entry-level position as a *fabric specialist*.

Buffie

Buffie is a college student majoring in merchandising. For the past two summers she has found a job in a fabric store. Buffie was hired because she sews well. She studied home economics in high school and was also a 4-H Club member. In 4-H she won prizes for clothing she sewed and modeled.

Buffie lives in a beautiful old country home that has been in her family for more than a century. She has to commute to her job and the hours are long, but she is always attractively groomed and always pleasant and helpful with her customers. She makes suggestions for pattern selection, proper care of fabric, and construction techniques. She also helps people gather together all the supplies, called *notions*, that they need.

Buffie does routine office work—answering the telephone, taking messages, and filing. She orders patterns, handles customer complaints, and records incoming shipments of fabrics, notions, and patterns.

She also spends a lot of time keeping the store neat. She straightens pattern drawers, replaces bolts of fabric, and helps in other ways to keep the store orderly and the merchandise displayed in an appealing way.

CARE OF CLOTHING AND TEXTILES

About one-third of the workers in the clothing care industry are employed in drycleaning plants, and one-third in laundries, including coin-operated laundromats. Most others work for firms renting uniforms, towels, and other linens. Many firms are owner-operated, so that one in seven of the industry's workers are self-employed.

In typical drycleaning and laundry businesses you will find *route drivers* and *counterclerks* who receive soiled items from customers. They separate the items and send them to the cleaners or launderers.

In the plant, *markers, spotters, machine washers,* or *drycleaners* put the items through the appropriate processes. *Finishers* and *sewers* press the garments and make any needed repairs. *Baggers* and *assemblers* prepare the finished items to be returned to the customers by the counterclerks and route drivers.

In institutional laundries, *linen sorters* and *launderers* weigh in, sort, launder, and keep records of all items received. *Pressers* using large machines for linens finish the laundered items and prepare them for return to the users.

In both commercial and institutional laundries, *managers* and *supervisors* are responsible for the supervision and training of workers and the proper operation of the machines and processes.

CAREER LADDERS

In factory production, sewing machine operators can advance to more skilled sewing and higher rates of pay. They can also become supervisors,

Figure 4-8. The designer-dressmaker, a top-level job in the clothing service field, prepares patterns, chooses fabrics, and sews clothing. (Kenneth Karp)

Table 4-6 CAREER LADDER: CLOTHING DESIGN

Levels	Titles	Work Descriptions	Minimum Qualifications
Professional/ managerial	Clothes designer	Creates designs and prepares patterns for new types and styles of men's, women's, and children's wearing apparel. Roughly sketches pattern; writes specifications describing construction, color scheme, and types of fabric to be used. Examines experimental garment on model.	Creative ability, ability to sketch, drape, stage fashion show. Thorough understanding of textiles and clothing construction.
	Designer-dressmaker	Performs all duties of clothes designer and dressmaker. Manages own business.	Same qualifications as for designer. Business ability.
Technician/ assistant	Master tailor	Designs and makes tailored garments such as suits and topcoats, applying principles of design, construction, and styling. May supervise other workers in tailoring shop.	Skill in tailoring, styling, and fitting.
	Copyist	Gathers information on current trends in fashion and sketches examples of competitor's garments. May design original garments, incorporating features of observed garments.	Ability to judge trends, sketch, copy observed garments.
	Dressmaker	Makes women's garments, such as dresses, coats, and suits, according to the customer's specifications and measurements. Discusses with customer type of material, pattern, or style to be used. May draft pattern. May make garment according to picture furnished by customer.	Skill in garment construction, pattern, and style selection. Ability to alter or draft patterns.
Entry	Sewer	Alters ready-to-wear as instructed; sews to fit customer measurements.	Basic sewing skills.

Adapted from *Career Ladders and Lattices in Home Economics and Related Areas: Possibilities for Upgrading Household Employment*, American Home Economics Association, 2010 Massachusetts Avenue, N.W., Washington 20036, pp. 56–57.

Table 4-7 CAREER LADDER: CLOTHING ALTERATION

Levels	Titles	Work Descriptions	Minimum Qualifications
Professional/ managerial	Alteration specialist	Supervises sewing staff. Handles personnel matters. Confers with buyers or department heads on consumer complaints.	Formal education and/or work experience in field.
Assistant	Alteration tailor	Alters clothing to fit individual customers or repairs defective garments.	Highly skilled in tailoring techniques. Experience or formal education.
	Sewer	Makes, alters, repairs garments according to pattern or customer specifications, using sewing machine or sewing by hand.	Highly skilled in fitting and alterations, mending. Business, industry, or home sewing experience.
	Garment fitter	Fits ready-to-wear garments on customer.	Experience or training in fitting.
Entry	Stock clerk	Refolds garments, or places them on hangers. May sew on missing and loose buttons, hooks, and loops. May account for garments tried on by customers.	Must be observant, have initiative. Hand-sewing ability.

Adapted from *Career Ladders and Lattices in Home Economics and Related Areas: Possibilities for Upgrading Household Employment*, American Home Economics Association, 2010 Massachusetts Avenue, N.W., Washington 20036, pp. 54–55.

tailors, or dressmakers. Tailors, dressmakers, and sample makers sometimes advance to designer. They could also move sideways on a career lattice to custom production or to alteration. Similarly, pressers could move from the production of clothing to drycleaning. Table 4-6 shows a career ladder for designers; Table 4-7, a career ladder for alteration specialists.

The merchandising career ladder (Table 4-8) shows that salesworkers can advance to management positions on the basis of talent and experience as well as through formal training. In advertising, copywriters, display workers, models, and photographers can also advance to management jobs. Some establish their own businesses and agencies. Sales and advertising workers can also move sideways on career lattices to similar jobs in other job clusters, such as interior design or foods marketing.

Advancement opportunities for most workers in care of clothing (launderers, hand pressers) are limited. However, some workers may be given special technical or managerial training. Experienced workers can move up to become supervisors and managers. Some start their own businesses.

A job description for an entry-level worker (hand presser[7]) in this cluster is shown below.

Job Description: HAND PRESSER

Overall Duties: Using hand iron, presses parts of garments and finished garments to remove wrinkles, flatten seams, and give shape to article. Lays aside ironed parts for returning to sewing-machine operator and places finished garments on hangers on conveyor line.

Overall Selection Factors: No specific formal education, only elementary reading and counting. Could function following training by demonstration—ability to hear or speak not necessary. Able to stand throughout shift. Able to grasp iron, which is swinging in mid-air from spring, without burning hand. Able to stretch arms at full length and bend elbows. No severe allergy to steam—humidity not excessive. Depending on height, may need to bend slightly from the waist. Free movement of shoulders. Normal (adjusted) vision. Form perception needed to check visual accuracy of pressing. Eye-hand coordination. Willing to accept routine, repetitive tasks.

REQUIREMENTS FOR EMPLOYMENT

Entry into beginning hand- or machine-sewing jobs is relatively easy. Skilled cutting room jobs require considerable experience, but advancement in some factories can be speeded by apprentice or special training programs.

For beginning tailor or dressmaking jobs vocational training is often required. Designers usually need some college training before they can be employed, and they also need experience in mass production—as sample makers, for instance—to help them understand production techniques.

Requirements for entry-level jobs in alteration and repair are much the same as for beginning tailor and dressmaker jobs in factories. In addition, workers must maintain a pleasant appearance and manner.

Salespersons must also have the ability to deal tactfully with customers, a pleasant appearance, and skill in arithmetic. Many employers prefer high school graduates, especially those who have had courses in selling, commercial arithmetic, and home economics.

Most advertising jobs require some creative ability in speaking or writing, and ability to work in a team. Typing skills are also helpful. Management positions in sales and advertising usually require some college.

---

[7]Adapted from *Specifications,* New York State Department of Labor.

Table 4-8 CAREER LADDER: MERCHANDISING

Levels	Titles	Work Descriptions	Minimum Qualifications
Professional/ managerial	Store Manager	Hires, trains, and discharges employees. Plans work schedules and supervises workers. Prepares purchase orders. Sets price policies, approves advertising and display work, checks inventories, handles receipts, compiles reports.	Formal education and/or experience.
	Training director, textiles and clothing	Advises various department buyers on textile fibers, finishes, fabrics, labels, sewing techniques, care.	College degree in home economics.
	Department manager	Supervises activities of workers in one department of store. Recommends purchase or reordering of stock.	Formal education in home economics and business or may learn from work experience and training programs.
	Buyer	Purchases merchandise for resale. Selects from showings of manufacturing representatives. May price items for retail.	Same as for department manager.
	Fashion coordinator	Promotes new fashions and coordinates promotional activities, such as fashion shows.	Same as for department manager.

Many entry-level jobs in the clothing care field require little experience or training, and can be quickly learned on the job. Spotters and drycleaners require some advanced training. Sometimes people who begin in entry-level positions work their way into a top-level position. Turn to page 88 for the story of Charles K., who did just that.

TABLE 4-8 CAREER LADDER: MERCHANDISING (CONTINUED)

Levels	Titles	Work Descriptions	Minimum Qualifications
Assistant	Assistant buyer	Checks quantity and quality of stock received from manufacturer. Authorizes payment of invoices or return of shipment. Approves advertising. Gives markers information, such as price.	Same as for department manager.
	Personal shopper	Selects and purchases merchandise for department store customers according to mail or telephone requests.	Ability to understand people and select merchandise as directed.
	Comparison shopper	Compares prices, quality, and styles of merchandise in competing stores. Visits stores to observe details.	Ability to recognize qualities of merchandise, write reports.
	Salesperson	Displays, describes, and sells to individuals. Emphasizes selling point of articles, such as quality, style, and use. Receives payment from customers. Prepares inventory of stock from stockroom.	Knowledge of merchandise. Understanding of people.
Entry	Stock clerk	Refolds or hangs garments on hangers. May sew on loose and missing buttons, hooks, and loops. May account for garments tried on by customers.	Must be observant, have initiative. Hand-sewing ability.

Adapted from *Career Ladders and Lattices in Home Economics and Related Areas: Possibilities for Upgrading Household Employment*, American Home Economics Association, 2010 Massachusetts Avenue, N.W., Washington 20036, pp. 50–51.

Charles K.

From the time Mr. K. was a little boy he liked to work in his uncle's department store. First he swept floors and ran errands. As he grew older, he became a stock clerk and then a salesman. He earned a degree in journalism at a large university, continuing to work summers and vacations at his uncle's store and advancing to assistant department manager.

After he graduated from college, Mr. K. worked as a reporter on a large southern newspaper and then as an advertising copywriter in New York. His work led him to Paris, where he eventually became a designer himself. He worked several years with a famous Paris "couturier" or couture designer, and later with a great American designer. After a few years he opened his own couture studio.

Today Mr. K. designs original gowns for private clients and also for the designer salons of department stores throughout the United States. But that's not all.

As a visiting consultant for American pattern companies and fabric industries, he conducts home-sewing clinics in major cities, demonstrating couture sewing techniques. He is also a visiting professor, and he teaches in colleges specializing in dress design, giving lectures and demonstrations and assisting students with their original designs.

In his own studio Mr. K. selects the fabrics for use in his designs, supervises his staff of assistant designers, and oversees the workroom where the gowns are sewed. He works with his private clients and with buyers from retail stores which carry his gowns, develops his own publicity and, of course, designs his beautiful gowns.

Mr. K. is a gracious, superbly skilled man who is extremely successful with the students, professors, and other audiences with whom he works. At the top of his profession, he is dedicated to beautiful design and construction.

COMPETENCIES

The knowledge, skills, and attitudes which are basic to home economics and also essential for many workers in the clothing and textiles cluster include the abilities to:

· Apply art elements and principles of design to buying and use of clothing and textile products.
· Analyze cultural, social, and psychological influences of clothing on the individual.
· Identify characteristics of clothing that will provide safety, protection, and comfort as they relate to age, health, occupation, and lifestyle.
· Analyze characteristics of fibers, yarns, fabrics, and finishes as they relate to cost, durability, use, and care.

· Demonstrate ability to select, care for, and use equipment for constructing and maintaining personal and family clothing.
· Consider relevant information when deciding whether or not to make, repair, alter, or recycle clothing.
· Recognize how research and laws have improved standards for clothing and textile products.

The people in this field help improve the appearance and comfort of the interiors of homes and public buildings. Three main areas of work in interior design and furnishings are production, sales and advertising, and care and repair.

INTERIOR DESIGN AND FURNISHINGS

PRODUCTION

The textile products, furniture, and other furnishings used in interior design are produced either in factories by mass production methods, or in shops and private homes by individual craftworkers. Some typical job titles are *sewing machine operators, assemblers, finishers, pressers,* and *inspectors.* Skilled and artistic craftworkers who design such items as lamps and art objects are also part of production.

Furniture finishers who apply the final covering of polish or varnish to wooden or metal parts of furniture and *upholsterers* who construct the padded, fabric-covered parts of furniture are important figures in production. They also restore used furniture and antiques.

Drapery makers construct window coverings. In custom work they also make pillows, slipcovers, and bedspreads. *Floor mechanics* install, replace, and repair tile, linoleum, and carpeting. They are usually employed by flooring contractors or retailers of floor coverings. Here is the story of John, a floor mechanic aide who enjoys his job.

John

John works as a floor mechanic aide in a retail store selling floor coverings, paints, and other building supplies. John helps the floor mechanics lay carpet and floor tile in area homes and businesses. He started working with the company while still in high school and has continued after graduation. He likes his job because he is learning a trade on the job. He hopes to establish his own small business some day, when he has learned to estimate costs on his own and has mastered the fine points of installation.

The work John does now is sometimes heavy. There's a lot of tile and carpet to be moved from the store to the work site. Clients' furniture must be moved, and old tile and carpet removed. But John enjoys driving the pickup truck, helping the workers, and talking with the families in the homes being built or renovated.

Much of his work at the store is of a maintenance type: keeping things clean and in order, unpacking and storing merchandise. But John has a chance to work alongside craftworkers and is learning to become one himself.

SALES AND ADVERTISING

Many sales jobs in interior design and furnishings resemble those in the clothing and textiles cluster. Manufacturers of textiles and furnishings need *sales representatives* to display and sell their products. In retail stores, *salespersons* are needed to help customers. However, a notable difference in this cluster is that the materials and items sold are generally more expensive than those sold in the clothing and textiles cluster. Salespersons need more background knowledge about what they are selling, because customers and retailers expect more help and advice.

For example, appliance salespersons must be able to demonstrate the appliances; furniture salespersons must be able to point out evidences of good construction; floor covering salespersons must be able to discuss the various qualities of different kinds of floor coverings; and fabric salespersons must be able to answer many questions about materials and techniques.

Buyers, stock clerks, and *personal shoppers* in this job cluster perform the same kinds of tasks as those with the same job titles in the clothing and textile cluster.

The same is mostly true of advertising workers. However, display workers in design and furnishings often need special knowledge. For example, a worker arranging a window display of Early American furniture must know what styles, fabrics, colors, and art objects are suitable to go along with that style of furniture.

Interior designers are very important figures in the sales and advertising part of this job cluster. They help customers select furnishings, estimate the costs, and make sketches so that customers can see what the final results will be.

Designers may also arrange for the buying and construction of these furnishings and supervise the work of those who install and arrange them.

Interior designers may own their own businesses or agencies or work for large department or furniture stores. They may be employed by large industrial corporations, restaurant and hotel chains, antique dealers, or furniture and textile manufacturers. Some work for magazines specializing in interior design. Some designers specialize in theatre design or in the design of airplane or ship interiors.

Other specialized salesworkers in the cluster are household equipment specialists. Their job titles may be *sales agents* for gas or electric appliances, *home service representatives,* or *home lighting advisers* or *demonstrators*. They may work in retail stores, or for manufacturers, or for public utilities (for example, gas and electric companies).

CARE AND REPAIR

Care of many household textiles and furnishings is basically the same as for clothing. It is provided by many of the same businesses which launder and dryclean clothing or upholster and finish furniture. Therefore, job titles and requirements for employment are similar to those explained in the clothing and textiles cluster. Carpet cleaning and large-scale maintenance are part of the institution and household maintenance cluster.

CAREER LADDERS

Some career ladders in production are short, because workers who have become skilled upholsterers, drapery makers, furniture finishers, and floor mechanics usually remain in these same occupations. Often they establish their own businesses. However, these occupations have a place on the career ladder for interior design. In factories and institutions, operators and craftworkers are on a career ladder to management and supervisory positions. Salespersons in this job cluster are on career ladders in both merchandising and interior design. A career ladder for positions in interior design is shown in Table 4-9.

REQUIREMENTS FOR EMPLOYMENT

It takes several years of training and experience to become a skilled upholsterer or floor mechanic. Drapery makers and furniture finishers also require experience and specialized training. But the skilled craftworkers sometimes need helpers. So beginning workers are started on the simpler jobs, such as removing old padding and fabric, or thoroughly cleaning the floors and other surfaces to be covered. They can often learn more complex tasks on the job. Vocational or apprentice training is available in many communities.

For most of these jobs considerable skill in using your hands is needed, plus some physical strength to lift heavy furniture and materials. For workers who frequently do their jobs in people's homes and offices, a pleasant and neat appearance and an ability to get along with others are also very important.

Salespersons in interior design and furnishings must also have a pleasant appearance and manner. As we have mentioned, they need a thorough knowledge of the products and materials they are selling. Therefore, salespersons in this cluster have a better chance of employment if they have received some training in basic home economics, such as principles of design, study of materials such as wood and fabrics, and have some knowledge of styles and furnishings. Like all salespersons, they must be able to speak clearly, write legibly, and do routine clerical work. Turn to page 93 for the story of Mary A., who finds her top-level job as an interior designer very satisfying.

Table 4-9 CAREER LADDER: INTERIOR DESIGN

Levels	Titles	Work Descriptions	Minimum Qualifications
Professional/ Managerial	Interior design educator	Teaches in college or university.	Master's degree or doctorate plus experience.
	Interior designer	Plans and designs artistic interiors for homes, ships, commercial, and institutional structures and other establishments based on clients' needs and preferences. Estimates costs. Selects and buys decorative, functional materials and accessories. Directs painting, laying of carpets, etc.	Bachelor's degree plus 2 years experience required for membership in professional associations. Alternative is solid experience in own business.
	Buyer, home furnishings	(See Table 4-8, Career Ladder: Merchandising.)	
Assistant	Junior designer	Assists interior designer.	Some college courses; on-the-job experience.
	Drafter, commercial	All-around drafting, such as laying out location of buildings; planning of arrangements in offices, large rooms, and factories; and drawing charts, forms, and records.	Courses in advanced drafting; work experience.
	Floor mechanic, upholsterer, drapery maker, furniture finisher		
Entry	Apprentice drafter	Assists drafter.	High school or vocational school generally required.
	Floor mechanic aide	Assists floor mechanic.	
	Upholsterer aide	Assists upholsterer.	
	Drapery maker aide	Assists drapery maker.	
	Furniture finisher aide	Assists furniture finisher.	

Adapted from *Career Ladders and Lattices in Home Economics and Related Areas: Possibilities for Upgrading Household Employment,* American Home Economics Association, 2010 Massachusetts Avenue, N.W., Washington 20036, pp. 90–91.

Figure 4-9. The drafter, an assistant-level job, plans the floor layout and furniture arrangement for homes, offices, schools, and so on. (German Information Center)

Mary A.

Mrs. A. is an interior designer with a furniture company in a large city. She graduated from college with a degree in home economics and is a member of the Interior Design Society, a new national organization for people in her profession. Mrs. A. enjoys her job designing interiors for homes, businesses, and even large pleasure boats since her city is located on a waterway. She talks with clients, finds out their tastes and interests, and assembles colors, fabrics, and furniture into a design for their approval. Since "a room is never finished until it is accessorized," lamps, pictures, and art objects are also part of the scheme. A simple room diagram or floor plan, done with a ruler and pencil, helps the client understand the design. Then cost estimates are prepared. Mrs. A. also acts as buyer for her store, selecting furniture, carpets, draperies, and accessories to be used with her designs. She gives overall supervision to the laying of carpet or other floor covering and painting to make sure the correct methods and colors are being used.

Mrs. A. finds her job a real challenge, since she must work within the tastes and money of her clients. She enjoys meeting and working with many people. The job requires many long hours, often 60 a week, and includes evenings, weekends, and holidays, since the interior designer must meet with clients at their convenience. Sometimes clients who like the design plans in her office change their minds when the plans are carried out in their home, boat, or business. But Mrs. A. recognizes that the job has its ups and downs and she has learned to live with this.

COMPETENCIES

Many of the same competencies required in the clothing and textile cluster are necessary in this cluster. In addition, workers in interior design and furnishings must be able to:

· Explain the effect of design on people at home and at work.
· Plan the use of available living space to satisfy the needs of people for comfort, convenience, beauty, health, and safety.
· Demonstrate skill in use of sewing machine and basic construction techniques.
· Describe community services related to living environments.
· Compare ease of care and cost of upkeep when buying furnishings and equipment.
· Appreciate human development, individual and family values, and different lifestyles.
· Show concern for the effect of people on the environment as well as concern for the effect of the environment on people.

Figure 4-10. The interior designer, a top-level job in the interior design field, selects furniture, carpeting, draperies, wallpaper, and accessories for clients' homes and offices. (Kenneth Karp)

In this cluster we find people who are skilled at cleaning and maintaining homes, hotels, businesses, and institutions such as hospitals or schools. Skill in working with people is important, especially where workers not only maintain the institution and manage the home, but also work with families, business employees, medical staff, customers, or school children.

INSTITUTION AND HOUSEHOLD MAINTENANCE

INSTITUTION MAINTENANCE

Top-level jobs in institution maintenance are held by executive *housekeepers* and *institution maintenance managers*. The executive housekeeper may be assisted by *floor housekeepers* who supervise work on one or more floors of the building. Large hotels may employ an *assistant executive housekeeper*.

The responsibilities of the *supervising housekeeper* in an institution are much the same as those of an executive housekeeper in a hotel. A typical job description is shown below.[8]

Job Description: INSTITUTION MAINTENANCE

Supervising Janitor: Supervises the care and cleaning of one or more public buildings and attached grounds; supervises janitors, cleaners, building service aides, and occasionally grounds and maintenance employees. Schedules cleaning services; inspects buildings daily to see that work assigned has been satisfactorily performed; checks operation of lights, heating equipment, plumbing fixtures and sanitary conditions, and the condition of fire protection equipment; distributes cleaning and maintenance supplies; supervises minor maintenance repairs to building and equipment. Reports conditions requiring services of journeymen mechanics; may supervise the care of grounds including mowing lawns and snow removal; may supervise the care of athletic fields; may receive, record, and distribute mail and supplies.

Supervising Housekeeper: Directs cleaning and housekeeping activities: assigns duties to and supervises employees under such titles as cleaner, housekeeper, and sewer; makes regular inspections of the institution; supervises the collection and distribution of laundry and may supervise laundry operations; prepares requisitions for household supplies, linen, and clothing. Requests necessary building maintenance and repairs; inspects premises for good housekeeping and for condition of furniture and fixtures; maintains inventories of supplies and furnishings; maintains time records for housekeeping employees; prepares reports. The work is performed under general administrative supervision from the head of the institution, the business officer, or the institution steward.

---

[8]New York State Department of Civil Service.

Institution maintenance managers supervise workers who maintain hotels, hospitals, office buildings, apartment buildings, factories, retail stores, schools, and colleges. Managers are sometimes called *building and grounds superintendent, building engineer,* or by the older titles, *custodian* and *janitor.* The job description for a supervising janitor suggests the important responsibilities assumed at the higher levels on this career ladder.

As you can see, these jobs call for many skills, and very often institution managers supervise and train large staffs. Entry-level workers on these staffs may be called *building service aides* or *cleaners.* Gary, a student who holds a part-time entry-level position as a building service aide, finds his job very convenient. Here is his story.

Gary

Gary is a building service aide who works part-time in the home economics center in a college. He is a college student himself, majoring in political science. Gary is an Army veteran and he likes his job because it gives him enough extra money to rent a nice apartment near the campus. He works 3 hours a day, 5 days a week. Three of those days he works from 10 a.m. to 1 p.m. But he has to come in at 6:30 a.m. the other days, and it is hard for him to get up early in the morning.

The work is not hard and Gary likes the housekeeper who supervises him. On a typical day Gary dust-mops three of the large classrooms and vacuums the rugs at building entrances and the carpet in the nursery school. Sometimes there is furniture to be moved and cartons to be carried.

Since his is a part-time job, there aren't as many benefits as for housekeepers. Gary does have a coffee break on his early days and half an hour for lunch on the other days. Uniforms are not furnished, but Gary wears his usual shirt and jeans and goes to class from work.

Hotels provide other opportunities for maintenance workers. There are three general types of hotels: commercial, resort, and residential. Many have recreational facilities such as swimming pools, boating marinas, golf courses, and tennis courts—all of which require maintenance. Additionally, craftworkers such as carpenters, electricians, and plumbers may be employed by hotels and other large operations.

Other maintenance workers may have specialized jobs. Examples are sewing machine mechanics in clothing factories, kitchen porters in large restaurants and hotels, and mechanics in bakeries, dry cleaning plants and laundries.

HOUSEHOLD MAINTENANCE

Jobs in household maintenance are often thought of as opportunities for the entry-level worker to gain work experience, earn money for further training, and move on to other occupations. And many people do just that. There are, however, other opportunities in the job cluster. Career ladders have been developed by the American Home Economics Association (AHEA) for the *homemaker/home health aide* and the *household manager*. The homemaker/home health aide is a job title which can be discussed both in this cluster and in the family and community services cluster.

In addition to household manager, homemaker/home health aide, and *housekeeping aide,* other workers in household maintenance are launderers, child care workers, gardeners, chauffeurs, private secretaries, and nurses.

CAREER LADDERS

The housekeeping career ladder starts off with a job as housekeeping aide, then moves up to assistant housekeeper, and then to executive or supervising housekeeper. In institution maintenance, a worker may begin as a cleaner or building services aide, climb to assistant custodian, and then to institution maintenance manager.

Figure 4-11. The building service aide, an entry-level position in the household maintenance cluster, does general cleaning chores. (Kenneth Karp)

Another path of advancement is for skilled and experienced workers in this cluster to develop their own cleaning or maintenance agencies or business. Many smaller businesses do not need and cannot afford full staffs. They make contracts, or formal business arrangements, with an agency or maintenance business to supply them with part-time maintenance and cleaning services. Table 4-10 shows the career ladder for institution maintenance.

REQUIREMENTS FOR EMPLOYMENT

High school graduation is not usually required for private household employment. More important is competence in homemaking skills and the ability to get along well with others.

Management skills are needed, since workers must be able to plan and organize their work. Workers employed by businesses that regularly clean offices and stores or private homes need similar management and human relations skills.

Beginners in institution management need simple arithmetic skills, ability to follow directions, and such personal traits as neatness, courtesy, and tact in dealing with the public. High school shop courses are helpful.

Executive housekeepers and their assistants often take courses in housekeeping procedures and interior decorating. Other workers in the clus-

Table 4-10 CAREER LADDER: INSTITUTION MAINTENANCE

Levels	Titles	Minimum Qualifications
Professional/ Managerial	Chief janitor, Grade 16	One year of continuous service as head janitor.
	Head janitor, Grade 12	One year of continuous service as supervising janitor. Open Competitive: 3 years of experience in care and maintenance of buildings and grounds, including 1 year in supervisory capacity.
Supervisory	Supervising janitor, Grade 9	Two years of experience in the care and maintenance of a large building.
Assistant	Custodian, Grade 7	One year of building maintenance or janitorial experience.
	Janitor, Grade 6	Must be able to speak, read, and write English.
Entry	Cleaner, Grade 4	No examination required

SOURCE: New York State Department of Civil Service.

ter may receive training offered by unions and government agencies. Here is the story of Mr. Harold G., who holds a top-level position as a building and grounds superintendent.

Harold G.

Mr. G. is building and grounds superintendent for seven buildings and their surroundings, which make up an area vocational school campus. He supervises a staff of four men who, assisted by some paid student aides, provide 24-hour-a-day maintenance of the property.

Mr. G. first learned the basic skills needed for the job from his electrician uncle and also from his early experiences as a farmer. Through the years he has taken advantage of short courses in lighting, refrigeration, and other special areas made available both by private corporations and adult education programs in area vocational schools such as the one he maintains.

Mr. G. was custodian of a rural central school for a number of years. During that time, he was a guest speaker in home economics classes dealing with heating, plumbing, wiring, and lighting of homes. A Scout leader and camper, he also taught classes in camping and survival techniques. At that time in his career Mr. G. did some private electrical contracting. Eventually he had to choose between developing his own business and moving into his present job.

Mr. G. loves to work with students and serves occasionally as busdriver and chaperone for students on field trips. One recent day he drove a busload of vocational students to New York City. He often takes handicapped children on bus trips to give them more experience in the outside world.

Mr. G. has a private office now and a secretary, and he is expected to wear business suits on the job. He still really prefers to do the work himself rather than to supervise others. He carefully trains new workers, including bus drivers, and expects the work he supervises to be done well.

In addition to maintenance he is responsible for ordering, delivering, and storing the many supplies used in the school. He likes his job, especially his work with teachers and students, and he gets a lot of satisfaction from training new workers in the many skills he himself possesses.

COMPETENCIES

Successful homemakers and workers in this job cluster can:

· Demonstrate knowledge and skill in care and maintenance of living space, furnishings, and equipment.
· Recognize ways to increase human resources available, such as energy and skills.

· Cite examples of ways to improve storage.

· Describe ways to minimize heat loss in winter and cooling in summer.

· Explain how to select and use equipment to save time and energy.

· Respect the privacy of others.

· Appreciate differences in individual and family values and lifestyles.

· Demonstrate knowledge of sanitary practices and willingness to follow them.

· Appreciate that order and cleanliness add to the sense of well-being of children and families, the ill, aged, customers, and workers in business and industry.

The home health aide must also be able to:

· Demonstrate knowledge of nutrition, food buying, storage, and preparation.

· Demonstrate knowledge and skill in child guidance.

FAMILY AND COMMUNITY SERVICES

Workers in this cluster assist individuals and families with health, money, and housing problems. *Homemaker/home health aides* help individuals and families improve their skills in shopping, cleaning, sewing, budgeting, family health, child care, meal planning and preparation, and use of community services. They may instruct groups of people at neighborhood centers, or they may provide services in people's homes. They may be assigned to a home when there is a family emergency such as sudden illness, or they may assist homemakers who are aged or disabled.

Figure 4-12. The nutrition aide, an entry-level job in the family service cluster, helps families plan and prepare nutritious meals. (Kenneth Karp)

Nutrition aides work with individuals and families who need help with nutrition, food buying, and meal preparation. They are trained and supervised by *extension home economists*. Geri is a nutrition aide who works for the county home economics extension program. Here is her story.

Geri

Geri is a nutrition aide in a federal program designed to help low-income people select and prepare more nutritious meals. Geri knows how important nutrition is to health, especially for the pregnant woman and her developing baby.

Geri works in a rural area where transportation is a problem for many of the people she serves. She receives a mileage allowance from the government and uses her own car to take people shopping for food. She helps them to analyze their eating habits, plan nutritious meals, and get the most for their money.

Geri receives training and supervision from one of two extension home economists in her county. She is also given teaching materials for use with the individuals and families she serves.

Part of Geri's job is to knock on doors to tell people about her program. She also encourages them to receive the help available to them from other agencies. Another part of Geri's job is working with groups of children, teaching them about nutrition and how to prepare simple foods.

Another new job title is the *community worker*, who works with people who are unemployed or in job training programs. The community worker gives advice on training programs available, and on "supportive" services the trainee might need. These include child care and transportation. Trainees are encouraged and assisted during their job training and after they are employed.

The *counselor on alcoholism* helps families and individuals with alcohol-related problems. *Housing management aides* assist both managers and tenants in housing projects.

Other job titles in this cluster are the *family planning health aide,* who gives advice on birth control and other health problems, and the *deputy juvenile probation officer aide,* who provides advice and help to young people in trouble with the law. These aides work with the police, foster homes, schools, and social workers to help the young people solve their various problems. They also work with the families of the young people and community groups.

Social worker aides act as go-betweens for schools, families, and agencies. They make home visits where there are problems, and they work with the school psychologist and staff.

Mental hygiene therapy aides assist in the treatment of people who are emotionally ill. Shown below is a job description for an entry-level therapy aide.[9] *Therapists* are highly skilled professionals who provide activities which help to ease, relieve, or even cure mental and emotional illness. There are also *recreational therapy assistants,* who lead activities like games, sports, and entertainments. *Occupational therapy assistants* help by instructing patients in skills and crafts which can lead to jobs, such as weaving, ceramics, and plant care.

Job Description: MENTAL HYGIENE ASSISTANT THERAPY AIDE

Encourages, guides, and assists patients/residents in the performance of daily living and personal activities, either in an institution or community setting. Assists patients/residents in dressing, grooming, and exercising. Ensures adequate rest periods; participates in play and recreation activities. Works with and assists patients/residents with such daily living activities as changing beds and washing, ironing, and mending clothes. Escorts patients/residents as necessary to treatment and recreational activities either inside or outside the institution. Assists medical personnel in performing routine nursing and physical care tasks. May deliver medication under supervision. Observes and becomes familiar with techniques and principles applied by higher-level treatment personnel.

Family management counselors help people who find themselves over their heads in debt. They help families to analyze their spending habits, show them how to get out and stay out of debt, and give advice on buying. If needed, they work with credit agencies and legal agencies to try to keep people in debt from being taken to court.

CAREER LADDERS

Career ladders have been developed by AHEA which show how home economics competency can help beginners in social work, public housing management, extension, and homemaker services. In some states there are civil service career ladders for jobs in this cluster. They are designed to encourage and assist advancement from entry-level jobs to more responsible and better-paying positions. Examples of career ladders in this cluster are shown in Table 4-11 and 4-12.

[9]New York State Department of Mental Hygiene.

Table 4-11 CAREER LADDER: HOMEMAKER SERVICES

Levels	Titles	Work Descriptions	Minimum Qualifications
Professional/ managerial	Homemaker services administrator	Administers programs, carries out policies, integrates program with related community efforts. Provides temporary emergency help.	Bachelor's degree in public health, experience in administration.
	Homemaker/ home health aide trainer	Organizes and carries out training for aides; provides in-service upgrading for staff.	Bachelor's degree in nursing, home economics, or related field.
Supervisory	Homemaker/ home health aide associate	Performs tasks requiring intermediate skills. May train aides.	Associate degree with background as above.
	Homemaker/ home health aide supervisor	Schedules visits, makes home visits to supervise H/HHA, determines routines, explains programs to H/HHA and clients. Orients new employees to agency.	Training as supervisor plus experience as H/HHA.
Assistant	Homemaker/ home health aide 3	Assumes partial or full responsibility for management of home and care of family, may have specialty area such as child care, nursing, consumer education, family planning, nutrition, diets, elderly, retarded, mental health, clothing, or home management. May assist supervisor.	Advanced on-the-job training and special course work, experience beyond that of aide 2.
	Homemaker/ home health aide 2	Assumes increasing responsibility, gaining skills and experience as above.	Special training in health care, specialized training in selecting personnel, health care on the job or in regular education program.
	Homemaker/ home health aide, 1	Performs as above with less management responsibility.	High school equivalency may be earned, plus on-the-job training.
Entry	Homemaker/ home health aide trainee	Participates in training program. Works in home situations under supervision.	High school diploma helpful; training in home maintenance helpful; ability to read, write, and follow instructions.

Adapted from *Career Ladders and Lattices in Home Economics and Related Areas: Possibilities for Upgrading Household Employment,* American Home Economics Association, 2010 Massachusetts Avenue, N.W., Washington 20036, pp. 82–83.

REQUIREMENTS FOR EMPLOYMENT

Many entry-level jobs in this cluster need little special training beyond basic home economics competencies. Personnel qualities of tact, patience, courtesy, sensitivity to others, and ability to work as a team member are more important. Knowledge of a foreign language will also be helpful, in order to help people who know little or no English.

Most jobs in this cluster will require that you keep records and files, fill out or help others fill out application forms, and make referrals to other agencies. Therefore, you will need some clerical skills. In more advanced positions, you will probably be expected to write reports, prepare budgets, and present educational talks.

Figure 4-13. The extension home economist, a top-level job in the family and community service cluster, may teach cooking and sewing classes for adults. (German Information Center)

Table 4-12 CAREER LADDER: PUBLIC HOUSING

Levels	Titles	Work Descriptions	Minimum Qualifications
Professional/ managerial	Public housing consultant	Gives advice and technical assistance to housing authorities.	Professional home economist, college degree.
	Housing management officer	Develops policy and standards. Studies operations, notes trends and needs, evaluates efficiency of projects, advises managers.	College preparation. Previous experience.
	Manager, housing project	Directs operations of housing projects such as low-rent housing, house trailers and trailer parks for families of military personnel, and rooming facilities for eligible individuals. May supervise other managers in large housing projects having commercial shops, libraries, and recreation facilities.	Previous social agency experience. In-service training on maintenance, supervision, housing regulations, insurance, tenant relations.
Supervisory	Interviewer, housing project	Interviews applicants seeking admission to public housing project to determine eligibility, presents findings to superior.	In-service training or course work, communication skills.
	Assistant manager, housing project	Directs office or maintenance personnel, keeps records, orders supplies. (Can perform duties in above description.)	Experience in assigning and inspecting work of others; ability to keep records.
Assistant	Assistant	Hears complaints, refers them to maintenance or other personnel. Assists with credit records and other data. Schedules and directs moving tenants.	Some clerical skills; ability to communicate with others. Experience.
Entry	Housing management aide	Assist management personnel, performs clerical and monitoring duties.	Ability to read and write and indications of a desire to work and train in this field.

Adapted from *Career Ladders and Lattices in Home Economics and Related Areas: Possibilities for Upgrading Household Employment,* American Home Economics Association, 2010 Massachusetts Avenue, N.W., Washington 20036, pp. 80–81.

For advancement to the assistant level, some formal training may be needed. Advancement to the top, or professional level, in this job cluster usually requires a four-year college degree, and possibly advanced degrees. Here is the story of Ruth, a college graduate who holds a top-level job as an extension home economist.

Ruth

Ruth is an extension home economist for a small, rural county in Appalachia. There are two other home economists in Ruth's office. She is a home economics graduate of a nearby state college, is married, and has a small daughter. Ruth's job is to work mostly with 4-H clubs, but she also teaches clothing classes to adults.

Her job is always interesting. She trains leaders of 4-H groups, often through workshops. The leaders may learn a craft like tie-dye or batik, and then go back to teach the craft to their 4-H clubs. Ruth teaches some classes herself, and recruits experts to come in to teach other classes. She is not expected to know how to do everything herself but *is* expected to work with her leaders and students, finding out their interests and providing the training for these interests. Popular 4-H programs range from fashion shows to horse shows, child care to dog training.

Sometimes Ruth is assisted by college students who are learning to become home economics teachers or extension educators. At all times she is backed up by a large state university, which provides instructional materials for use in adult education and 4-H classes.

The university also provides *inservice* training for extension agents, to keep them informed of new developments in home economics which they, in turn, carry back to their counties. Ruth enjoys this extra training and she expects to start work on her master's degree before long.

COMPETENCIES

Basic home economics competencies which help workers in this job cluster include the abilities to:

· Appreciate varying kinds of family units and lifestyles.
· Compare human development at different stages in the life-cycle: infant, preschooler, school-age child, adolescent, adult, and aged.
· Analyze the impact of different values (community, religious, family, friends) on an individual's behavior.
· Recognize the effects of crisis situations (death, divorce, separation, drug abuse, job loss, illness) on individuals and families, and identify community resources which can provide assistance.

· Describe the services available in the community and how to get them: housing, legal aid, recreation, education, consumer aid, health agencies, day care, job training.

· Demonstrate communication skills and a helping relationship.

· Explain the effect of environmental influences on individuals and families and the effect of individuals and families on the environment.

· Respect the rights of all people to privacy and dignified treatment.

· Appreciate order, cleanliness, nutrition, and management of time, energy, and money, as essential to people's well-being.

· Describe rights and responsibilities of both the tenant and the landlord.

· Recognize ways individuals and groups can work to improve living conditions.

Where can you get more information about jobs? Probably some of you already hold jobs in home economics. You can start by sharing what information you have from your own experiences.

ADDITIONAL INFORMATION

WHERE TO LOOK

Another way to learn about jobs in a cluster is to read job descriptions or the more complete job specifications. Your state employment service will have job specifications to share with you. You can ask major employers in your community about their job descriptions. And, of course, you can read job descriptions in the *Occupational Outlook Handbook* and *D.O.T.* Even classified ads in newspapers may tell you the tasks or responsibilities involved in a particular job.

Most occupational reports in the *Occupational Outlook Handbook* suggest organizations you can write to for added career information. Trade unions, employer's groups, and professional societies in your community will be helpful.

Best of all, you can observe people who are working at jobs of interest to you. You can talk to them and to other workers about their jobs.

FUTURE HOMEMAKERS OF AMERICA/HOME ECONOMICS RELATED OCCUPATIONS

Your local chapter of FHA/HERO might sponsor a career fair, where you can talk with employers and workers in home economics occupations. Or your club might cooperate with other vocational education student organizations like Future Farmers of America (FFA), Vocational Industrial Clubs of America (VICA), and Distributive Education Clubs of America (DECA) to include other occupations also.

Figure 4-14 Sometimes the local chapter of FHA/HERO sponsors a career fair, where students can talk with employers and workers in home economics occupations. (Future Homemakers of America)

Career education focuses on two things: knowledge of and preparation for the world of work *and* self-understanding and self-development. FHA and HERO chapters have similar goals: to strengthen personal growth, family life, vocational preparation, and community development.

The organization gives you a chance for extra experiences in exploring jobs in your community. It provides opportunities to develop your leadership and followership abilities, and help plan and carry out action programs of interest to you and other youth.

In Part I of this book we have discussed the changing world of work and lifestyles. We have looked at you and at some jobs in home economics. Next we'll learn how to go about getting the job of your choice.

CHAPTER SUMMARY

1. There are many *entry-level job titles* to choose from in home economics occupations, and a wide variety of places to work. Some job titles are very old, some are new, and others are being developed every day.

2. There are *career ladders* in all the clusters, not always "official" and built-in, but clear steps to advancement to higher-level positions. *On-the-job training* is common in home economics job clusters. Top-level jobs usually require college education, but some can be reached after on-the-job experience.

3. There are jobs in *production, sales, and care* in several job clusters. Some jobs are in mass production (clothing, laundry, fast-food restaurants). Others are of the most individual type, caring for a child or custom design and tailoring.

4. There are quiet jobs and jobs with a lot of competition. Jobs often carry a lot of *responsibility*, and may have rush periods.

5. *Requirements for employment* usually stress: ability to get along with others, good health, communication and management skills, reliability, respect for the rights of others to their own ideas and lifestyles, and ability to work as a member of a team. There are jobs for people with handicaps.

6. Home economics competencies are needed in all seven occupations, from the unpaid occupation of homemaking through the last of six job clusters. Some workers are generalists, using many home economics competencies. Others are specialists, needing just a few.

7. Readers interested in *additional information* can get it from reading job descriptions and specifications, occupational reports, and classified ads. You can talk to people employed in jobs of interest. You can visit workers on the job.

8. Your *HERO chapter* will provide other chances to learn about jobs, and opportunities for self-development, too. Employers, trade unions, and professional societies are other sources of information about jobs.

• FOLLOW-UP PROJECTS

1. Many of you have already worked. Are you on a career ladder now? What step are you on? Have you already moved sideways on a career lattice? What is the next step?

2. Working in small groups, prepare job specifications for jobs members hold *now* or have held in the past. Consider:
   a. Job description (tasks performed on the job)
   b. Education required
   c. Experience needed or desired
   d. Physical requirements
   e. Worker traits (interests and abilities)
   f. Working conditions, hours, wages, and opportunities for advancement

3. As a class, observe workers on the job in the school or community.

4. Divide the class into groups who are interested in the same job cluster. Prepare a list of questions to be answered about the chosen occupations, such as:
   a. What are the requirements for employment?
   b. What are working conditions in your community for the jobs chosen? Pay scale? Hours?
   c. What are the chances for advancement?

    d. If advanced training is needed, is it available in your community?

    e. What is the job outlook in your community for occupations in this cluster?

    Discuss and reach an agreement on strategies to be used to find answers to these questions. Such strategies may include visiting businesses, inviting guest speakers, and talking to workers.

5. When all this information has been compiled, debate the advantages and disadvantages of jobs in each cluster.

6. Rate jobs discussed as to their desirability for you. Which is best? Second best? Last?

7. Rate yourself on the basic home economics competencies which will help you get a job and be successful in a cluster of your choice. Talk over with your teacher ways to improve or enhance your basic skills in order to become more employable in entry-level jobs in home economics.

8. Have the class set up a Career Fair, a showcase, or another exhibit to share career information with others in the school.

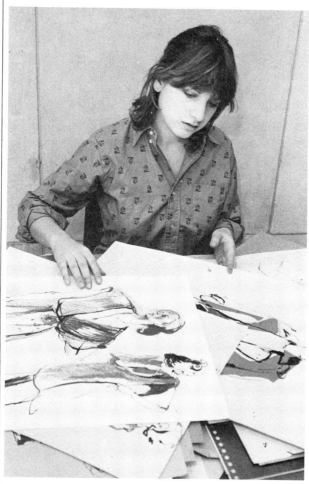

THE JOB SEARCH

You have looked at occupations and have selected a job cluster which meets your interests. Now you are ready to look for a job.

There are certain steps to take to prepare for your job search. They include knowing where to look and how to apply for a job as well as what to expect on your job interview. Part of your job know-how concerns an awareness of the laws designed to protect the worker and all the people ready to help and advise you.

Another part of your job search is deciding whether to accept a job which is offered you. Working conditions, hours, personal safety, pay, and fringe benefits are all part of this important decision.

In Part Two you will learn about the steps to take to find a job and how to decide which job offer is best for you.

5 | LOOKING FOR A JOB

After studying Chapter 5 you should be able to:

1. Explain where to look for job openings in home economics occupations.
2. Describe procedures applicants may expect at public and private employment agencies.
3. Contrast the advantages and disadvantages of using private or public employment agencies.
4. Fill out an application card for an employment agency.
5. List advantages civil service jobs have to offer the beginning worker.
6. Keep informed about the national economy and local job market.

When students are asked whether they have jobs, they often say "I want a job, but I don't know where to start." Knowing *where* to look for jobs is a very important job skill. Where to start is what this chapter is all about.

There are a number of places to look for a job. Sometimes just one look does the trick, and you find the job of your choice. More often, people look in several places before finding a job.

WHERE TO LOOK

SCHOOL PLACEMENT SERVICES

Most schools have someone who coordinates the working experience of their students. Schools may also have a placement office, which could be in a coordinator's office or guidance office. Where is it in your school? Find out, because this is where you start.

You will find information there about the kinds of jobs available in your community, about employers who regularly hire workers in entry-level jobs, and about how to apply. The coordinator may supervise you on the job, and help you understand your new job and adjust to it. Or your teacher may supervise your work experience.

Your guidance office will assist you with counseling and aptitude testing. Even when you are no longer in school, your school guidance office can still help you directly with counseling and testing, and it can refer you to others who can help you.

Supervised work experience while you are still in school is valuable. Part-time jobs can lead to full-time employment when your schooling is finished. They let you sample an occupation to see what it is like. They help you establish a work record for dependability, honesty, cooperation, and willingness to learn.

Counselors, coordinators, or instructors in your school have a keen interest in helping you get a job. Let them know you are looking for work and the kinds of jobs you would like.

FAMILY, FRIENDS, AND NEIGHBORS

When you are looking for work, let your friends and family know about it. Talk with them about their jobs, about working conditions, and about possible openings for you. Ask your neighbors about entry-level jobs where they work and how to apply.

WALK-IN VISITS TO EMPLOYERS

You probably know the names and addresses of some of the major employers in your community. It is often a good idea to go to their *personnel offices* and apply for a job. In large operations personnel offices specialize in hiring workers. They also look after your interests once you are hired, helping you to make claims for medical insurance and other benefits.

If you don't know all the major employers, your local Chamber of Commerce can supply you with the names and addresses of some of them. There may be industrial directories in your placement offices, and the yellow pages of your telephone directory can give you the names and addresses of others.

In small businesses you apply directly to the manager. You can still "walk in," but avoid rush hours. Choose a time when the manager is likely to be free to talk with you, or make an appointment to return.

Even if the employers cannot offer you a job right away, your application will tell them that you are available for work, and they may consider you in the future.

CLASSIFIED ADS

Advertisements for workers in the "Help Wanted" section of newspapers are a good source of information about entry-level jobs. Trade magazines may also have want ads for workers.

By studying lists of classified advertisements in your newspapers, you can learn the names of businesses and industries in your area and get an idea of the kinds and number of openings.

When you see a job described that you think you would be qualified for, apply at once. The employers have advertised because they need workers right now, and if you delay the jobs might very well already be taken.

Notice that many want ads list phone numbers to call. They may give hours to call and the person to ask for. Others request that you apply in person, or write to a post office box number.

EMPLOYMENT AGENCIES

Employment agencies are offices where employers who need workers can place *job orders* and where workers can go to look for jobs. Job orders are specifications which describe the jobs, indicate the skills required, wages, hours, and working conditions. An example of a job order is shown below.

> **Food Service Worker:**
>
> Beginning position, no experience necessary but good training required, must be able to use heavy-duty kitchen blenders, ovens, dishwashing equipment. Hours 6:00 am to 2:00 pm. Salary $130–150, depending on qualifications. Benefits excellent. Equal Opportunity Employer.

Workers who register with the employment agency may be sent to apply immediately if a job order is alrcady on file for someone with their skills. If no such job orders are on hand, workers may fill out application cards and leave them with the agency for future reference.

There are two main kinds of employment agencies: public agencies supported by taxes, whose services are free to workers and employers using them; and private agencies, which charge fees, either to the workers or to employers for the service they provide. Let's take a look at both kinds.

Public Agencies. Your state employment office is part of a network of agencies which makes up the U.S. Employment Service. Through the use of computers the agencies compile *job banks*. These are lists of jobs and workers for a large geographical area, so that both workers and employers can find out what work is available and who is available to do it. Some of the services these agencies offer are:

· Screening and selecting workers for suitable jobs
· Locating and recruiting skilled workers not available locally
· Helping employers develop job specifications
· Aptitude testing, to identify workers best suited for jobs and to help people discover their own abilities
· Counseling workers with problems interfere with the job performance

To visit your local employment agency, look for the address and phone number in your telephone directory under your state's Department of Labor. Before visiting you should phone to make an appointment or find out office hours. If you "drop in" you may have to wait to see an interviewer. You can make good use of the time by reading helpful pamphlets the agency has for you on subjects like how to get and hold a job, and by studying bulletin boards with notices of jobs that may interest you.

At the agency an interviewer will help you fill out an application card. You will need several kinds of information. One kind is your work history, that is, where you have worked (names and addresses of employers), the kind of work you did (job titles are important; the *D.O.T.* can help you with this if you do not know them), how long you worked (the exact dates), and why your employment ended.

You will need your social security number. You will be asked to list any special education or training you have had, and whether you belong to a union.

Other information needed includes whether or not you are a veteran, a member of a minority group, economically disadvantaged, or need special help with child care. You will be asked about any handicaps, schooling completed, and about your willingness or ability to move to another area to accept employment. All this information helps the employer determine if you are eligible for special programs, or need special help or training.

If you wish counseling about your occupational choice you will be referred to an expert in this line. Vocational counselors can help you find the right kinds of jobs for you or guide you toward further training if necessary. You may be tested in order to discover skills or abilities you may not know you have or to see if you can qualify for a particular job.

Test battery is a term used to indicate a group of tests. Table 5-1 shows the kinds of separate tests that make up a battery.

Table 5-1 KINDS OF APTITUDE TESTS

Test	Skill
Intelligence	General learning ability
Verbal	Ability to understand language and to present information and ideas accurately
Numerical	Ability to perform arithmetic operations
Spatial	Ability to understand space relationships
Form perception	Ability to see differences in shapes and lines
Clerical	Ability to see detail, to observe differences in words and numbers
Motor coordination	Ability to coordinate eyes and hands or fingers
Manual dexterity	Ability to use hands easily
Eye, hand, and foot coordination	Ability to move hand and foot together
Color	Ability to recognize similarities or differences in color

SOURCE: *Dictionary of Occupational Titles,* U.S. Department of Labor, 1977.

One set of tests is called the General Aptitude Test Battery. You may hear a counselor refer to these as the GATB. They are used to determine your potential for acquiring skills, with training, in occupational *groups.* The Specific Aptitude Test Battery (SATB) is given to determine ability for acquiring skills needed for a *specific* occupation.

You may be given "proficiency" tests, which measure skill or knowledge you have already acquired in an occupation, probably through work experience on the job. New tests, such as "work samples," are being developed to assess skills which cannot be shown by pen and paper tests. Sewing skills are an example. What kind of "work sample" do you think you might use to demonstrate your sewing skill? Your skill in quantity food preparation? Still other tests are especially designed for people who have special aptitudes but who cannot read or write well enough to show those skills in a written test.

Taking an aptitude test is something of an adventure. You're going to learn what *you* are good at doing.

If a job order for which you qualify is on hand, the interviewer will discuss the job specifications with you and will help you fill out the employer's application form. You will be given a *notice of referral* card, which will contain the employer's address, your name and social security number, and the date and time of your job interview. It will also include the job title you are applying for, and whether or not you were selected by tests as a qualified applicant for the job.

Figure 5-1. The notice of referral card is given to the employer when you go for the job interview.

NOTICE OF REFERRAL
FROM PENNSYLVANIA STATE EMPLOYMENT SERVICE

To *Henry O'Donnell*

Address *Cup o' Coffee Shop, 110 Market Street, Springfield*

Name *Anna Estes*   S.S. Acct. No. *000-00-0000*

is reporting to you *March 11*   *9 AM*   to apply for employ-
             DATE   TIME

ment as *Busser*   Test Selected ☐

ESARS Job Order Number _____

Occ. Code _____ Representative *Janet Pelham*

For Employer's Use Please note your decision and return this card as soon as possible.

Date applicant reported for interview _____

Hired ☐   Date applicant started work _____

Reason not Hired: Not Suitable ☐   Job Filled ☐   Refused Job ☐

                      Failed to Report on Job ☐   Will Hire Later ☐

Date _____ Employer's Signature _____

COMMONWEALTH OF PENNSYLVANIA
ES-508 REV 1-73   DEPARTMENT OF LABOR AND INDUSTRY   BUREAU OF EMPLOYMENT SECURITY

Give the card to the employer when you go for the job interview. After the interview the employer will return the card to the agency after marking down whether or not you were hired, and if not, why not. (You, of course, do not have to take the job unless you want to.)

Keeping in touch with the agency is important once your application is on file. You are asked to contact the office at once when you receive a mail or telephone message. When employers have job openings, they want to fill them right away. Find out how often the office wants you to contact them, even when you have not received messages about job openings. If the agency does not hear from you regularly it will assume you have a job or have moved, and are no longer interested in its services.

Private Agencies. Private employment agencies operate much as public agencies do, except that they are not supported by tax money. Private agencies earn their money by providing services to workers and employers, whose payment for these services is called a *fee*. The amount of the fee is based on the salary or wages the worker is paid by the employer.

Public employment services are required by law to serve all people, but private agencies are not. Since they need to make money to stay in business, private agencies must keep both employers and workers pleased with their services. Therefore, they only accept workers whom they feel are acceptable to employers. That is, if you do not give them solid evidence of being employable, they will not encourage you to use their services.

Since the amount of fee an agency can collect depends on the salary or wages of the jobs offered, entry-level workers are often not preferred by private agencies. The fees paid would be too small to make such business profitable for them. However, some private agencies make a specialty of household employment, and are happy to provide services to entry-level workers.

Perhaps you would like to work over the summer for a family that vacations on the ocean or in the mountains. You may want to consult a private agency. Or things are difficult at home, and you would like a live-in position. Agencies specializing in household employment also place workers who do not wish to live in.

Fees may be paid by employers. Some agree to pay the fees of any workers they hire. This information must always be told to the workers, that is, that a position is "fee-paid."

Where the workers must pay the fees, the agency will show you a scale of fees so that you know exactly what you will owe them in the event you are hired for any of their jobs. You will be required to sign a contract in which you agree to pay the fee according to a schedule. Take time to read the contract and be certain that you understand it before you sign. A reliable agency will not pressure you to sign until you have had time to read the fine print. If in doubt, check with your instructor or counselor, your legal aid society, or your family lawyer, just as you would before signing any other contract. Also be sure to get a copy of the signed contract.

As in any business or industry, some private agencies will be very reliable and effective, while others will charge too much or misrepresent jobs. Because of this, private employment agencies are regulated by state and city laws regarding their advertising, their fees, and their services. You can find out about the regulations from the closest office of the Department of Labor or your Consumer Protection agency. Your local Chamber of Commerce can tell you which agencies enjoy a good reputation. In many states, private employment agencies must be licensed.

When visiting a private agency you can expect the same kind of procedures as at a public agency. You will fill out an application card. Interviewers and counselors will talk with you about your qualifications and advise you about the job market—who is hiring at the moment, the starting salary you can expect, and general requirements of the job.

Some offices are part of nationwide networks which offer many job openings. Local offices have up-to-the-minute computer printouts of job openings for a large area of the United States.

Why do people use private employment agencies when there are free public services available? Maybe they do not know about their public employment service. Maybe the state employment service has been unable to place them in a job. Maybe the job they want is fee-paid, so that the services of the private agency are free to the worker. Maybe the private agency has more jobs and more desirable job openings, so that paying the fee is worth it to the worker.

Private agencies can be useful to you at the stage in your career when you are experienced or have higher education. The service is confidential. Perhaps you would like to change jobs but do not want your present employer to know you are looking. Maybe you are just curious about the job market. You can check out the job situation, take a new job, or continue in the one you have in a happier frame of mind.

CIVIL SERVICE OFFICES

Another important place to look for jobs is in civil service. One in every five people employed in the United States works for the federal, state, or local government, many of them in home economics occupations.

Civil service jobs usually offer:

· Fringe benefits, such as retirement plans, sick leave, and paid vacations
· A fixed salary schedule that gives you increased pay after certain periods of time and good performance on the job
· Built-in career ladders and assistance with advanced training for higher-level positions
· Programs for people with special needs

Under the civil service *merit system,* people get jobs on the basis of their ability to do the work. The positions are called *competitive* because sometimes workers compete for them on the basis of written tests. All qualified candidates are considered for the jobs regardless of race, religion, color, national origin, sex, politics, age, or handicaps.

Federal Civil Service. The federal government has thousands of different kinds of jobs for which it employs people. Only 11 per cent of the federal jobs are in Washington, D.C. Other federal workers are scattered throughout this country and its territories, and some are in foreign countries. The U.S. Civil Service Commission, which has charge of the hiring of the federal government workers, has offices throughout the United States. There is at least one in every state.

These offices announce and conduct examinations. They check your work experience, training, and aptitudes. They send the names of people who meet the requirements to federal agencies that are seeking new workers. Each office also provides, through its Federal Job Information Center (FJIC) a free, one-stop, complete information service about job opportunities in its local area, as well as in other locations. To find your closest office, look in the phone book under U.S. Civil Service Commission. Every FJIC has a toll-free number for calls made from any place within the state.

Announcements are printed when job openings exist. They tell you what experience or education is needed, whether a written test is required, where the job is located, and the pay. You can call the toll-free number to request announcements in occupations of interest to you, along with application forms and pamphlets describing employment programs for people with special needs.

Check the announcements carefully to make sure you are qualified and willing to work in the area where the job is. At first, you may only fill out a small card, but sooner or later you will be asked to complete a 2- or 4- page application.

Counselors remind you to answer every question on the application. Otherwise, the office will have to write you for the missing information, which will take time and delay action. They advise you to put down all your training and experience, since written tests are not required for many positions, and people are hired on the basis of training, experience, and volunteer work in the community.

If a test is required, the announcement will tell you when and where you can take it. You can usually take a test more than once, in order to improve your score.

In regard to civil service tests, the government warns:

> It is not necessary to prepare for the test by taking a "Civil Service" course. No school can guarantee that you will be found qualified or that you will be offered a job.[1]

[1]*Working for the USA*, U.S. Civil Service Commission, 1973, p. 12.

Figure 5-2. Fill out job applications fully; you can't get a job unless the employer knows what you can do.

If you meet the requirements in the announcement your name is put on a list of *eligibles*. Your chances of getting a job will depend on how high you stand on the list and how fast agencies are filling jobs from the list.

Some jobs are *temporary* or *term* appointments. Others are career appointments, once the worker demonstrates acceptable performance on the job. During a trial period you will be given a chance to learn and adjust to the work. You will also be rated by your supervisor on such things as accuracy, neatness, skill and knowledge, amount of work produced, cooperation, initiative, attendance, dependability, and work habits.

Before you are hired, or immediately after, a check is made to determine your "reliability, trustworthiness, good conduct, character, and loyalty to the United States." You may have to have a security clearance. In any case, you will be asked to swear that you will support and defend the Constitution. (The oath is much like the one the President takes.)

In addition to the FJIC you can also get information about federal civil service jobs from post offices, state employment service offices, national and state headquarters of veteran's organizations, placement offices at schools and colleges, and by going directly to personnel offices in government agencies near you. You can also write for information to the U.S. Civil Service Commission, Washington, D.C. 20415.

State Civil Service. Jobs in state civil service (and possibly in your county and city, too) are very much like those in federal civil service. You can expect *fringe benefits* (health and life insurance, paid vacation, sick leave, pension), competitive examinations, and job opportunities in many occupations, including home economics. State institutions and programs need food service workers, people who can work in maintenance jobs, paraprofessionals in child care and family and community services, launderers, and others.

The best place to find out about opportunities in state civil service is from your state employment office, which can advise you about examinations that have been scheduled and help you with application forms. Or you can go to the personnel office of any state institution near you, such as schools and universities, departments of health and mental hygiene, social service agencies, and so on.

Once you've found out what the opportunities are, you proceed as usual. You will fill out application forms, be interviewed in some cases, possibly take some tests, follow up any leads immediately, and keep in contact with the employers or personnel offices to make sure they will consider you for future job openings.

NONPROFIT ORGANIZATIONS

Sometimes nonprofit organizations such as a YWCA or YMCA serve as informal employment agencies. Although not a regular agency, a ''Y'' may have job orders from employers. Staff members at the ''Y'' counsel young people regarding occupational choice and other matters. You can write, phone, or walk in for assistance of this type.

UNION OFFICES

Many workers belong to a union, or trade or professional association. Whatever its name, the organization protects and promotes the welfare of its workers, and also helps them get jobs. You can find out if there is a trade union or association for the occupations you have in mind by asking workers already employed about their union. Or you can look up the occupation in the *Occupational Outlook Handbook,* to find names of its associations or unions.

If there is a local union office, employees there can give you information about the union and the advantages of membership. They can also give experienced advice on how you can enter the occupation they represent. Because they are in contact with employers in that occupation, they may have knowledge of new openings or training programs for which you might qualify.

Deciding whether or not to join a union is a big choice to make. You have to pay dues to belong to a union. In some businesses, management and union members are often at odds. Get all the facts you can, weigh the advantages and disadvantages, and then decide.

When times are "good," that is, when the national economy is healthy, local businesses and industries are probably hiring more people. People buy more clothing, furniture, and services. They eat meals in restaurants. There are more jobs for salespersons, operators, and craftworkers, and for the large numbers of people employed in the service occupational group.

When times are "bad," when a recession hits, jobs are harder to find. Vocational counselors point out that there *are* jobs, but workers have to know how to look and where to look. They may need to relocate or take a different job from the one they had in mind.

In times of recession the greatest danger you will face is discouragement and loss of confidence in yourself. Being turned down for a job is a blow to your self-esteem.

A weapon against discouragement is to be informed regarding the national employment picture. When you know that things are "tough all over," you are not so quick to blame yourself for your lack of success. Don't give up. Make use of the counseling, training, and placement help available to you from many people. Be informed about the national economy and the local job market. You can find up-to-date information about the employment picture in U.S. Department of Labor publications: the *Monthly Labor Review, Manpower,* and *Occupational Outlook Quarterly.* These may suggest occupations you had not known about and which have expanding job opportunities. The publications should be available in your school guidance office and in your public library.

Figure 5-3. Stay informed about the national economy so you know how the local job market is affected. (Kenneth Karp)

**CHAPTER
SUMMARY**

1. Knowing where to look for jobs is an important *job skill*. A good place to begin is with your *school placement service*. *Family, friends,* and *neighbors* may be able to tell you about job openings. *Walk-in visits* to employers and *classified ads* in newspapers are other sources of information about job openings.

2. *Employment agencies* are offices where workers look for jobs and where employers who need workers place *job orders*. Workers who register with an employment agency may be sent to apply for a job immediately if a job order is already on file for someone with their skills. If no such job orders are on hand, workers fill out *application cards* and leave them with the agency.

3. There are two main kinds of employment agencies: *public agencies* whose services are free and *private agencies* which charge fees. Private agencies do not accept all people looking for a job, but public agencies are required to do so.

4. Your *state employment service* is a public agency. It is part of a network of offices which share information about jobs, called *job banks*. You can request *counseling* at your state employment service.

5. You may be *tested*, to find out your aptitudes and kinds of jobs you can expect to do well.

6. When a job order is on hand for which you qualify you will be given a *notice of referral card* with the employer's name and address, your name and social security number, and the date and time of your *job interview*.

7. Another place to look for jobs is in *civil service,* which is employment by the federal, state, or local government. Civil service jobs usually offer *fringe benefits,* a *salary schedule* that gives you increased pay after certain periods of time, and built-in *career ladders*. There may be programs for people with *special needs*. When job openings exist *announcements* are posted in public buildings. You can also get announcements from your *Federal Job Information Center (FJIC)*.

8. Other places to check for job openings are *union offices* and *nonprofit organizations* like the YMCA, which help young people get jobs.

9. The *national economy* affects the local job market; that is, when times are "good," local businesses and agencies are probably hiring more people. When there is a recession, jobs are harder to find. By *keeping informed* you can avoid becoming discouraged, and you will know when you must try harder in order to get a job.

● **FOLLOW-UP PROJECTS**

1. Visit your state employment service, or invite a counselor to class. Ask about job banks, special programs for youth, and other services. Also ask about aptitude tests used at the agency. Practice taking aptitude tests.

2. If your school has a cooperative work/study program, invite the coordinator to class to explain the program, employment opportunities, and how students are supervised.

3. Make a list of abbreviations commonly used in newspaper want ads. Look up their meanings in a dictionary, under the section called "Abbreviations."

4. Get copies of application cards used to register at the state employment agency and practice filling them in. Check your Self-Analysis sheet, to be sure you have ready the information you need.

5. Ask your local consumer protection agency for information about private employment services. Ask about regulation of the agencies, legal fee schedules, and guidelines to follow when using a private agency. Look in the yellow pages of your telephone book under "Employment Agencies" for the names, addresses, and phone numbers of private employment agencies in your area.

6. Phone the toll-free number for your nearest FJIC for a list of announcements about job openings. Ask about services offered by the center, such as programs for people with special needs, testing, and placement.

7. Check with your local school placement office, state employment service, or post office for announcements of city and state civil service jobs. Are there any jobs for entry-level workers in home economics? What are the requirements for employment?

8. Add to your job folder the names, addresses, and phone numbers of major employers in your area, the state employment service, and FJIC.

9. Ask friends and neighbors about job openings for entry-level workers in the places where they work. Compare findings. Is this a good source of job leads for you?

10. Collect magazine and newspaper articles on the state of the national economy. Form a committee to read articles in *Monthly Labor Review* and other publications of the Department of Labor. Report to the class. Discuss how nationwide business conditions affect the local job market.

11. In small groups, visit:
    a. Major employers, such as a large business or institution
    b. Union offices
    c. Nonprofit organizations such as YMCA/YWCA

    What kinds of jobs in home economics are available?
    What advice do they have to offer the beginning worker?

6 | LAWS ABOUT WORK AND WORKERS

After studying Chapter 6 you should be able to:

1. List kinds of responsibilities the Department of Labor and its units have for workers.
2. Explain laws governing working conditions, wages, affirmative action, and employment of minors for specific jobs held by or of interest to you.
3. Demonstrate ability to obtain working papers and a social security number and ability to fill in proper income tax withholding form.
4. Explain basic purpose of the Social Security Act, list persons protected by the program, and explain how to become insured.
5. Willingly follow work laws and regulations set up for your protection.

There are many laws about work and workers. There are laws regulating who can work, and how, when, and where they can do what. All the laws have one major purpose: to protect the safety and rights of the worker.

There are also laws about worker benefits and worker responsibilities. These include social security and income tax.

As a result, there is a certain amount of paperwork to be done before you can start a job. Getting your papers in order is another vital job skill.

UNITED STATES DEPARTMENT OF LABOR

The United States Department of Labor (USDOL), created in 1913, is a federal agency which looks after the interests of workers. It is headed by the Secretary of Labor, who is a member of the President's Cabinet and his chief advisor on matters concerning workers.

The following list of the main departments—called *administrations*—of the Department of Labor gives a good overall view of its activities on behalf of workers. In Chapter 1 we mentioned the Bureau of Labor Statistics of the USDOL. Four other main units are:

· Occupational Safety and Health Administration: responsible for preventing illness and injury in the workplace, and for insuring that both employers and workers obey health and safety regulations.
· Labor-Management Services Administration: to strengthen free collective

bargaining by employers and workers over wages and working conditions; to protect veterans' reemployment rights; to supervise pension (retirement) plans.

· Employment Standards Administration: concerned with enforcing laws which set minimum wage, overtime pay, and child labor standards; with compensations (payment) for job-related injury, disease, and death; and responsible for the welfare of women workers.

· Manpower Administration: helps people out of work or seeking new work to receive training, placement, or unemployment compensation. The U.S. Employment Service, discussed in Chapter 5, is a unit in this administration.

The important thing to remember is that the Department of Labor looks after the safety and rights of workers. If you have questions regarding these rights you can find the address of the nearest office of the appropriate administration by contacting your State Employment Service or looking in your phone book under *United States Government—Department of Labor*. Let us look in general terms at the responsibilities of the USDOL and its units which will especially affect you as you plan your life.

YOUTH AND THE LAW

Although children work in many parts of the world today, use of child labor in America is restricted, to protect youth from danger and loss of educational opportunities. Federal laws set standards for the employment of minors, and so do the laws of every state. Whenever federal and state child labor laws differ, the one which sets the higher standard must be observed.

Federal child labor laws cover employment in interstate and foreign commerce and in the production of goods for such commerce. Such employment is defined as work in the telephone, telegraph, radio, television, importing, exporting, and transportation industries; in wholesaling, manufacturing, or occupations essential to the production of such goods. Included also are work in hotels, motels, restaurants, hospitals, institutions for the care of the aged, laundries and drycleaning establishments, other retail and service establishments, and schools. Thus, you see that home economics occupations are subject to these laws.

Working Papers. Most young workers must have working papers, called age or employment certificates or working permits. An employment certificate is granted after you submit proof of age and a statement from the employer describing the work you are to do and the hours you will work. Over half the states also require a statement from a physician showing physical fitness to do the intended work.

Age certificates have two purposes: to protect young people from harmful employment and to protect employers from hiring young workers illegally, for which they can be heavily fined.

Working papers are needed by young workers for most jobs. There may be exceptions, such as for golf caddies and babysitters. Your school counselor or principal can advise you on whether or not you need working papers, and on how to get them.

Minimum Age. The basic minimum age for employment in most jobs is 16 years. Younger workers may be employed in a few occupations, but only after school hours or during vacations unless the workers are enrolled in special work training programs. There are special rules for youth employed in agriculture.

Workers 14-15 years old are allowed, under federal law, to work in retail, food service and gasoline service establishments at such occupations as:

· Office and sales work
· Cashiering and comparative shopping
· Tagging and shelving
· Bagging and carrying out customers' orders
· Kitchen work
· Car washing
· Dispensing gas and oil

Figure 6-1. The basic minimum age for employment in most jobs is 16 years. However, 14- and 15-year-olds are allowed to hold certain jobs at food service establishments. (McDonald's)

In these same establishments 14- and 15-year-old workers may *not*:

· Operate or clean power-driven food slicers, grinders, or automatic bakery mixers
· Cook, except at snack bars and cafeteria counters
· Bake
· Work in freezers or boiler rooms, on scaffolds or ladders, or near pits and racks in service stations

They may not be employed in manufacturing, mining, construction, or any other hazardous occupations.

Workers 14 to 15 years old may not be employed before 7 a.m. or after 7 p.m. except during the summer. They may work only 3 hours a day on school days and 18 hours a week in school weeks. When school is not in session they may work up to 8 hours a day and 40 hours a week.

Workers 16 to 18 years old may do factory work, but may not work in hazardous occupations such as mining, logging, wrecking and demolition, meat packing, roofing, excavating, or in occupations where they work with explosives, radioactive substances, or certain power-driven machines. There are exceptions for apprentices and student-learners who have had safety training and are under the close supervision of qualified persons.

Getting Paid. Workers are entitled to receive promptly and regularly the wages they have earned. Most states have laws dealing with payment of wages, although few of them protect all workers.

If workers are not paid the wages due them, many state departments of labor offer help in collecting them. Your state employment office is part of the Department of Labor and can tell you how to get this help.

MINIMUM WAGES AND OVERTIME PAY

The Fair Labor Standards Act provides for minimum wages and overtime pay in many, but not all, occupations. Some occupations are covered by minimum wage regulations but not by regulations about extra pay for overtime; for example, private household workers who live where they work do not receive overtime pay, nor do companions for aged persons. Minimum wage rates are sometimes changed to reflect changes in the economic conditions of the nation. You should know what the minimum wages are that apply to you and the job you hold.

Overtime pay is at least one and one-half times the worker's regular pay, and in most jobs it must be paid for every hour beyond 40 worked in a week. Tips count as wages, as do meals.

Full-time students may be employed on a part-time basis in certain jobs and under special conditions at 85 percent of the minimum wage.

For information about minimum wages, exemptions, and hours, contact the nearest office of the Wage and Hour Division of the Department of Labor. Look in the phone book for the phone number and address, or ask at your state employment office or local post office.

Figure 6-2. The Equal Pay Act requires that women receive equal pay for performing the same work as men.

WOMEN, MINORITIES, AND THE PHYSICALLY HANDICAPPED

Federal laws of special importance to women and minorities are the Equal Pay Act of 1963 and the Civil Rights Act of 1964. Of importance to physically handicapped workers is the Rehabilitation Act of 1973.

The Equal Pay Act requires equal pay for women performing the same work as men. State equal-pay laws are also significant since they cover more industries and occupations than the federal law. However, standards vary from state to state.

The Civil Rights Act prohibits employment discrimination based on sex, race, religion, or national origin in industries engaged in interstate commerce, and in labor unions and employment agencies. Also, *executive orders* (regulations coming from the executive or presidential branch of government rather than from laws passed by Congress) prohibit discrimination in federal employment or employment in programs assisted by federal funds. One-third of the nation's work force is covered by these executive orders. Employers are required to take "affirmative action" to ensure equal employment opportunity. They must actively seek to employ, train, and advance minority workers and women, and set up timetables for doing so.

Employers in jobs that are partly or wholly supported by federal funds cannot discriminate against workers with a physical handicap unless the handicap would clearly interfere with job performance or be dangerous. Some states have similar laws.

SOCIAL SECURITY

You will need a social security number before you can begin work in most jobs.

You may already have a social security number. If not, you can apply for one at any social security office. (Look in the phone book for the number of the office closest to you, or ask at your local post office.) It usually takes about three or four weeks for your social security card, which bears your number, to be issued.

Your social security number is used to keep a work record for you. The record includes the number of years you work and the amount of pay you receive, both of which affect the benefits you can receive. You also use your social security number in other important ways, for example, on your income tax return and on your driver's license.

Before you apply for your social security number, find out what proof you need of your age, identity, and citizenship. The rules are different for people under 18 who were born in the United States and for those who are senior citizens or who were born in another country.

When you apply, ask about any special provisions applying to the work you plan to do; for example, for workers receiving cash tips and for those working in private households and on farms.

Social Security Benefits. Social security helps to protect workers and their families against loss of income when earnings are reduced or stopped because of retirement, disability, or death. Today, nine out of ten workers earn protection under the Social Security Act, and one out of every seven Americans receives a social security check each month.

Social security benefits in the form of monthly payments may apply to young people. Some examples are:

· Young workers who are disabled
· Young workers' widows and widowers
· Children of workers who are disabled, retired, or dead

These children are protected until they are 18 or, if they are fulltime students, until they are 22.

Are you such a child? Did you know you could receive this help to get an education?

Figure 6-3. You will need a social security card and number before you can begin working in most jobs.

The money to pay social security benefits comes from workers and employers. Deductions are made from workers' paychecks, and the employers contribute equal amounts. The amount of the deduction is based on workers' income.

You build up *credits* for social security for each "quarter" (3-month period) that you work. A worker who has earned ten years of credit is "fully insured" for life. But a worker who has worked less than ten years but at least one and one-half years out of the past three is "currently insured." Some benefits may be paid that worker's family if the worker dies. Also, there are special provisions for young disabled workers.

The amount of benefits a worker receives is based on the worker's contributions to the system during the years worked. The higher your income, the more you will contribute to the system and the higher your benefits will be.

Here are some other important things to remember about social security:

· If you are entitled to any benefits, you must apply for them by contacting your local social security office.

· Sometimes too large a deduction is taken from a worker's paycheck. Your employer must give you a statement of the deductions made from your pay at the end of each year or when you stop working for him. If you have paid too much the employer can make adjustments, or the Internal Revenue Service will give you credit on your income tax.

· You can check your work record for accuracy, and should do so every three years. Secure a "Request for Statement of Earnings" from your local office. This card is preaddressed to the Social Security Administration, P.O. Box 57, Baltimore, Md. 21203. At the same time, you can request a statement of the quarters of coverage that you have.

· Full-time students between the ages of 18 and 22 lose their benefit checks if they marry.

· Once earned, social security protection stays with you when you move or change jobs. Also, your credits will wait for you if you stop working for a while, and you can add to them when you are again employed.

- Most jobs are covered, including self-employment and service in the armed forces.
- Your social security number remains the same through life. If your name changes, however, apply for a new card. (When a woman marries she can continue to use her maiden name if she wishes. But she should choose between her married and maiden names and use one or the other for all legal papers.)

When to Contact Your Social Security Office. There are certain times when you should contact your social security office. They include:

- When you need a social security number
- If you or someone in your family reaches 62 years of age or more and stops working
- When you or someone in your family are nearly 65 years old, to see about Medicare health insurance
- If someone in your family dies
- If you or someone in your family becomes sick or hurt and can't work for a long time

Counselors in social security offices are especially trained to help you and are glad to answer your questions. Do not hesitate to call on them.

FORM W-4E

As soon as you are employed you will be asked to fill in a W-4 or W-4E form, so your employer will know how much income tax to deduct from your paychecks. The money that is withheld is counted toward the tax you owe at the end of the year.

Many entry-level workers do not earn enough money to owe any tax at all, but they must still file a return in order to have any money they have paid returned to them. If you will not earn enough to owe any tax, you can make sure that no tax will be withheld by filling out Form W-4E, *Exemption from Withholding of Federal Income Tax*.

When you do expect to earn enough money to pay federal income tax, you fill out Form W-4, *Employee's Withholding Allowance Certificate*. In this case, the employer estimates how much tax you will owe from specially prepared tax tables. The amount withheld will depend on your income and the number of *exemptions*, people who are considered dependent on that income.

You will be wise to get answers to any questions you have about the number of exemptions to claim when you start looking for work. Your teacher may be able to help you or you can contact your nearest Internal Revenue Service (IRS) office. Then you will be able to fill in the proper number of exemptions on the W-4 form as soon as you are employed. In Part Four we'll learn more about income tax.

Form W-4
(Rev. May 1977)
Department of the Treasury
Internal Revenue Service

Employee's Withholding Allowance Certificate
(Use for Wages Paid After May 31, 1977)

This certificate is for income tax withholding purposes only. It will remain in effect until you change it. If you claim exemption from withholding, you will have to file a new certificate on or before April 30 of next year.

Type or print your full name
RAUL MENDEZ

Your social security number
000—00—0000

Home address (number and street or rural route)
35 PEACHTREE LANE

City or town, State, and ZIP code
MERTON, PA

Marital Status

☒ Single ☐ Married
☐ Married, but withhold at higher Single rate

Note: If married, but legally separated, or spouse is a nonresident alien, check the single block.

1 Total number of allowances you are claiming . . . .
2 Additional amount, if any, you want deducted from each pay (if your employer agrees) . . . . $
3 I claim exemption from withholding (see instructions). Enter "Exempt" . . . .

Under the penalties of perjury, I certify that the number of withholding exemptions and allowances claimed on this certificate does not exceed the number to which I am entitled. If claiming exemption from withholding, I certify that I incurred no liability for Federal income tax for last year and that I anticipate that I will incur no liability for Federal income tax for this year.

Signature ▶ Raul Mendez   Date ▶ 6/23 , 19 78

For Company Payroll information, please supply the additonal information: Date of Birth 11/6/58   Sex ☒ Male ☐ Female

Figure 6-4. Using the information supplied by your W-4 form, the employer can figure out how much federal tax to deduct from your paycheck.

CREDENTIALS

You can see that paperwork plays a big part in getting a job: social security card, age certificate, W-4 or W-4E forms. Another paper the worker may need before being employed is a *credential*, a certificate or diploma proving the worker's qualifications for the job. The credential might be a certificate showing successful completion of an occupational home economics course. It might be a high school diploma, a college degree, a license, or a similar document indicating that the holder has basic skills needed for employment in certain jobs.

Fortunately, not all jobs require credentials, especially entry-level jobs. You can often earn income while continuing your education. And that is what most people do, until they have earned the credential needed for their chosen career.

CHAPTER SUMMARY

1. There are many *laws* about work and workers. Some have as their purpose the *protection* of the safety and rights of workers. Others provide for *worker benefits*, such as social security, and *worker responsibilities*, such as income tax. As a result, there is a certain amount of *paperwork* to be done before you can start work.

2. *The United States Department of Labor (USDOL)* looks after the interests of workers. There are units which are responsible for *preventing illness and injury* in the workplace; strengthening free *collective bargaining* by employers and workers; enforcing laws which set *minimum wage, overtime pay*, and *child labor standards*; and helping people who are *out of work* or seeking new work.

3. Most young workers must have age certificates or working permits.

There are strict laws about the kinds of jobs young people may hold. There are also laws against *discrimination* in employment.

4. You will need a *social security number* before you can begin to work in most jobs. Your number is used to keep a work record for you, which is the basis of *benefits*. The money for social security benefits comes from workers and employers.

5. Social security benefits may apply to young people; for example, to those who are disabled, are widows or widowers at a young age, or are children of those who are disabled, retired, or dead. If you are entitled to any benefits you *must apply* for them.

6. As soon as you are employed you will be asked to fill in a *W-4 or W-4E form* for income tax. You may need to know how many *exemptions* you have.

7. Another paper the worker may need before being employed is a *credential*. A credential is a certificate or diploma which proves your qualifications for a job.

• FOLLOW-UP PROJECTS

1. Get your working papers in order. Obtain an age certificate and a physical examination where needed. Apply for a social security number or obtain a card to check record of earnings.

2. Practice filling in W-4 and W-4E forms.

3. Develop a list of phone numbers and addresses of importance to workers, such as social security office, Wage-Hour Administration, Internal Revenue Service. Place it in your job folder.

4. Place in your job folder a list of the times when you should contact your social security office.

5. Invite a representative from the social security office to class, or visit the office. Ask about social security benefits for someone who is retired, disabled, or widowed. Ask about special provisions for workers who receive tips, or who are employed in private households or by parents. Collect brochures on programs such as benefits for students and information of special interest to women.

6. Prepare a bulletin board or transparency on the President's Cabinet. Who is Secretary of Labor at present? Show the relationship of labor to other interests. Show how management is represented in the Cabinet.

7. Develop a checklist of labor laws which apply in your community: child labor, minimum wage, equal pay, etc. Compare with the standards of other states. How does your state rate? If you are working, are you being paid the legal wage? Are you working legal hours?

8. Discuss with your class the rights and responsibilities of workers in complying with labor laws. Are they the same as the rights and responsibilities of employers? Have you had some on-the-job experiences which indicate to you that work laws are needed?

7 PREPARING FOR A JOB INTERVIEW

After studying Chapter 7 you will be able to:

1. Prepare a resume, cover letter, and portfolio.
2. Select business and character references.
3. Fill in an application form for a job.
4. Explain how to dress for and what to expect at a job interview.
5. Accept responsibility for establishing a good school and work record.

What do you have to do to become employable? To get and hold a job? By now the steps are pretty clear to you. You must:

· Take a good look at yourself.
· Match your abilities and interests to an occupation.
· Know where to look for jobs.
· Get your working papers in order.

You can see that the point you have reached in your job know-how is preparing for an interview.

YOUR RESUME

A resume (pronounced rez'-oo-mā) is a summary of your job qualifications presented in a one- or two-page, easy-to-read form. It gives you a chance to introduce yourself to an employer in a business-like way and to make very clear what you have to offer. Also, the resume provides a handy record for employers, to help them remember the information about you.

Your resume includes your career goals, education and special training, records of any work experience, and other information about you as a worker. The following is a suggested outline for your resume.

HEADING

The information telling who you are should always come first:

Name

Address

Telephone Number

OCCUPATIONAL INTEREST AND GOAL

Put here the kind of job or field of work you want. If you are qualified for several jobs list them in order of preference:

1. Child care aide
2. Home health aide or
3. Food service worker in a nursery school

1. Short-order cook or
2. Kitchen helper or
3. Pantry worker

1. Garment inspector or
2. Power sewer

You may want to list your present goal (the job you are qualified for now) and your future goal.

> Future goal: Department store buyer
> Present goal: Salesperson, children's clothing

WORK EXPERIENCE

You can organize your work history either by job or by the kinds of experience you have had.

By Job. If you choose to present your work experience according to jobs you have held, list the following information about each job, starting with the last job you held and going backward through time:

> Dates of employment
>
> Employer's name and nature of the business
>
> Employer's business address
>
> Name and title of your supervisor, if different from the employer listed
>
> Your job title and duties

Describe the tasks you performed for each job. Emphasize those requiring the most skill and good judgment. Include any special tools or equipment you used on the job. An example might be:

> September, 1977–June, 1978. American Elementary School. Front and Fourth Streets, Independence, Pa. Supervisor: Mrs. Harry Doe, Kindergarten teacher. Teacher aide. Assisted with child care routines and supervision of outside play.
>
> Summer, 1977. Employer: Mrs. Lee Chang, 1776 American Avenue, Independence, Pa. Mother's helper. Assisted with meal preparation, light housework, and care of three children: 1, 3, and 5 years old.

Figure 7-1. When you sit down to draw up your resume, begin by making a list of all your talents and abilities.

By Kinds of Experience. The same work experience can be described in this way:

> *Child care:* Assisted with care of children 1 to 6 years old in private household and in kindergarten. Supervised routines: bathing, naptime, meals, and snacks. Supervised outdoor play for small groups. Prepared materials for art and dramatic play activities. Selected books and read stories. Stored supplies, kept play areas neat, prepared snacks and simple meals.

The next entry is military experience, if any.

> *Military experience*
>> Length of service
>>
>> Branch of service
>>
>> Duties performed which relate to job applied for

EDUCATION AND TRAINING

If you are still in school, give your present grade. After you graduate, list the date of high school graduation and name of the school. If you have a college degree, list major subject, degree, and date received. Include also:

> Additional training
>
> Professional certificate or license
>
> Courses related to your occupational choice
>
> Scholarships and honors
>
> Extracurricular activities

Were you president of your class? Captain of the football team? Here is your chance to show the employer you have leadership ability. Do you belong to organizations which help others? This kind of membership demonstrates a commitment of service to others. Have you worked on committees for school projects? This activity suggests cooperation. If you belong to FHA/HERO you will want to highlight your membership and activities in the group.

Under this heading you can place any special skills or abilities you have. For example, can you speak, write, or read a second language? Being able to communicate with people who do not easily understand English is important in any occupation, but especially so in the people occupations. Be sure to let possible employers know that you have this valuable skill.

Other special skills are knowing how to drive a car, or type, or operate equipment used in large-quantity cookery. Is photography a hobby? (Helpful in many jobs.) Can you paint or draw? (Important for an assistant interior designer.) Can you operate a movie projector? (Teacher aides need this skill.) What about power sewing machines? Look over your self-inventory and be sure that every special skill which adds to your employability has found a place on your resume.

PERSONAL DATA

Date of birth (optional)

Marital status and dependents (optional)

Preferred location, or willingness to relocate

REFERENCES

A reference is a person to whom employers can *refer* to find out more about you. Your references should be people who have known you at school or at work, but not relatives. There are *character references*—people who can testify to your honesty, reliability, and other character traits. There are also *business references* who can testify to your performance and experience at work or to your qualifications.

Below are some people who are good references. A few of them could be used as both character and business references:

Character references
· Minister, priest, rabbi
· Doctor, dentist
· Teacher, principal
· Neighbor, friend
· Banker, if you have had a student or car loan

Business references
· Vocational teacher
· Guidance counselor
· Former employer, supervisor
· Coworker who has a responsible job

Before you give the names of persons as references, ask their permission. Not only is this the courteous thing to do but it is also a chance to check to be sure you have the correct addresses and telephone numbers. (Use the business, not the home, address of your employer.)

References are handled in different ways. A common practice is to add to your resume the line: "References will be provided upon request." This option lets you select references with a particular job and employer in mind.

Your placement office may keep on file for you a folder of credentials which includes personal information, courses you have taken, and your references. If so, state on your resume that your folder of credentials, including letters of reference, is available and give the name and address of the placement office.

Sometimes the names and addresses of your references are typed on your resume, or a separate card can be prepared to leave with an employer at the time of your interview.

After you have drawn up a rough draft of your resume, check it out with your employment counselor at school or the state employment service. After you have received their polishing-up advice, you are ready to carefully prepare as many copies as you need. A copy of a sample resume is shown in Figure 7-2.

```
Lou Garcia
1220 Fifth Street
Greenlee, Arizona  85224
602: 756-4692

TYPE OF WORK DESIRED:      Florist Aide

EXPERIENCE:                Sands Nursery and Garden Supply (1977-1978)
                           Florist Aide, part-time
                             Assisted with care of plants and general maintenance.

TRAINING AND EDUCATION:

Schools Attended:          Hartford Elementary, Hartford, Illinois (1965-1968)
                           Cleveland Elementary, Greenlee, Arizona (1968-1972)
                           Chandler Junior High, Greenlee, Arizona (1972-1975)
                           Chandler High, Greenlee, Arizona (1975-1977)

Subjects:                  Typing 1 (B average)
                           2 years home economics (B average)
                           3 years mathematics (C average)
                           3 years English (B average)
                           1 year science (C average)

Student Activities:        Student Council (1977)
                           Baseball Diamondbell - assistant manager (1976-1977)
                           HERO (1975-1977)

Other:                     Speak and write Spanish
                           Driver's License

PERSONAL DATA:             Age:  17
                           Present Occupation:  Student
                           Health:  Excellent

REFERENCES:                Ms. Vern Serrano
                           Sands Nursery and Garden Supply
                           West Jay Street
                           Greenlee, Arizona  85224

                           Ms. Bobby Smith
                           865 West Galveston
                           Greenlee, Arizona  85224

                           Mrs. Jack I. Brown
                           817 West Galveston
                           Greenlee, Arizona  85224
```

Figure 7-2. This resume shows you one format for presenting important information about yourself.

Your resume should be typed but carbon copies should not be used. Using a carbon copy suggests that you sent the original to someone you considered more important.

Mimeographed or photo-offset copies are acceptable if you need a number of copies and these processes are available to you. Check with your print shop, if there is one in your school, to find out the best method to use. The employer will appreciate being able to quickly review your qualifications. It goes without saying that any resume you use must be neat, with no smudges, strikeovers, or crossed-out words.

USING YOUR RESUME

Once you have your resume just the way you want it, use it! You can leave copies of your resume with your school placement office and with friends and neighbors who may be able to help you find jobs. Take copies of your resume along on job interviews and leave one with the employer. Quickly refer to your resume yourself as a reminder of dates or names of employers. Include resumes when you send letters applying for available jobs or with letters inquiring about job openings in places where you would like to work.

A PORTFOLIO

A portfolio is a collection of samples of your work. Depending on your imagination and skill, it could be the most important element in getting a job. If you are looking for a job in interior design, for example, some samples of sketches you have drawn could show very clearly your ability in this field.

You might have to create some materials to put in a portfolio. For instance, if you were looking for a job as a teacher's aide, you could prepare some descriptions of activities for children.

Not every kind of work can have a portfolio made for it, but, in more cases than you might think, some samples of your abilities can be developed into a portfolio. Newspaper clippings about your school activities and photographs of you as a volunteer or on the job also have a place in your portfolio.

The usual procedure is to indicate on your resume that your portfolio is available upon request. And you would expect to take your portfolio along with you on job interviews.

According to employers, a portfolio makes a good impression. It helps present your abilities in a good light. It is often the extra feature that gets the job for you even though other applicants may be as well qualified.

COVER LETTERS

Always enclose a cover letter when you mail out a resume. The cover letter may be either a *letter of inquiry* or a *letter of application*. A letter of inquiry is used when you would like to work for a particular employer but you do not know whether there are any vacancies. A letter of application is used when a vacancy has been advertised. Samples of the two kinds of letters are shown in Figures 7-3 and 7-4. Be sure to keep the following points in mind as you write your cover letter:

- Type or write in ink.
- Use standard-size white paper.
- Keep your letter brief. Your resume will have the details.
- State your purpose for writing.
- Make clear when you will be available to work.
- Indicate your occupational choice.
- State that interview arrangements can be made at the employer's convenience. Suggest that *you* telephone for an interview.
- Address your letter to a specific person by name, when possible.
- Don't forget to sign your name.

The cover letter is usually your first contact with the employer. It should be carefully prepared to help you make a good first impression and to encourage the employer to look over your resume. Again, the letter should be typed, if at all possible. But a neatly handwritten letter is better than one sloppily typed. The letter should be correctly folded and sent in a business-size envelope.

Notice that you do not send letters of reference or your folder of credentials along with an application letter. Business manners require that you wait to be asked for these materials. Your resume, however, *can* be sent, and that is why it is so valuable.

APPLICATION FORMS

For nearly any job you will have to fill out an application form. Application forms contain questions about the same kinds of information that are in your resume. They serve the same purpose, to tell an employer quickly what your qualifications are.

Because employers are trying to get a lot of information in a small space, application forms are very condensed. A lot of abbreviations are used, and you have little space in which to write. It is a good idea to practice filling in application forms. When you actually must fill out an application form for an employer, fill in the blanks first lightly in pencil, and then go over your answers in ink.

The kinds of information you'll be asked for are listed below. You will recognize most of this information as part of your resume or self-analysis inventory.

747 Jones Avenue
Phoenix, AZ 85287
June 12, 1978

Mr. R.W. Smith, Personnel Director
Glory Food Service Corporation
112 Sky Avenue
Phoenix, AZ 85008

Dear Mr. Smith:

On the advice of my HERO coordinator, Ms. Sue Smith, at York High
School, I am writing to you regarding employment with your food
company.

York High School offers courses in food and nutrition, and I have taken
all three of them. I have completed Beginning Foods, Meal Management,
and Advanced Foods and earned a B average in these classes. In addition,
I have held a part-time job at The Beanery for the last three months.

Enclosed with this letter is my resume which will give you more
information about myself. Since I plan a career in the food service
field, I am eager to affiliate with a food service company of your
reputation.

I would welcome the opportunity to come to your Phoenix office for
a personal interview at your convenience. If it is more convenient
for you to call me, my telephone number is 797-8389.

Yours truly,

Mary R. Black

Mary R. Black

Figure 7-3. This is a sample letter of inquiry; it includes general information about
yourself and asks for a personal interview.

128 Dearborn Place
Ithaca, New York 14580
January 1, 1978

Ms. Ann Fogarty
Personnel Manager
Apex Corporation
27 Broad Street
Syracuse, New York   13210

Dear Ms. Fogarty:

The placement office at Ithaca High School informed me of the vacancy
at your day care center. I would appreciate your consideration of my
candidacy for the position.

Enclosed is a copy of my resume. My folder of credentials, including
letters of reference, is available at the Placement Office, Ithaca
High School, Ithaca, New York 14850.

I shall be happy to make arrangements for an interview at your
convenience.

Thank you for your consideration. I look forward to hearing from you.

                                        Sincerely,

                                        Robert L. Hankins

                                        Robert L. Hankins

Figure 7-4. This is a sample letter of application; it includes more specific information
about yourself and also suggests an interview.

· Name, address, telephone number
· Military status
· Social security number
· Education
· Work experience; reasons for leaving previous jobs
· Reference sources
· Honors and awards

Be honest and thorough. For example, if you were laid off from a previous job because the department closed down, include that information on the application.

If you have a mark on your record such as being fired for being undependable, it's better to explain the situation and tell the employer that you recognize the problem and will not continue the same behavior on this job.

The employer may check the facts on the application with your references and previous employers. It is much worse for an employer to learn that you were not honest in completing the application than it is to give the facts, even if they are not what you would like them to be.

INTERVIEWS

A job interview is a face-to-face meeting between the person looking for the job and the employer, or a representative of the employer. It gives the employers or their representatives a chance to follow up on some of the information in your application form or resume, to judge for themselves your appearance, manners, personal qualities, and interest in the job. It gives *you* a chance to find out more about the job you've applied for, and to get some impressions of the employers.

QUESTIONS TO EXPECT

The point of an interviewer's questions is to discover the person and the reasons behind the facts given on resumes and application forms. Therefore, many of their questions are apt to be probing and personal. They may even make you feel uncomfortable. That's partly intentional, because the interviewer wants to see how you react to some stress. Here are some questions that interviewers ask. Think about how you would answer them, and ask your teacher or your school counselor about those you aren't sure about.

· Why did you decide to get training in this particular field?
· What can you do in addition to what this job calls for?
· What can you tell me about yourself?
· Where do you see yourself in five or ten years?
· Why did you leave your last job?
· Do you have any problems getting along with other people?

- Why would you like to work for us?
- Do you have any personal or family problems that might interfere with your job?
- How much do you want to earn on this job?
- What questions would you like to ask?

To help you answer the last question, learn as much as you can beforehand about the business or agency to which you will apply. Find out what kinds of jobs the organization has available and the kind of product or service offered. Learn the area pay scale for the type of job you are seeking so that you will know whether you are being offered fair pay. Your employment counselor or someone already employed by the organization can give you this information.

WHAT TO WEAR

Clothing has a psychological meaning for people of all ages. Appropriate and attractive clothing that does not make people feel different or conspicuous gives a sense of well-being and confidence. Clothing influences behavior. When people feel confident about how they look, they can act in a confident way.

What you wear will matter when you go on job interviews and you will want to start planning now. First impressions are created by clothing. Your employer, in most cases, is getting a first impression of you.

Avoid clothes which are too fancy or too casual. Being *businesslike* is the key.

Even when you know you will be wearing a uniform or work clothes on the job you are applying for, the usual advice is to dress for the interview as you would for an office job. A rule of thumb is to choose clothes that are attractive but not odd or unusual for an office.

Employers know that clothing tells a lot about self-image, about how you feel about yourself. When your clothing is right for the occasion, you communicate pride, know-how, and confidence, the qualities the employer wants.

**CHAPTER
SUMMARY**

1. A *resume* is a summary of your job qualifications presented in a short, easy-to-read form. It includes your *career goals, education and training, work experience*, and other information about you as a worker.

2. When you apply for a job you need *references*, persons to whom employers can refer to find out more about you. *Character references* can testify to your honesty and reliability; *business references* can testify to your job performance or qualifications. Before you give names of persons as references, ask their *permission*.

3. A *portfolio* is a collection of samples of your work. A portfolio makes

Figure 7-5. During an interview, your clothes can give others a strong first impression; try to avoid wearing odd or unusual clothes.

a good impression and shows you are willing to make extra effort in your search for a job.

4. You always enclose a *cover letter* when you mail out a resume. A *letter of inquiry* is sent when you do not know whether there are any vacancies at the place where you want to work. When a definite job has been advertised, you send a *letter of application*.

5. For nearly any job you are asked to fill out an *application form*. Take along a copy of your resume to be sure you have the information you need.

6. A *job interview* is a face-to-face meeting between the person looking for the job and the employer, or someone representing the employer. It gives employers a chance to follow up on some of the information in your application form or resume, and to judge for themselves your appearance, manners, personal qualities, and interest in the job. It gives you a chance to find out more about the job.

7. There are *certain questions* you can expect to be asked on an interview. You can *prepare* answers ahead of time, and *practice* giving them. It is also important to *plan ahead* your grooming and your clothing.

• FOLLOW-UP PROJECTS

1. Prepare a resume. Decide whom to ask to be your references. Get their permission to use their names and check their business addresses.

   Decide how many copies of your resume you will need. Investigate photo-offset and other methods of copying the original.

2. Write a cover letter for your resume. Inquire about chances for a job or apply for a position which has been advertised.

3. Working in small groups, prepare sample portfolios for typical entry-level workers in home economics occupations. Exhibit the portfolios in a school showcase.

4. Practice filling in job application forms.

5. Prepare answers to questions commonly asked by interviewers. Practice interviewing with a friend, before a mirror, or using a videotape recorder.

6. Make a list of papers you need to take with you on a job interview. Talk this over with your teacher or counselor so you are sure you have everything you need.

7. Students preparing for interviews they expect to have soon should investigate the businesses or institutions they have in mind. Find out job title, prevailing wage rates, working hours, and other information from people already employed, the personnel office, or your counselor.

8. Plan your dress and grooming for an interview. Discuss hair styles, beards and mustaches, and what you will wear.

8 | THE JOB INTERVIEW

After studying Chapter 8 you should be able to:

1. Demonstrate how to respond during a job interview.
2. Explain why some people fail to get the jobs they want.
3. Describe how to follow up an interview.
4. Enjoy a job interview.

The moment you have been waiting for has come: an appointment for an interview for a job. You have been preparing for a long time. You have practiced filling in application forms. You have prepared a resume and maybe a portfolio. You have tried to build a good reputation at school.

Before you leave for the interview, check your appearance. You know when you are called for an interview that you are being seriously considered for a job. You also know that the employer will be observing you and listening to you carefully. The employer is interested in hiring someone who is neat, well organized, and polite.

When you arrive for your interview you may be greeted by the employer, an interviewer in a personnel office, or a receptionist. Tell whomever greets you who you are and why you are there. If you have to wait, do so graciously.

AT THE INTERVIEW

During your interview, try to be your natural self. Looking your best, feeling prepared, and having some idea of what to expect will give you confidence.

The following are some *dos* and *don'ts* suggested by employment counselors.

Do:

· Be pleasant and friendly, but businesslike.
· Let the employer control the interview. Give frank and complete answers, but keep them short.
· Be flexible and willing, but give the employer a clear idea of jobs of most interest to you. Have definite job titles in mind, to show you have done your homework and know something about the organization.

Figure 8-1. If you dress neatly, arrive on time, and try to act naturally, you'll look and feel more confident. (Freda Leinwand, Monkmeyer)

· Have your papers arranged for easy reference—your resume, your driver's license or health certificate, or other necessary papers.
· Be prepared to state the pay you expect, but not until the employer brings up the subject.
· Speak clearly and distinctly. What you have to say is important, and how you say it is, too.
· Have confidence in what you can do. In most cases, you will not be interviewed unless the employer thinks you can do the job.
· Tell the interviewer if you plan to take extra courses to help you on the job.
· Show off your good manners. Be polite and tactful.
· Sit up straight. Your posture is as important as how you dress.
· Be prepared to take an aptitude test if asked to do so.
· Thank the employer for the interview, even if you don't get the job. There may be a job for you sometime in the future, or the employer may refer you to another job opening.
· Smile.

Don't:

· Criticize former employers or fellow workers.
· Chew gum or mints, or smoke.

· Discuss your personal, family, or financial problems unless you are directly asked about them.
· Be in a hurry to ask questions unless the employer invites them. But don't be afraid to ask what you need to know—the job description, for instance.

AFTER THE INTERVIEW

Look back over the interview and try to see what went well for you and what you would do differently. As long as you were neatly groomed and dressed, well-mannered and polite, and answered the interviewer's questions clearly and accurately in a pleasant tone of voice, then the chances are excellent that any little slip-ups you might have made will not matter at all. Interviewers understand that most people are nervous during an interview, and they certainly make allowances for young workers who have had little experience with interviews.

Employers are eager to find qualified people to fill their job openings, so probably you will hear fairly soon after the interview whether or not you have been chosen. But if you do not hear within two or three days and you really want the job, send a *follow-up letter* to the person who interviewed you, thanking the employer and indicating your continuing interest in the job. Even if you are not hired for this job, your letter will help to create a favorable impression and may help you with future job openings. The letter may even be a deciding factor in getting you the present job. It shows you have good manners and that you are willing to give a little more and do a little better, which is so very important to employers.

IF YOU DON'T GET A JOB OFFER

Employers are not required to tell you why they don't hire you, and they usually don't tell you. There may have been several candidates for the job and another person was more qualified. Just as a check, review your activities in applying for the job and see if you could have improved your letter of application, resume, or list of references.

Ask yourself how the interview went. What things seemed to interest the employer? Did you present your qualifications well? Did you overlook strong points you could have mentioned? Did you pass up clues to the best way to "sell" yourself? How can you improve your next interview?

If you are satisfied that you have done everything you could, keep looking. Keep learning. Try to adopt the philosophy that everything works out for the best. Expect another job opening to be a better opportunity for you.

WHY PEOPLE FAIL TO GET THE JOBS THEY WANT

The following people did not get the jobs they wanted. Can you see why? Is your story like any of these?

Tom wanted a job as a counterworker in a fast-food restaurant. He knew he would wear a uniform on the job, so he did not bother to change his

Figure 8-2. Tom went to his interview straight from school—in sneakers, patched jeans, and wrinkled shirt.

clothes before going on his interview. He went straight from school in a wrinkled shirt and patched jeans. Also, he had to hurry, and didn't take time to comb his hair.

Jane was well trained in her school as a power-machine sewer. She asked many questions at her interview, but they were all about the pay and fringe benefits. She did not ask how she could help the company or seem interested in the job itself.

Josephine wanted a job as a cocktail waitress, but she was only 16 years old. She applied for a job, writing on her application form that she was 19. When the employer checked her records, she discovered that Josephine had lied about her age.

Jerry was interviewed for a job as a floor mechanic aide. Jerry had not prepared for his interview by finding out the going rate for his job title. He asked for too much money, and was not hired.

Mary wanted a job as an interior designer's assistant. She looked in all the right places for a job opening, but was not hired because she did not have enough training. One interviewer referred her to a job opening as a stock clerk and suggested she enroll in night school at her vocational-technical school.

Peter had a job interview for a job he wanted as a teacher's aide. But he forgot to write down the time and did not show up for his interview.

Sue did not prepare for her interview as a salesperson for children's clothing. She did not get her papers in order and also knew that she did not look her best. As a result, she felt ill at ease and her natural, friendly personality did not show through. Instead, she seemed unfriendly and disorganized as she struggled to answer the interviewer's questions and to remember dates, places, and other information about her work and school record.

Sally took two friends along on her interview as a nutrition aide. This indicated to the employer that Sally lacked self-confidence and was not mature enough for the job.

George did not like school, but he really wanted to succeed at his job interview. He had dreamed for a long time of being a short-order cook. But George has a poor attendance record at school. Any employer in the food service industry will tell you that workers have to be reliable. George did not appear to be a reliable person, and he did not get the job.

Figure 8-3. Josephine tried to look older and more sophisticated for her interview as a cocktail waitress.

Figure 8-4. Peter forgot to show up for his interview for a job as a teacher aide.

Figure 8-5. Sally took two friends along on her interview.

Figure 8-6. Kurt was careless in filling out his job application—he made many mistakes and left many blanks.

Marcia had a job interview as a worker for a cleaning service. She thought she would enjoy working with a team that did weekly cleaning for families and small businesses. But Marcia was always in trouble with her teachers and principal. She even argued with the interviewer. As a result, the employer decided Marcia could not work well on a team, and she was not employed.

Kurt hates paperwork. He wanted a job as a therapy aide in a state hospital but did not take seriously the application form he was asked to fill in. He was careless and left many blanks. Since there were several other applicants, the interviewer hired one who had supplied all the necessary information.

IF YOU DO GET A JOB OFFER

Sometimes an employer will offer you a job during the interview. More often, you will be notified in a few days whether you have been chosen for the job. There are many things to consider when deciding whether or not to take a job.

Deciding whether or not to accept a position is the subject of the next chapter.

CHAPTER SUMMARY

1. Before you leave for an interview, check your *appearance*. You know when you are called for an interview that you are being considered seriously for a job. And you know that the employer is interested in hiring someone who is *neat, well-organized*, and *polite*.

2. Allow plenty of time so you can arrive a bit early. When you arrive, tell whoever greets you who you are and why you are there. During your interview, try to be your natural self. *Looking your best, feeling prepared*, and *knowing what to expect* will give you confidence.

3. Employment counselors have developed *dos* and *don'ts* which can help you in your interview. *Do* be business-like, have your papers arranged for easy reference, and give frank and complete answers to questions. Be prepared to take an aptitude test if asked to do so. Thank the employer for the interview. *Don't* criticize others, discuss personal problems, chew gum or smoke.

4. After the interview, *review* what happened to try to see what went well and what you would do differently another time. If you really want the job, send a *follow-up* letter thanking the interviewer and indicating your continuing interest in the job.

5. People *fail to get the jobs they want* because they: are not neatly dressed, give the impression they are more interested in the money than the job, lie about their age, expect too much money, are not qualified, are not organized, take someone along on the interview, have a poor school record, cannot work well on a team, or are careless in filling in application forms.

6. If you feel your interview went well, but you do not get a job offer, don't give up. Keep looking. If you do get a job offer, you have to decide whether or not to take it.

• FOLLOW-UP PROJECTS

1. Invite the school principal or an employer to class. Role-play a job interview, with the principal acting the part of the employer and class members the persons being interviewed. Videotape if possible.

   Analyze the questions, responses, appearance, and behavior of the person being interviewed. Would the job applicant be hired? Discuss.

2. Write a sample follow-up letter, thanking an employer for the job interview. Put a copy in your job folder for future reference.

3. Discuss reasons why people fail to get the jobs they want. Consider the stories on pages 153-157. Why were the people not hired? What could they have done differently to be successful?

9 | DECIDING ON A JOB

After studying Chapter 9 you should be able to:

1. List working conditions to consider when deciding whether or not to take a job.
2. Compare fringe benefits.
3. List costs of working.
4. Identify procedures to follow when changing from one job to another.
5. Accept responsibility for making a job choice.

What is a good job? How do you decide whether to take a job which is offered you? In the first excitement of being chosen for a job, you run the risk of accepting a job which may later turn out to be unsatisfactory. What things will you consider when deciding whether to take a job?

How many times have you heard someone say, ''You couldn't pay me to do that,'' or ''I wouldn't take that job for a million dollars''? This tells you that working conditions are a very large factor in whether or not a job is considered a good one. Many things go into making up working conditions— hours, safety, people you work with or for, the pressure of the work load, the physical surroundings like noise, dust, heat, or steam.

WORKING CONDITIONS

HOURS

The number of hours you work are important, because too many hours on the job can prevent you from keeping up with your school work. (Remember, too, that the number of hours young workers may work is regulated by law.)

Split shifts, where you work a few hours in one part of the day and then have several hours off before returning for the rest of your day's work, may add to the cost of your transportation to work. You have to make two round trips to work each day instead of one. On the other hand, a split shift may be an advantage if it allows you to schedule your work around your school classes or to work part-time.

Very late or very early working hours may pose problems for your personal safety. In some seasonal jobs workers can expect to work extra hours

Figure 9-1. The number of hours you will have to work should influence whether or not you take the job. For example, too many hours can be exhausting and prevent you from keeping up with school work.

and to receive overtime pay. Examples are food service jobs in areas which cater to tourists and sales jobs during the holidays.

Some jobs include a certain amount of weekend and holiday hours. Airline pilots, police officers, and doctors are in this category. So are many jobs in child care and food service.

PERSONAL SAFETY

Does the job you are considering affect your safety? There are several points to consider. One is your safety in getting back and forth to work. Do you have a reliable car? Do you accept any risks because of where you catch the bus? Do you ride with others? How good are the drivers? Does the job require you to work alone in situations where you are in danger?

The following practices are recommended to protect yourself on the way to and from work:

· When arriving at or leaving from work, try to do so in the company of at least one other person. Employ this "buddy system" when walking to and from your car or the subway. Avoid using shortcuts. Stay on well-lighted and well-traveled throughways.

· If you are threatened, noise will discourage a would-be attacker. Passers-by will be alerted by a scream. Loud buzzers and whistles can be carried for use when needed. Should you be trapped in a car, sound the horn.

· Keep your auto locked. Before entering, look it over for signs of a break-in or persons in the rear seat or floor area.

· Try not to carry large amounts of cash or display large amounts of money. If women carry a purse, it should be held close to your body or under your coat.

· When walking on deserted streets, walk near the curb rather than near buildings where people could be lurking in doorways. Watch alleyways also.

Ask yourself such questions as:

· Are you aware of strangers who might be following or watching you?

· Do you walk with poise and confidence, as if you knew exactly where you were going?

· Are you aware of how you appear to others?

· Do you stand out in a crowd?

· Do you wear clothing that will allow you to move freely and run if necessary?

· Can you get a taxi quickly if you need one?

· Can your employer be trusted?

Some young people like the idea of hitchhiking to work, especially around college towns and army bases. Records show, however, that a high proportion of hitchhikers have criminal records. Police records also show the considerable danger of assault for both hitchhiking men and women.

There is some element of risk in almost every situation in life. Your own good sense plus some advice from more experienced persons will prevent you from taking jobs where your safety is not reasonably assured.

ECOLOGY

Ecology means your relationship with your environment, how your surroundings relate to you and you to your surroundings. Your ecology at work has a lot to do with how much you like your job.

In home economics occupations you often work directly with people—aged and sick people, infants and children, troubled people. All these people have special needs and ways of behaving which you must understand.

In every job there are coworkers and supervisors to get along with. Being human, they all have *their* special ways.

People can be grateful, interesting, attractive, friendly, funny, and fun to be with. But they can also be insulting, demanding, intoxicated, cranky, unreasonable, and impatient.

Jobs working with people may be in beautifully decorated restaurants, hotels, or stores; but they may also be in crowded or run-down buildings, neighborhoods, or homes. In jobs where workers produce food or clothing or reupholstered furniture there may be heat or noise or dust.

In addition to different kinds of people and different kinds of surroundings, your work place may have a fast or slow work pace. There may be a pleasant, relaxed atmosphere or a constant sense of pressure and rush.

All these conditions affect your satisfaction with your job. Finding out about the ecology at work is a factor in deciding which jobs you would like to try.

INCOME   After working conditions, the income a job will give you is probably one of your biggest considerations in deciding which job to take. Finding out your pay scale is the beginning. But you must also *add* the benefits and *subtract* the costs of working in order to judge the wages.

Wages consist of how much your employers pay you. For most entry-level jobs, wages are paid at an hourly rate. Your employer should tell you before you begin work what the hourly wage is, how many hours you will work each week, and whether payday is weekly, twice a month, or monthly.

In some jobs the hourly rate may be less because part of your wages will come in the form of *tips* from customers. In some jobs you might be able to earn *commissions*. A commission is a percentage of the price of an item you sell, which is paid back to you. For example, people who sell furniture may receive commissions as part of their wages.

On some jobs, there are *bonuses*. A bonus is an extra sum of money given to workers for a special reason. For example, some employers give their workers bonuses at Christmas. Or workers may earn bonuses because of extra effort or efficiency. You already know about overtime pay, that it is at least one and one-half the amount of regular hourly pay. Some jobs offer many chances for overtime pay, others may have little or none.

Regular wages, tips, commissions, bonuses, and overtime are all considered part of your pay and are subject to income tax.

FRINGE BENEFITS

Fringe benefits are those extras workers gain from jobs which do not add to their paychecks but can be of much value to them. Employers may be contributing 30 percent of your pay to programs which provide your fringe benefits. That means that the cost of hiring you, if you are paid $100 a month, is actually $130. Some fringe benefits, such as pension plans or insurance, may require contributions from the worker too.

Unemployment Compensation. Unemployment compensation is a government insurance system which may give you some income if you lose your job through no fault of your own and are doing everything you can to get a new one. Its main objective is to provide income for a period long enough to tide most workers over spells of unemployment.

The unemployment insurance program is financed through a tax on employers. In most states, no deductions are made from a worker's pay. Not all jobs are covered by unemployment compensation, but many home economics occupations are.

Health Benefits. Benefits related to health can be an important part of your total income from a job. In some jobs, for instance, you are allowed to have a certain amount of time off for sickness and still be paid for it.

There may be the chance to take part in health insurance plans. The advantages for the workers are that they can get coverage under such insurance programs at a cheaper price than if they were covered as individuals.

In addition, many employers, especially large companies or places of business, have some medical services provided free to their workers right on the job. For example, a large factory, plant, or office may have a doctor, nurse, or both right in the building, and also a small clinic where workers with health problems can receive medical advice and certain kinds of care.

Social Security. Both workers and employers contribute toward the funds that pay out social security benefits. Whenever you are in a job covered by social security, your contributions earn you *credits* in the system, and when you have earned enough credits, you will be eligible for social security benefits throughout your life. So it is important to you to start earning your credits.

Retirement Benefits and Pensions. In addition to social security, employers may have their own retirement programs. Employers may make all the payments into these private programs, but the usual thing is for workers to contribute also. Under the programs, workers who retire receive a monthly check for life. The amount the person (or survivor) receives depends on the number of years worked and the salary earned.

At one time workers enrolled in private retirement programs lost their pension rights when they moved to another job. A new federal law, the Employment Retirement Income Security Act of 1974, was passed to protect those benefits. Federal law also allows people who are self-employed, or those whose employers do not provide retirement programs, to put aside part of their own earnings toward a pension fund. You do not have to pay income tax on all money you put into these funds, called Keogh Plans or Individual Retirement Accounts (IRAs).

To young people just beginning their working careers, retirement and pensions seem far off. However, these contributions are a form of savings for you and will be a large factor in your future income. Before the new law, employees often had to wait for many years before starting to build pension credits. Today, a person 25-years old, who has worked for the employer for one year, is eligible to take part in a pension plan.

Paid Vacations and Holidays. In many jobs certain holidays are given to workers and they are paid as if they had worked those days. In most full-time jobs workers are guaranteed a certain amount of paid vacation time also.

Often, the longer you have worked for an organization, the more paid vacation you earn. In 1975 technical, clerical, and salesworkers averaged 3–4 weeks of paid vacation and service workers, operators and craftworkers, 2–3 weeks.

Workmen's Compensation. Workmen's compensation is an insurance for persons injured or killed at work. This insurance, paid for by the employer, gives weekly cash benefits and furnishes medical care to a worker who is disabled because of a work-connected injury or occupational disease. In the event of death resulting from disease or injury, workmen's compensation includes weekly cash benefits to dependents of the victim. Most jobs are covered by workmen's compensation.

Training and Career Development. Some jobs, especially those with federal or state governments, have on-the-job training opportunities. There may be career ladders leading to better-paying and more interesting jobs. Many large businesses have similar programs. In any job you will want to consider the chance for advancement.

Other Fringe Benefits. Examples of other fringe benefits are:

· *Union protection*—opportunity to join a union which, through collective bargaining, looks after worker interests
· *Tenure*—a job where you can work for a lifetime once you pass a trial period
· *Incentive awards*—cash prizes for suggestions that save the organization money. *Bonus plans* or *profit-sharing*
· *Credit union*—where you can save money and borrow at reasonable rates
· *Discounts*—where you can buy products at a lower price
· *Employee cafeterias*
  and
· *Recreation programs* and *daycare* for *children of employees*

Figure 9-2. An on-the-job training program is one of the benefits you should consider when taking a job. (Bruce A. Dart)

In some jobs, almost every dollar you earn is profit. In others, costs for transportation, moving to a new location, or child care may eat up much of your pay. Other costs of working are meals away from home, clothing, and personal care such as hair styling.

COSTS OF WORKING

You may want to move into a room or apartment of your own. You may want very much to buy a car. You look forward to having money for a new wardrobe and expensive haircuts. These are some of your reasons for working. Still, you will want to compare the costs of working at different jobs. Consider your goals. Are you also working to save money for college or to travel or buy a home? Is it better to take a job near home so that you can save more of your pay? Should you take a job where uniforms are provided rather than one where you will need to spend much of your pay on clothing?

Thinking through the expenses involved in a job opportunity is part of choosing a job. Later in this book, costs of working will be looked at more closely and suggestions made for keeping them under control.

CHANGING JOBS

Deciding on a job may mean leaving the job you already have. Changing jobs becomes a job skill, since it is almost always to your advantage to leave a job on friendly terms. You probably want to use the old employer as a reference. You may even want to return to work there someday in a different job.

A rule of thumb is to give two weeks' notice. If that is impossible, give as much notice as you can. It may be a good idea to put your resignation in writing. Date it and keep a copy in case someone questions your responsibility in this matter.

Sometimes workers just fail to show up, with no explanation, when they decide to leave a job. By doing so they forfeit a good reference. Also, there may be arrangements to be made, such as transferring pension rights and finding out how to continue insurance coverage which may have been provided on the job. Your employer may have specific procedures to follow. You may be asked to give an "exit interview," to explain to a supervisor or personnel officer your reasons for leaving.

Unless a job is truly unbearable, you are usually advised to stick with it until you have another job. The fact that you are already employed is a plus factor in your search for a new job. In extreme cases, perhaps fear of physical harm, workers cannot be expected to continue on a job. This is the time to make immediate contact with an employment counselor, a union representative, or a legal aid society for advice.

Where you have been fairly treated, be fair to your employer. Give as much notice as you can. Your new employer will understand and respect your thoughtfulness.

CHAPTER SUMMARY

1. What will you consider when deciding whether or not to take a job offered you? *Working conditions* play a part in your decision. They include *hours, safety, people you work with and for*, the *pressure* of the work load, and physical *surroundings*.

2. Consider the *number* of hours, *split shifts*, and possibilities of *overtime* pay. Consider also your *personal safety* on the job and getting to and from work.

3. People, places, and work pace make up your *ecology* at work. They all affect your satisfaction with your job.

4. To find the *income* a job will give you, *add* fringe benefits to your wages and *subtract* the costs of working. For entry-level jobs most *wages* are paid at an hourly rate. There may also be *tips, commissions*, and *bonuses*.

5. *Fringe benefits* are those extras workers gain from jobs which do not add to their paychecks, but can be of much value to them. They include *unemployment compensation, health benefits, social security, pension credits, paid vacations* and *holidays, training for advancement*, and others.

6. In some jobs, almost every dollar you earn is profit. In others, costs of working eat up much of your pay. *Costs of working* are *transportation, meals away from home, clothing, child care, moving to a new location*, and *personal care*. Thinking through the costs involved in a job opportunity is part of choosing a job.

7. When deciding on a job means leaving one you already have, *changing jobs* becomes a skill. Try to leave on friendly terms. You will probably want to use your old employer as a reference. Also, there may be arrangements to be made, such as transfer of pension rights and continuing insurance coverage. You may be asked to give an *exit interview* to explain your reasons for leaving.

8. Where you have been fairly treated, *be fair* to your employer. Your new employer will understand and respect your thoughtfulness.

● FOLLOW-UP PROJECTS

1. Discuss jobs you now hold, whether volunteer work, work at home, or work for an outside employer. Consider working conditions, costs of working, income, and chance for advancement.

2. Make a checklist for your job folder of fringe benefits which can add to your income on a job.

3. Invite a banker or insurance agent to class to explain how workers who are self-employed or who work where there is no company pension plan can set up a personal retirement account.

4. Employed students should find out whether they are covered by unemployment compensation on their jobs and what they must do to be eligible for benefits. Report to class and discuss.

   Practice filling in unemployment insurance claim forms.

5. Working in small groups, investigate fringe benefits of major employers in your community: your school, a hospital, college, department store, or other large private business. Ask about:
   a. Pension plans
   b. Career development and training
   c. Workmen's compensation
   d. Unemployment insurance
   e. Health benefits
   f. Personal services
   g. Other fringe benefits

6. Role-play procedures to follow when changing jobs.

7. Invite a police officer to class to discuss personal safety on the job and going to and from work. Ask how to protect your personal belongings at work and on the job.

PART THREE

YOU AND YOUR JOB

Once you have decided on a job, the next challenge is to be successful at work. Personal qualities play a big part in that success. Much depends on your appearance, manner of behavior, and ability to get along with your supervisor, coworkers, and the families, customers, or patients with whom you work.

Getting along with others requires listening to them and expressing yourself clearly so that you understand each other. Listening and speaking, along with writing reports and reading directions, are *communication* skills. Communication skills are very important in home economics occupations.

Task analysis showed that workers in home economics also use *computation* skills. They take measurements, keep records, and estimate costs. In most job clusters skills necessary for *safe and sanitary performance* are also required.

Skills in relationships, communication, computation, and safe and sanitary practices make people more employable and more successful on their jobs. Skills can be improved with practice. In Part Three we will show how these skills relate to home economics occupations and provide some opportunities for practicing and developing them.

10 PERFORMING ON THE JOB

After studying Chapter 10 you should be able to:

1. Describe what the employer expects of you on the job in regard to image, relationships, production, and dependability.
2. Relate your values to your job performance at work and school.
3. Demonstrate in class your ability to accept supervision, get along with coworkers, and contribute to the school's image.
4. Explain your responsibility to yourself and others to get more training and where to get it.
5. Explain how personal problems, poor health, drug abuse, and wasting time limit productivity.
6. Find pleasure in cooperating with others and in producing a fair amount of work.

How can you be successful at work? What does your employer expect of you?

Employers have been asked these questions many times, and many times their answers are the same. They say appearance and manner of behavior are important. They like workers who are optimistic and confident. They say attitudes make the difference and a positive attitude is the key to success.

One employer of waiters and waitresses said she looked for interest in the work, humor, enthusiasm, good will, and friendliness. Do you have these qualities?

Another employer was shown a list of qualities thought to help people be successful at work. Can you guess which of the following he said were important?

· Appearance on the job
· Cooperation with coworkers
· Attention to regulations
· Acceptance of supervision
· Management on the job
· Dependability
· Loyalty
· Honesty

· Adaptability

· Initiative

· Attitude toward the public

· Pride in job

· Quality of work produced

· Quantity of work produced

· Aptitude for the work

You're right. He said *all* of them are important. And he added another: Alertness. He expects his workers to be alert to the needs of others, whether fellow workers or the public.

Employers know they are hiring human beings, not machines. They hire a whole person, a whole personality, not just a pair of hands and eyes. They know your attitudes and personality help get things done or slow down the work. They know your image gives atmosphere to the business or institution and can help sell products like hamburgers or services like care of the elderly. As a result, the whole person, everything you are, counts.

IMAGE Appearance has subtle effects on others. You can't depend on employers letting you know how they feel about appearance. Criticism may be unspoken or even unconscious on the part of the employer. A waitress wearing too much make-up or jewelry on the job is fired for giving a restaurant the wrong image. A pantry worker may produce well on the job, but his poor appearance projects an image of carelessness. Some other worker is promoted to assistant cook instead of him.

The demands of the job enter in. Long hair has to be tied back in food service in the interest of sanitation and, in factories, to prevent its being caught in machines.

When employers emphasize that they want enthusiastic workers, they mean people who are proud of themselves and proud of the organization and their place in it. Good appearance is a way of showing pride and maturity. Besides, nothing can quite match the self-confidence you feel when you know you look your best.

INTERPERSONAL RELATIONSHIPS Skill in getting along with others is part of image, part of public relations, part of being successful at work. In most jobs you have to cope with co-workers, supervisors, and the public. In addition, sometimes you work with government inspectors.

ACCEPTING SUPERVISION

Employers expect workers to produce as *many* products or services as *well* as the employer wants them done. How you produce on the job depends on your ability to follow directions and accept supervision.

Figure 10-1. Getting along with others on the job requires listening and understanding, and is part of being successful at work.

· Can you work independently?
· Or do you require constant supervision?
· Do you cooperate with your supervisor?
· Are you willing to follow directions?

Employers of entry-level workers often have their own way of doing things and prefer to do their own special training, as long as you have the basic aptitude for the job. This can work to your advantage since in this way an unskilled person can get a job. But you must expect and accept supervision and be able to adapt to the demands of the job, whether they are the respect for sanitation and safety required in food service or the patience and understanding required in community jobs.

COPING WITH COWORKERS

Many jobs in the people occupations are jobs as a member of a team. The team in health services may be a doctor, registered nurse, dietician, and tray worker. The team may be chef, cook, and kitchen helper. Or home economist, assistant teacher, and child care aide. Every team member performs well or the team fails in its job. Members of a team have to work together.

Not all jobs in home economics are organized into teams, but they still require cooperation among workers.

Working closely together contributes to job satisfaction and to a sense of companionship and belonging. Skills which help you cope with coworkers and build morale can be learned. Have you had that kind of instruction?

PLEASING THE PUBLIC

The public counts. They're the reason your job exists. No annoyance can match standing in line trying to buy something or pay somebody while employees visit among themselves. Such behavior may well cost you your job. People are better consumers today. They do not hesitate to make themselves heard, and a complaint to your supervisor can cost you your job and be a blot on your record.

Employers expect their workers to be courteous always. There is no other way. The child or patient or customer comes first, no matter how unfair that may sometimes seem to you. In the real world the old saying "the customer is always right," is right.

GETTING ALONG WITH GOVERNMENT INSPECTORS

Remember all those laws that protect you, the worker? There are laws that protect the consumer, too, against unsanitary restaurants, unsafe child care centers, and overcrowded nursing homes. Both as a member of a team and as an individual worker you may find that your job involves contacts with government inspectors whose job is to see that protective regulations are enforced. As a worker you have a right to know what the regulations are and a responsibility to carry them out and to be courteous to the inspectors.

MANNERS MATTER

Manners matter. They smooth relationships rather than stir up annoyances and trouble. They are contagious; you get back what you give. They are the easy way to friendship; they show grace and good will. They give you style.

When you decide on job training or are employed you will probably receive specific instruction in manners expected in your occupation. For example, there are accepted phone manners required in many jobs.

For the most part, manners are simply consideration for others, making people feel comfortable, being sure not to embarrass or humiliate others, and respecting the privacy of others.

Thoughtfulness, kindness, and showing more interest in others than in yourself all help keep the atmosphere pleasant. As a result, everyone has a greater sense of well being, especially you. Knowing how to act adds to your self-confidence.

Successful workers are dependable and honest. Dependability has different definitions in different occupations. Food service is an occupation where absenteeism is not tolerated. The work cannot wait. Workers have to show up. This special dependability might be called an ethic of the food service industry. Special dependability is also required in other home economics occupations. Children must be cared for in a responsible, dependable way. It is a matter of life and death. The same is true for the physically ill, the aged and disabled, or the emotionally disturbed.

YOUR VALUES AND YOUR JOB

Honesty in employment means a number of things. One is getting to work on time: for your shift, after coffee break, and after meals. It also means being careful with expensive machines and equipment and with company supplies. Did you know employees have been known to shoplift their business *out* of business and themselves out of a job?

Maybe your job is in food service, health service, or child care, where there are regulations requiring frequent hand washing. Your supervisor isn't around, but you follow regulations. Why? Because you do not want to spread disease, because you recognize and accept a responsibility for others beyond yourself, because it is the right thing to do.

Doing the right thing in these ways does not amount to a lot of separate acts, but, these acts add up. Every time you do the right thing you build a little more pride in yourself, a little more self-respect. You can ask yourself how you feel as a person and the answer is, "Good."

In some occupations the worker has a responsibility *to others* to obtain further education. Such an occupation is that of the child care aide, who is responsible for the happiness, safety, and development of children. All workers owe it to themselves to get as much training and education as they can.

There are many opportunities for advanced training and education. Some are low-cost or even free. These include vocational-technical schools, community or junior colleges, on-the-job training, and programs under the Department of Labor. In certain cases trainees receive a support allowance while they learn.

Apprenticeship is another route to advanced training. In apprenticeship programs a person learns a skilled trade on-the-job, working under an experienced craftworker. There is related classroom instruction. These programs are conducted by employers, often jointly by labor unions.

You have your whole lifetime to continue your education. Schools and colleges are making it easier for older people to enroll, and the median age of college students is rising noticeably as many older persons are going back to college or entering for the first time.

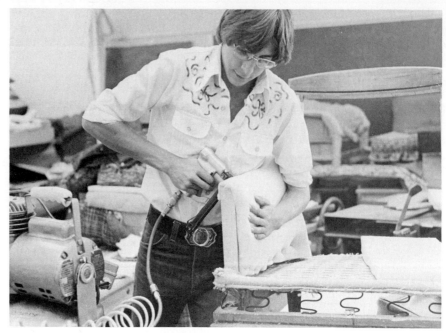

Figure 10-2. Your enthusiasm and dedication result in a good product; your employer will appreciate both. (Future Homemakers of America)

Choose your training program with care. Not all schools provide the training *or* the jobs they advertise. If in doubt, check with your counselor or consumer protection agency.

Dependability, honesty, responsibility, education. Are these your values? If so, they will help you be a success at work.

THINGS THAT LIMIT PRODUCTIVITY

The employer is concerned with production: the number of trays served in a hospital, beds made in a motel, or meals served in a fast-food operation. And so is the operator in a clothing factory whose pay depends on the number of bundles sewed.

When productivity falls, business profits fall and firms may go bankrupt. In nonprofit organizations such as hospitals and schools, people do not get the services they need.

PROBLEMS AT HOME AND SCHOOL

All human beings require security, love, and recognition. Trouble in your personal and family life—divorcing parents, alcoholism, failing grades, breaking up with someone you have loved—can affect your performance at work. As a result, you are not as employable *with* problems as you are without them.

Employers and coworkers on the job care about you. But depression over personal problems and time spent talking over these problems with others at work limits productivity. It interferes with getting the work done.

HEALTH

Poor health can limit your productivity on the job. Some home economics occupations require unusually good mental and physical health. For example, home health aides and child care workers must be emotionally stable. There is no place for the worker who abuses children or the elderly. Physical stamina is a requirement for the hospitality industry, if your focus is food service or maintenance.

Preventive Medicine and Nutrition. The idea behind preventive medicine is to prevent medical problems from starting by such means as yearly physical examinations, immunizations, and regular dental care. Mental health clinics and good nutrition are other elements of preventive medicine.

Table 10-1 reviews the major nutrients and ways they are used in the body. As you look over the list of foods supplying nutrients, you see Basic Four foods repeated over and over: the milk group; meat, fish, poultry, and eggs; fruits and vegetables; and cereal and bread.

In addition to choosing the right kinds of food, good nutrition means selecting the right amounts of food for weight control. You may want to gain, lose, or maintain your present weight. The challenge is to balance the energy value of food, measured by calories, with the energy that bodies use to move and for processes like breathing, heartbeat, digestion, and warmth.

Drug Abuse. Alcohol and marijuana are often called the most widely abused mind or mood drugs. People known to abuse them stand little chance of being hired. The day they go to work "under the influence" may be the last day on that job. A recommendation for another job cannot be expected, no matter how good the worker has been up until then. Is it worth the risk?

WASTING TIME

Most workers in any job are judged according to the way they use and manage time. To waste time is to limit your own productivity and, often, that of your fellow workers.

What are the major time wasters on a job? Drop-in visitors and needless telephone calls lead the list.

Unless they are customers, friends cannot expect you to stop to talk with them while you are on the job. As for coworkers, you can discuss personal matters with them at lunch or on coffee breaks.

Don't tie up the agency or company phone with personal calls. No one may be using the phone at work, but you have no way of knowing how many people are trying to phone in.

Table 10-1 NUTRITION IN A NUTSHELL

Nutrients	Uses in the Body	Major Food Sources
Proteins	Build bones, muscles, and blood Fight infection Supply energy	Meat Fish Poultry Eggs Milk Dried peas and beans Nuts Cereals
Carbohydrates (sugar and starch)	Energy	Breads Cereals Dried Fruits Starchy vegetables Sugar
Vitamins*		
Vitamin A	Healthy skin and mucous membrane	Yellow and green vegetables Egg yolk Cream, butter
Vitamin B	Healthy nerves, digestion, and skin	Whole grain cereals Green leafy vegetables Meat Milk Eggs
Vitamin C	Prevents infection Promotes healing Healthy blood vessels	Citrus fruits Tomatoes Cabbage
Vitamin D	Helps build bones	Vitamin D milk Fish liver oil
Minerals*		
Calcium	Helps build bones, teeth Helps blood to clot	Milk Leafy green vegetables
Iodine	Healthy thyroid (prevents goiter)	Iodized salt Seafood
Iron	Builds blood	Meat Eggs Green leafy vegetables
Fat	Energy Keeps skin smooth	Butter, cream Salad oils, margarine

*Note: There are other vitamins and minerals. If your diet provides the major nutrients given here, you can expect it to provide the others also.

Another time waster is a cluttered work station where time is spent looking for something which is lost in the confusion.

Fatigue wastes time, when the tired person makes mistakes or has accidents which take time to correct. Get proper rest before going to work.

Failing to plan ahead wastes time. If the worker can't decide what to do next, he or she should try to become organized.

Poor instructions are time wasters. If you give directions on the job, be sure they are clear. When you are the receiver, be sure you understand what is expected.

HOW YOU RATE

Table 10-2 shows an evaluation chart used by employers to evaluate workers. The chart shows a range of employee behavior. In the safety area, for example, if workers are a hazard to themselves or others, they deserve a score of (1) or "unsatisfactory." If workers are alert to hazards then they deserve a score of (5) or "superior." How do you rate?

Notice the personal qualities most prized by employers. Appearance is one, along with skill in relationships and dependability. Initiative, being able to go ahead on your own once you know what to do, is rewarded with a high rating.

Figure 10-3. Needless personal phone calls waste time and can interfere with getting your work done.

The worker who demonstrates these personal qualities and produces careful, high-quality work is a success on the job. You feel a sense of pride in your work and, best of all, in yourself.

Table 10-2 EMPLOYEE EVALUATION CHART

	1*	3	5
Appearance	Sloppy, unattractive.	Meets minimum requirements of job.	Attractive, adds to business image.
Relationships Supervisor	Resists criticism and direction.	Accepts supervision, follows directions.	Invites criticism, quickly understands directions.
Coworkers	Source of friction.	Cooperates with others.	Contributes to group morale.
Public	Discourteous, neglects patrons.	Courteous, puts patrons first.	Enjoys people; can handle difficult patrons.
Production Quantity	Rarely finishes assigned task.	Reasonable work pace; requires occasional help.	Consistently on top of job; helps others.
Quality	Careless, sloppy.	Meets minimum standards.	Does careful work of high quality.
Safety	A hazard to himself and others.	Needs occasional warning.	Alert to hazards to himself and others.
Initiative	Dependent upon direction.	Shows initiative in routine matters.	Consistently goes ahead on own.
Dependability Integrity	Questionable honesty about time, money, supplies.	Honest about money and supplies. Rarely wastes time.	Completely honest about time, money, supplies.
Loyalty	Criticizes company on and off job	Accepts company facilities and policies.	Promotes company, shows pride.
Absenteeism	Late and/or excessive absenteeism.	Usually punctual; rarely absent.	Consistently present and punctual.
Key: 1*—Unsatisfactory; 3—Acceptable; 5—Superior			

Adapted from: H. Y. Nelson, and G. P. Jacoby, *Evaluation of Secondary School Programs to Prepare Students for Wage Earning in Occupations Related to Home Economics,* Department of Health, Education, and Welfare, Washington, 1967.

1. According to employers, *appearance, manner of behavior,* and *attitudes* on the job make the difference between failure and success. They like *confidence, enthusiasm,* and *alertness* to the needs of others, whether to fellow workers or the public.

2. Skill in *getting along with others* is part of being successful at work. In most jobs you have to cope with *coworkers, supervisors,* and the *public.* Sometimes you also have to be able to get along with *government inspectors.*

3. How you *produce* on the job depends on your ability to *follow directions, accept supervision,* and work *independently.*

4. In many home economics jobs you are a member of a *team.* Every team member must perform well if the team is to succeed. In any job, *cooperation* among workers contributes to job satisfaction.

5. The *public* counts. They are the reason your job exists. The child, patient, or customer comes first, and workers are expected to always be *courteous.*

6. *Thoughtfulness, kindness,* and showing more *interest* in others than yourself are all part of your manner of behavior. These qualities smooth relationships with the public, coworkers, supervisors, and inspectors.

7. *Dependability, honesty, responsibility,* and *education* are values which lead to success on the job. There are many opportunities for advanced training and education. Some are low-cost or free. In some cases trainees receive support allowances while they learn.

8. Things that *limit productivity* are personal problems, poor health, drug abuse, and wasting time. *Drop-in visitors* and *needless phone calls* are time wasters. Other time wasters are fatigue, which can cause accidents and mistakes, and a cluttered work space, where time is spent looking for something lost in the confusion.

9. Business-like appearance, skill in relationships, dependability, and careful work of high quality all result in a high rating from the employer. They lead to success on the job and a sense of pride.

● FOLLOW-UP PROJECTS

1. What is your image? How do you appear to others? The instructor should videotape students or take photographs. How does your image contribute to public relations on your volunteer or paid job?

2. If your are employed, rate yourself on the evaluation chart shown in Table 10-2. If you are not yet employed, rate your personal employability qualities (see the student workbook). Talk over your rating with your teacher. What are your strengths? Where is there room for improvement?

3. Invite a panel of employers to class. Ask them what they expect from their beginning workers.

4. Develop a checklist of manners that matter on the job, at school, on dates, and at home. Role-play, showing how consideration for others and respect for their privacy can smooth relationships.

5. Working in small groups, prepare meals which demonstrate ways to save the nutrients in food. Prepare and share meals which help with weight control: for persons wishing to lose weight, to gain weight, to maintain weight.

6. Find out what vocational training is available in your community, such as manpower programs, apprentice programs, vocational-technical schools, courses offered in community and 4-year colleges. Find out the costs, lengths of time the training takes, whether graduates get jobs, and the kinds of jobs they get. Interview graduates regarding their satisfaction with the training, their jobs, and chances for advancement. Find out average starting pay.

7. Watch in your local papers and on television for training school advertisements. Do any of them make misleading claims? Could graduates get the same jobs without the course?

8. As a class, develop learning centers on simple clothing repair, spot removal, and laundry for use by students who do not already know these techniques.

11 COMMUNICATING WITH OTHERS

After studying Chapter 11 you should be better able to:

1. Follow oral and written directions.
2. Record a complete and accurate message.
3. Explain the contribution of every worker to public relations.
4. Demonstrate through role playing a capacity for empathy with a customer, child, or client without passing judgment or imposing your own values.
5. Give a demonstration combining good verbal, nonverbal, and visual communication.
6. Demonstrate standard telephone manners.
7. Handle complaints tactfully.

To communicate is to send and receive messages. Sometimes you send a message and have to wait for the reply. This is true when you write a letter or send a telegram.

Sometimes you just receive messages: through television, radio, newspapers, or direct-mail advertising. You may send back a reply: Write a letter to the editor, answer a want ad, or order from a mail-order catalogue. Mostly people just receive the messages sent, sort out what is important to them, and forget the rest.

At other times, communication means *interacting,* both giving messages and receiving immediate answers. This might be face to face or by telephone or CB radio. Some interaction is merely a brief encounter; other, a deep sharing of ideas and feelings.

In many home economics occupations, services or products are offered for sale. Successful communication puts the customer in a favorable frame of mind to buy. We speak of maintaining good public relations, of projecting a positive image so that the customers buy from us or people needing help come to our agency.

In sales, interaction is usually brief and impersonal. The salesperson is expected to be courteous and business-like. In interior design or clothing alteration, where the designer or tailor gives more attention to tastes and wants, the interaction is longer and more intimate. In child care or community services, communication is open and trusting so the child can be taught and the client counseled.

**HOW PEOPLE
COMMUNICATE**

How, exactly, do people communicate with each other? How do they give and receive messages? Languages were invented for just that purpose, to convey meanings through speech and the written word. But words are just the beginning. Babies communicate long before they can use words. Everyone who owns a pet knows that they communicate very well without using languages. How do you know when your cat is hungry? Wants attention? Does your dog sit up, shake hands, bark, nudge your hand as a means of communicating with you? Are you ever very much in doubt about what your pet is "saying"?

Communicating without words is sometimes called nonverbal communication or *body language*. Body language refers to the messages people send and receive through gestures, facial expressions, posture, and dress.

Gestures that convey a lot of meaning are things like finger drumming, hand twisting, squirming, and foot shuffling. Unfortunately, the messages these gestures send are negative: they express nervousness, impatience, or boredom. The sender may not even be aware of them.

Gestures can be used in a positive way. They can clarify the message you are trying to send. You point to explain, pat on the back to congratulate, and shake hands to demonstrate friendliness.

Another kind of body language is called *social distance*. Social distance refers to the space you keep between yourself and others when you speak with them. It means drawing close to or moving away from people. Have you noticed how uneasy you become when someone stands closer than feels comfortable to you? You automatically move away. Animals have what is called the *territorial imperative,* which means staking out their territory and warning other animals to stay off it. Apparently the human animal does the same thing. This kind of body language may be friendly, saying "I like you. I want to be close to you." Or it may seem threatening and aggressive and seem to be saying, "I'm in charge here and you will do as I say."

Eye contact is body language also: looking people right in the eye, blinking, or looking away. According to recent research, the pupils of the eye dilate or open wider when you like what you see, and constrict or get smaller when you don't like what you see. Of course the amount of light causes the pupils of the eyes to react in the same way, to widen in the dark and narrow in the glare of the sun.

Facial expression is more easily controlled, but sometimes surprise, fear, or dislike is mirrored in a face for an instant before that particular message is hidden. Smiling, looking alert and interested, lifting eyebrows, and frowning are all ways that people use to accent the words they are saying. (Or use when they want to communicate without words in church, in class, through a bus or plane window.) A smile can show appreciation, approval,

Figure 11-1. Do you feel uncomfortable when someone seems to stand unusually close to you?

respect, and encouragement, but it can also be a sneer, a laughing *at* rather than *with* the other person. It can be a sign of rebellion ("you and who else?") and ridicule ("you must be kidding!"). These examples of facial expressions are just the beginning. There are many more made possible by different combinations of eyebrow, eyelid, and mouth positions, the thrust of the chin, and the tilt of the head.

Body stance or posture can send a message of pride, confidence, and interest or one of depression and despair, of defiance, fear, or "couldn't care less." Think of the waitress or waiter standing attentively, pencil and pad poised to receive your order. Or of the angry 4-year old, feet planted far apart, hands on hip, chin thrust out. Or of the dejected and lonely aged person, shoulders rounded, head nodding forward, resting on the hands. Or the salesclerk slouched behind the counter, gazing toward the clock.

The messages your *style of dress* send are much like those of your posture. Do your clothes say pride, confidence, and self-respect? Or the opposite?

Tone of voice and how fast or slowly you speak also affect the meaning of what you say. The words you accent are significant. So are giggling, yawning, groaning, and sniffing.

Body language has different meanings depending on regions of the country, cultures, and age groups. This is important to remember in home economics occupations, where you often serve people with backgrounds different from yours. Others may be older or younger, richer or poorer, more or less educated, and more or less experienced. Your business often caters to tourists from other parts of the country or of the world.

Consciously or unconsciously, people are always sending and receiving messages through body language. It often gets in the way of the words being spoken. People may attend so closely to body language they do not hear the words. At other times people hear only the words and miss the subtle messages of body language. You will want to spend some time in front of a mirror studying your own body language. Are you communicating what you intend to?

COMMUNICATION SKILLS IMPORTANT IN HOME ECONOMICS OCCUPATIONS

What communication skills are important on the job? Skill in *listening* is essential, in order to follow directions, receive orders, handle complaints, answer the phone, counsel clients, and guide children. *Speaking* clearly is just as important, in order to give directions, answer questions, and advise customers. Understanding what *body language* is and being able to receive its messages is crucial for teacher aides, counselors, and home health aides. They must also use body language to better communicate what they want to say. *Reading* skills are needed in order to follow written directions, read stories to children, and read reports about clients.

Writing business letters and reports and recording telephone messages are often part of the worker's responsibilities. *Visual* communications are prepared by child care and teacher aides to assist instruction. They are used also in advertising and commercial displays and in other ways. Let's take a closer look at each of these skills.

LISTENING

There is a human need for someone to listen, to care, to understand what is clearly expressed and what is left unspoken. Learning to listen can enrich everyone's personal life. At work, listening skills means being able to follow directions, to get along with fellow workers, and to help customers and clients. Employers value workers who listen to directions, quickly understand them, and accurately follow them. They know that once workers understand exactly what they are to do they can go ahead on their own.

Some jobs require special listening skills. The worker listens differently to children, parents, teachers, the aged, the ill, the intoxicated, and people with special needs who are not accustomed to expressing themselves. Think how many different people the teacher aide listens to, for example, or the flight attendant or floor mechanic or juvenile probation officer aide.

Why can't people listen? What gets in the way? Real language barriers, sometimes, like speaking another language, or speaking with a different accent, or using unfamiliar words. Another problem is that you can think faster than the other person can speak, so your mind wants to race on ahead. Or you may think you already know what the person is going to say. Or you are distracted by mannerisms or dress (body language). Or your own emotions intrude. You are nervous or upset and planning what to say next rather than hearing the words of the other person.

To be a good listener requires concentration on and sensitivity to what the other is saying and feeling. To improve your listening skills:

· Give immediate feedback. That is, repeat the directions given or rephrase in your own words what you think the other person has just said, to be sure you understand.
· Watch the body language of the other person and try to interpret it.
· Empathize with the other person.

Empathy has been described as walking a while in the other person's shoes, putting yourself in the other person's place. You do not need to agree or sympathize with the other person, but you do need to understand exactly how the other person feels. Thus you do not agree with an angry customer or a fearful child. But you do see the situation from his or her viewpoint. You send the message "I am with you" and the angry person becomes less angry, the fearful child less afraid. Empathy allows you to be more objective and less emotional. You can think more clearly.

There is an important difference between sympathy, "I feel as you do," and empathy, "I know how you feel." Sympathy is not always welcome. Empathy is more likely to be appreciated.

You can see that an essential part of empathy is to accept and respect the other person. The troubled child or sick adult senses this and views you as someone to be trusted. They do not feel rejected and defensive. They are able instead to express themselves more clearly. You are able to better understand their problem and suggest a solution.

Empathy reduces tension, frustration, anger, and fear but cannot be expected to do away with them altogether.

SPEAKING: PUBLIC RELATIONS BEGINS WITH YOU

What you as a worker say on the job and how you say it projects the public image of the company. You *are* the company or the agency as far as the customer or client is concerned. How a waitress or waiter speaks to a hungry and tired child, how a housing project aide speaks to a tenant worried about paying the rent, and how an appliance salesperson explains the workings of the refrigerator all influence the sale of food or equipment and the cooperation of the tenant. In home economics occupations, workers give a lot of advice: which fabric to select, how to care for a wall finish, what agency to contact. Such advice must be given in a helpful and pleasant way. Clear directions must often be given: food orders relayed from dining room to kitchen, for example, or instructions given new employees. There is a special voice tone, reassuring but firm, required when making sure a patient follows doctor's orders or when guiding a child's play or routine.

Figure 11-2. Good relations between your employer and the public begin with you. (Richard Watherwax, Nancy Palmer Photo Agency)

Information you give must be clear and accurate: when you explain how menu items are prepared, how to care for a fabric, how to apply to an agency for help. Your voice tone can show you are friendly, pleasant, and understanding. Use of correct grammer is always desirable when speaking to customers and is essential around children. Slang may be frowned on, depending on the job. Parents do not want you to teach their children poor speech habits. Profanity will disturb customers, and may be offensive to coworkers also. Speak slowly to people who are not familiar with English or who are hard of hearing.

ANSWERING THE PHONE

Answering the phone was a task mentioned as often performed by entry–level workers. Telephone manners are so important in the business world that definite rules have been worked out. In general:

· Use a pleasant tone of voice.
· Identify yourself and your office or company, according to your employer's instructions.
· Have pencil, paper, and calendar handy.
· Thank the person for calling.

TAKING A MESSAGE

When taking a message by phone or directly from a customer or parent, include the who, what, when, and where of the message:

Who: Make sure you spell the name right.

When: Record the date and time.

What: Write down all the details. Is the message a reservation for dinner? A request for an appointment? For repair service?

Where: Is the call to be returned (area code, number, and extension) or delivery made (street and number, and any special directions for lakeside, country, or apartment house)?

Make sure to write clearly, so someone else can read the message. Deliver it as soon as possible.

HANDLING COMPLAINTS

The entry-level worker rarely has to settle complaints but often has to receive them. The complaints are probably not directed at the worker personally and are probably beyond the control of a single worker to change. But the worker has the responsibility to receive the complaints graciously and in such a way as to create customer good will, to keep friends rather than make enemies. Since complaints are so much a part of the work world, rules have been developed for receiving complaints either by phone or in person.
In general:

· Make sure you understand what the complaint is about.
· Be cheerful and gracious.
· Refer the complainer to the proper person at once, or assure the caller that action will be taken promptly.
· Do not pass judgment on the complainant, just pass on the complaint to the appropriate person. This may be the executive housekeeper, host or hostess, nursery school director, or similar supervisor.

When a complaint is made the company has a chance to make amends or to correct a condition they might not otherwise know about. Many people do not complain when they are unhappy with a service or product. They just take their business somewhere else.

WRITING: WHEN ALL YOU HAVE IS THE WRITTEN WORD

Look at the last notes you took in class. Can anyone, including you, read them? What about the last telephone message you recorded? Is it clear enough for someone else to understand? A simple rule for writing messages for others is to make it clear, keep it neat.

Writing legibly is especially important when taking an order to be filled or keeping health or business records. Mistakes can mean lost customers or even more serious trouble. Sloppy handwriting can give your employer the impression that you are careless, even when you are not.

In addition to writing messages, keeping records, and taking orders, you may need to write business letters and reports. When all you have is the written word to report your achievements, request information, or sell a service or product, the message must be concise, clear, and attention getting. You do not have a chance to sell yourself or your product in person, and you are not on the spot to answer questions which may arise.

Writing letters and other messages does have one advantage. You can think through your message, organize the material, and make changes.

Writing is a chore for many people, but others like to express themselves in this way. In most businesses there is a place for the person with a flair for writing advertising. Every agency has to write reports. There are always records to be kept. The person who likes to write will find plenty of encouragement on the job.

VISUAL COMMUNICATION: BECOMING A MEDIA SPECIALIST

The worker in home economics occupations often uses visuals to teach or to tempt people to buy goods or services. Clothing salesworkers, interior designers, and food service workers all use visuals to sell their products: window and counter displays, model rooms, menu cards. Child care workers, teacher aides, and recreation aides use visuals to teach: a story book, bulletin board, craft sample, or game board. Whatever the media, the message should be clear. Each visual should have a point, a big idea.

A good visual, whether it is a menu, a child's book, or carpet display, has definite requirements: neatness, a color scheme, and good design. Color schemes are planned according to the purpose of the visual. If your major purpose is to attract attention, you'll use bright or contrasting colors. If your purpose is to sell infants' clothing, you will probably choose soft pastels instead of bright red for your counter display.

Good design can be achieved by following the principles of design you learned in art or home economics classes.

GIVING DEMONSTRATIONS

You may be called upon to give a demonstration to sell a product or teach others how to do something. You might demonstrate the use of a new product in a food store. You might demonstrate how to use an appliance. You might teach another worker how to polish furniture. You might teach school children a craft.

Giving a demonstration is a matter of preparation, planning, and practice. First, think through the purpose of the demonstration—what you want people to be able to do after watching your demonstration. Plan a list of the steps you will follow and all the materials you will need. Everything should be large enough to be seen by the audience, so you will probably need visuals. Plan time for the viewers to ask questions and be sure you can answer them.

You can see that giving a demonstration is a good way to check out your communication skill in speaking, listening, preparing a visual, and using body language. All communication skills can be developed through practice. The practice is sometimes tedious, but the skills increase your chances for personal happiness and success on the job.

CHAPTER SUMMARY

1. To *communicate* is to send and receive messages. People use *words* to communicate, but they also use *body language*. Body language refers to the messages people send and receive through *gestures, social distance, eye contact, facial expression, posture,* and *style of dress. Tone of voice* and how fast or slowly you speak also affect the message.

2. Body language has different meanings depending on *regions* of the country, *cultures,* and *age groups*. Successful workers in home economics occupations are aware of body language, their own and that of the public with whom they work.

3. Skill in *listening* is needed in order to follow directions, answer the phone, and counsel clients. *Empathy* helps you improve your listening skills. Empathy means to put yourself in the other person's place and understand how he or she feels.

Figure 11-3. When giving a demonstration, think through what you want to explain, plan a list of steps to follow, and make sure people can see what you're doing. Afterwards, allow your audience to ask questions. (Kenneth Karp)

4. *Speaking clearly* is important in order to give directions, answer questions, and reassure a child. When *taking a message,* record the who, what, when, and where. Make sure written messages are readable. Deliver a message as soon as possible.

5. Entry-level workers rarely have to settle *complaints* but often have to receive them. When customers or clients complain, the business or agency has a chance to make amends or correct a condition they did not know about. Complaints should be handled with courtesy and quickly passed on to your supervisor.

6. When all you have is the *written word,* be sure it is clear. Visuals should also be clear, neat, and of good *design.*

7. Giving a *demonstration* is a good way to practice speaking, listening, use of visuals, and body language. All communication skills can be improved with *practice.*

• FOLLOW-UP PROJECTS

1. Demonstrate how people communicate without words by using body language to express the following emotions: joy/sorrow; hope/despair; indifference/interest; fear/confidence; frustration/satisfaction; admiration/contempt; shyness/aggression; love/hate; helpfulness/rejection.

2. Prepare collages demonstrating positive and negative body language.

3. Role-play situations involving workers in home economics and the following: disruptive child, irate tenant, rude customer, fearful patient, troubled teenager. The worker should show empathy and courtesy. The class should observe body language of players and give feedback.

4. Study your own body language on videotape or before a mirror.

5. Play a listening game such as old-fashioned "Gossip." Class sits in circle. First student whispers a statement to next person. Each person repeats the statement, continuing around circle. Last person gives aloud the message received. Practice listening skill by repeating the game until the final message is the same as the original. Or have the circle respond to a controversial topic. Each person must repeat what neighbor has just said, then state own opinion.

6. Read directions for operating an unfamiliar appliance or piece of equipment, preparing a new recipe, or setting up a tray for a person on a special diet. Demonstrate ability to follow written directions by performing the activity exactly as directed.

7. Study your phone book for directions for direct dialing a long-distance call, placing a collect call, and reporting an emergency. Phone your local telephone company for a kit of materials to help practice these and other telephone skills.

8. Role-play phoning in answer to a want ad for a job.

9. Practice taking messages: from parent of a nursery school child, an order for room service in a hotel, request for appliance repair, doctor's instructions. Check to be sure to have who, what, when, where, and how or why.

10. Role-play handling a customer complaint.

11. Read a newspaper or magazine article related to a job cluster of interest. Summarize, in writing, the main idea of the article and one or two supporting points.

    or

    Read an advertisement. Give, in writing, an example of a fact presented in the advertisement and an example of an opinion.

    or

    Prepare a report of class activities for the student newspaper.

12. Visit a public library for information on jobs or consumer problem. Locate *D.O.T., Monthly Labor Review, Occupational Outlook Handbook,* and consumer magazines. Practice filling out form for library card.

13. Play a communication game: Sit in circle, all at same level on floor or in chairs. Only one person can talk at a time and must stick to the topic. Leader picks topics related to feelings and skills such as "The thing I do best is . . . ," "I feel sad when . . . ," "I feel angry at people when . . . ," and "I am happiest when. . . ."

14. Write a business letter: request information, invite a speaker to class, thank a speaker for attending a class session, make a consumer complaint.

15. Prepare a visual relevant to a job cluster of interest: a menu card, bulletin board, advertising flyer or poster, brochure with instructions for tenants, counter or window display. Critique each other's work, considering color, neatness, design, lighting. Does the "big idea" come across?

16. Prepare and give a demonstration performing a typical task such as: setting up a buffet table; garnishing food; hemming a pair of slacks; removing stains from clothing or upholstery; buffing a waxed floor; making finger paint, clay, or similar material for children's creative play; referring a client to an agency for help with a consumer or health problem; changing linen on an occupied bed; or removing old finish from furniture. Other students should watch demonstrations and then (a) give feedback on their impression of oral directions in demonstration. (b) Critique each other's work. (You may want to practice your demonstration before one or two friends before presenting it to the class.)

12 | WORKING WITH FIGURES

After studying Chapter 12 you will be better able to:

1. Compute your gross pay.
2. Make out a requisition.
3. Take inventory.
4. Make change.
5. Prepare a salescheck.
6. Price merchandise.
7. Estimate costs.
8. Use the metric system to weigh and measure.
9. Convert customary measure to metric measure.

To *compute* means to work with numbers, to use arithmetic. On the job in home economics you are often expected to perform tasks like "prepare salescheck," "accept payment," "take measurements," "price merchandise," and "estimate costs." You may do all the computing yourself, or there may be machines or charts to help you.

Chances are you will start computing your first day on the job. You will certainly want to add up the numbers of hours you work and multiply by your rate of pay to see how rich you have become.

COMPUTING YOUR PAY

You may be asked to punch a *time card* when you arrive and when you leave. That is, you will be asked to "punch in" and "punch out."

If you forget to punch your card, you will not be paid. If you are late, you lose pay. By the end of the week your card will show all the hours you have worked.

Your work week may be 35 or 40 hours. If you work less, you are paid for the exact hours you have worked. If you work more, you may make overtime pay. For example, some firms may pay you time and a half for overtime and double pay on Sundays and holidays.

Computing your pay in many jobs is simple. In others, overtime and piecework complicate things. Some workers, those in a typical clothing factory, for example, are paid by the hour, but piecework rates are set according to the difficulty of the operation being performed. Those who

Figure 12-1. On a time card you record the number of
hours you've worked during a certain time period. At
many businesses, a machine automatically prints the
time when the worker inserts the card at the beginning
and end of the day.

HARRY'S HAMBURGER

EMPLOYEE NAME

James Morrier

DEPARTMENT	PAY PERIOD ENDING
800	6-22-77

DAY	MORNING IN	NOON OUT	NOON IN	NIGHT OUT	EXTRA IN	EXTRA OUT	TOTAL
	7	12	1	3:30			7½
	7	12	1	3:30			7½
	7	12	1	3:30			7½
	7	12	1	3:30			7½
	7	12	1	3:30			7½

DAY	MORNING IN	NOON OUT	NOON IN	NIGHT OUT	EXTRA IN	EXTRA OUT	TOTAL
	7	12	1	3:30			7½
	7	12	1	3:30			7½
	7	12	1	3:30			7½
	7	12	1	3:30			7½
	7	12	1	3:30			7½

TOTAL ALL HOURS: _____ 75

"make the rate" get paid at a higher scale. To determine whether they make the rate, they keep tickets which give the size, shade, and lot number of bundles of clothing on which they work. At the end of the day the worker must add up, in dozens, the work completed. The worker who has completed enough work has "made the rate" and is paid the higher wage. In this way skilled workers are paid more than others who are slower.

The pay you earn is called your *gross pay.* If deductions are made for social security and income tax, your *take-home pay* will be less. (In a later chapter we'll learn more about deductions.)

FORMS MEAN BUSINESS

There are three types of forms often used in institutions, hotels, restaurants, and other business. They are the *requisition,* the *purchase order,* and the *invoice.* These forms all require similar computing skill—multiplying the amount of the item needed by the *unit price,* and adding up the total. The unit price is the cost of each can, box, pound, or similar unit.

REQUISITION

A requisition is a form used to request supplies from a storeroom. For example, if you are a cook needing certain foods not present in the kitchen, you will make out a requisition. On it you will list a description of each item and the amount you need. You sign the requisition and your supervisor may also need to sign it. Refer to Figure 12-2 for a sample requisition form. The purpose of the requisition is to show the person in charge of the storeroom (called a steward or clerk) exactly what you need. It is also a receipt for the material you have received, and it helps the steward keep a record of the supplies on hand (an inventory).

PURCHASE ORDER

When the storeroom runs low on supplies the clerk notifies the manager or purchasing agent, and another standard business form, the *purchase order,* is made out. Like the requisition, a purchase order is a "shopping list." When you make one out you describe the items you need and the amounts you want. You then fill in the prices, subtract any discounts you may be entitled to, add any taxes that may apply, and add it up for a total. The purchase order is then sent to the company which sells the supplies.

INVOICE

When delivery is made, the steward matches the delivered supplies with the order. Once assured that quantity and quality match the order, a receipt is signed. One copy of the receipt is returned to the seller, whose bookkeeper makes out a bill, an *invoice,* and sends it to your company for payment.

METROPOLITAN HOSPITAL REQUISITION

Charge To __#0639__   Date __2/22/78__

Amount	Unit	Item	Unit Price	Cost
3 DOZ	BOXES	FACIAL TISSUE	.45	16.20
6 DOZ	BOXES	COTTON SWABS	.98	70.56

Total _____ 86.76

Signed ___Helen Martello___

Approved ___R.D.Nietech___

Figure 12-2. A requisition is a form used to order supplies from a storeroom. On it you list the amount, unit, description, price, and total cost of the item.

INVENTORY

Stewards usually keep two kinds of inventories. Once a month, or more often, everything in the storeroom is actually counted. This is sometimes called the *physical inventory*. Another *perpetual inventory* is kept in a book or on cards to show the balance of supplies on hand at any one time. In this system items listed on requisitions are subtracted from the totals on hand and new items are added on when they are delivered. The actual count, or physical inventory, should match the totals in the perpetual inventory. When they do not agree the management is alerted to possible theft, careless work by the steward, or some other problem.

In large operations the whole inventory system is computerized. But you will be expected to make an entry for the computer and will be shown how to do so.

RECEIVING PAYMENTS In any job where you are dealing with customers, your job will include receiving payment for whatever they buy. In order to do this, your employer will show you how to make out a salescheck and receive cash, check, or credit card. You will also be expected to make change when necessary.

PREPARING A SALESCHECK

In home economics occupations many saleschecks are prepared. Examples are guest checks in a food service establishment, a salescheck for clothing in a department store, or a salescheck for fabric in a sewing center. The checks provide the management with a record of the day's sales. You may have a cash register or adding machine to help you.

If you are a waiter in a hotel dining room, you should also have tax tables handy for reference. You may have a lot of time to prepare a neat, handwritten check. If you work in a fast food operation, however, you may have preprinted checks for standard orders, which make checking easy and quick.

In many jobs you may have to work in haste and confusion. Whatever the case, you will be held responsible. You must initial each check you make, including listing or checking of everything ordered or purchased, in

Figure 12-3. Counting the supplies in the stockroom is called taking "physical inventory."

the proper amounts, and at the correct prices. The check must be totaled accurately and the correct tax added. Your check must be reasonably neat and readable, according to the standards set by your employer.

MAKING CHANGE

If the customer pays by cash, you must be able to make change properly if the amount you are given is larger than the amount to be paid.

Suppose, for example, the total to be paid is $4.51, and the customer hands you a $10 bill. Put the bill right in front of the open drawer of your cash register where both you and the customer can see that it is a ten. (If you put it right in the drawer along with the other $10 bills the customer may claim you were given a $20 bill, and then demand $10 more from you.)

Now give the customer 4 pennies, saying "Four fifty-five"; then 20 more cents in nickels or dimes, saying "Four seventy-five"; then a quarter, saying "Five," then a $5 bill, saying "And five are ten." Now you can put the $10 bill in the drawer and close the register.

ESTIMATING COSTS

Another exercise in computing is to estimate costs. Part of your job may be to estimate the cost of carpet to be laid, the cost of paint for a room, the cost of fabric for draperies, and the cost of labor (the workers' pay) to complete these jobs.

In food service, you often estimate the cost of a food item. Suppose you are costing a recipe for the pizza served in your carryout restaurant. You add up the food costs, then divide the total by the number of pizzas you get from the recipe to find the cost of each.

Costing recipes is a common computation for the chef or economy-minded homemaker. Figure 12-4 presents a format for this procedure.

PRICING MERCHANDISE

Pricing merchandise is a task in home economics. A restaurant must charge enough for meals to pay for the cost of raw food, labor, equipment, furnishings, rent, taxes, and all the other business expenses. A store must charge enough for carpeting or paint to cover the basic cost of the products plus business expenses.

This "markup," as it is called, sets the selling price of foods on a menu or merchandise in a store.

The restaurant where you work might have a policy of marking up the cost of meat dishes by two-thirds to get the selling price. Fractions can easily be converted to decimals, so you can use your pocket calculator or some other business machine. Two-thirds $(2/3) = .666$.

Suppose, for example, the cost of the raw food was $1.23. You would multiply 1.23×0.666 to get the markup, 82 cents.

Add the markup to the food cost to get the selling price:
$1.23 + 0.82 = $2.05

Item: __Meat Loaf__

Number of portions: __6__

Ingredients	Package Price	Quantity Used	Unit Price (in cents)	Cost for Quantity Used
ground chuck	$1.39 (pound)	1 lb	.09 (oz)	$1.39
eggs	.99 (dozen)	2	8.3 (each)	.17
rolled oats	1.29 (42-oz box)	1 C	3.0 (oz)	.24
milk	1.89 (gallon)	1 C	1.5 (oz)	.12
onion	1.39 (5-lb bag)	1	27.8 (lb)	.07
catsup	1.25 (32-oz bottle)	1/2 C	3.9 (oz)	.31

Total cost : __$2.30__

Cost per portion : __$ .38__

Figure 12-4. To cost a recipe, figure out the cost of each ingredient used, then add these, and divide by the number of servings.

METRIC MEASURES

Often workers in home economics estimate costs based on measurements. Measurements—length and width of a room, a child's temperature, weight of food portions—are taking on a new look as the metric system is adopted. You'll probably still want to be sure you can accurately measure in inches, quarts, pounds, and degrees Fahrenheit, but the time to think metric is here. Your state and city highway signs may already use metric language, listing kilometers as well as miles. You may buy soft drinks in liters instead of quarts. Your television station reports weather information in Celsius as well as Fahrenheit.

Why change to the metric system? Because the United States is the only industrial nation still using inches, pints, and pounds. Our products are shipped around the world, and success in international trade requires that weights and measures be the same.

Most of the new words are familiar to you. You watch the 200-meter race in the Olympics and view a 16-millimeter film in class. You see nutrients expressed in grams on your cereal box.

To think metric, remember:

· Weight is a measure related to heaviness.
· Length is a measure of extent or distance.

· Volume is a measure of space occupied.

· Temperature is a measure of hotness and coldness.

The basic metric units are the *gram* to measure weight, the *meter* to measure length, and the *liter* to measure volume. Notice in Table 12-1 that the prefixes *kilo- centi-*, and *milli-* mean the same thing whether the measure is weight, length, or volume. A *milli*gram = 0.001 gram. A *milli*meter = 0.001 meter. A *milli*liter = 0.001 liter.

Table 12-1 METRIC MEASUREMENTS

Weight	Length	Volume
1 kilogram (kg) = 1,000 grams	1 kilometer (km) = 1,000 meters	1 hectoliter (hL) = 100 liters
1 hectogram (hg) = 100 grams	1 hectometer (hm) = 100 meters	1 dekaliter (daL) = 10 liters
1 dekagram (dag) = 10 grams	1 dekameter (dam) = 10 meters	1 liter (L) = 1 liter
1 gram (g) or (gm) = 1 gram	1 meter (m) = 1 meter	1 deciliter (dL) = 0.1 liter
1 decigram (dg) = 0.1 gram	1 decimeter (dm) = 0.1 meter	1 centiliter (cL) = 0.01 liter
1 centigram (cg) = 0.01 gram	1 centimeter (cm) = 0.01 meter	1 milliliter (mL) = 0.001 liter
1 milligram (mg) = 0.001 gram	1 millimeter (mm) = 0.001 meter	

You might be asked on the job to convert a recipe to metric. Using the conversion chart, Table 12-2, you can convert an old recipe to new metric and get some practice in multiplying decimals at the same time.

Table 12-2 APPROXIMATE CONVERSIONS TO METRIC MEASURES

	When You Know	Multiply By	To Find
Length	inches	2.5	centimeters
	feet	30.	centimeters
	yards	0.9	meters
	miles	1.6	kilometers
Weight	ounces	28.	grams
	pounds	0.45	kilograms
Volume	teaspoons	5.	milliliters
	tablespoons	15.	milliliters
	fluid ounces	30.	milliliters
	cups	0.24	liters
	pints	0.47	liters
	quarts	0.95	liters
	gallons	3.8	liters
Temperature	Fahrenheit	5/9, after subtracting 32	Celsius

Adapted from: National Bureau of Standards.

Converting recipes means working mostly with volume. To practice weight and length measures, establish your own height and weight measurements in metric, using the conversion tables.

Temperatures are measured in degrees Celsius (formerly called centigrade) rather then Fahrenheit. Some important temperatures for workers in home economics are shown in Figure 12-5.

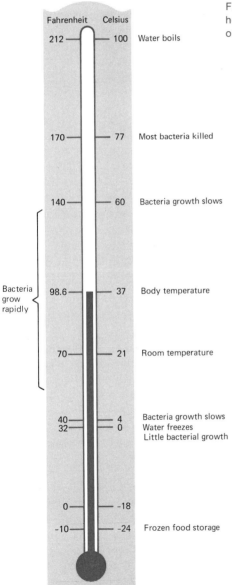

Figure 12-5. Here are some important temperatures for workers in home economics occupations. Notice that the temperatures are given on both the Fahrenheit and Celsius scales.

Fahrenheit	Celsius	
212	100	Water boils
170	77	Most bacteria killed
140	60	Bacteria growth slows
98.6	37	Body temperature
70	21	Room temperature
40	4	Bacteria growth slows
32	0	Water freezes
		Little bacterial growth
0	–18	
–10	–24	Frozen food storage

Bacteria grow rapidly

**CHAPTER
SUMMARY**

1. To *compute* means to work with numbers, to use arithmetic. Workers can compute their *gross* pay, to make sure they are paid what they earn. Your employer may ask you to punch a *time card,* which will show all the hours you have worked. Computing your pay can mean figuring *overtime* and *piecework rates.*

2. If deductions have been made for social security and income tax, your *take-home* pay will be less.

3. Three kinds of forms often used in businesses are the *requisition, purchase order,* and *invoice.* They all require similar computing: multiplying the amount of the item needed by the *unit price* and adding up the total. Unit price is the cost of each can, box, pound, or similar unit.

4. A storeroom clerk usually keeps two kinds of inventories. A *perpetual* inventory is kept in a book or on cards to show the balance of supplies on hand at any one time. The actual count, or *physical* inventory, should match the totals in the perpetual inventory. When they do not agree the management is alerted to theft, carelessness, or some other problem. In large operations the inventory system may be computerized, but you must make an *entry.*

5. Your employer will show you *how to receive* payment by cash, check, or credit card. You are expected to *make correct change* where needed.

6. *Saleschecks* may be preprinted or handwritten, prepared in haste and confusion or with time for careful thought. You are held responsible for each check you prepare. The check must be totaled accurately and the correct tax added.

7. Another computing skill is to *estimate costs* of food items, carpet, paint, fabric, and costs of the labor to make or install these products. You may help *price merchandise* by figuring *markup.* Markup is added to the basic costs to decide the selling price.

8. Measurements may be made using the metric system. The basic metric units are the *gram,* to measure weight, the *meter,* to measure length, and the *liter,* to measure volume. Temperature is measured in degrees Celsius.

• FOLLOW-UP PROJECTS

1. Visit a clothing factory, food processing plant, or similar large operation employing home economics workers. View a demonstration on use of a time clock. Interview manager or supervisor regarding piecework rates, job opportunities, and career ladder.

2. Ask school or local business officer for copies of a requisition, a purchase order, and an invoice form. Practice filling them in, checking each other's work for accuracy.

3. Set up a perpetual inventory of your personal wardrobe, stereo collection, sports equipment, or other possessions.

4. Discuss kinds of saleschecks used in places where you are employed. How are they alike? Different?

5. Using real menus and sample guest checks collected from local restaurants, practice taking orders, preparing and presenting guest checks, and making change.

6. Role-play accepting checks and credit cards from customers.

7. Using metric measures, estimate amount and cost of carpeting your home economics department.

8. Working in pairs, measure your height, body dimensions, and weight in metric.

9. Figure the markup and selling price on the following:

Cost	Rate of markup	Amount of markup	Selling price
$0.89	¾	_____	_____
1.26	80%	_____	_____
0.95	2½	_____	_____
2.34	.67	_____	_____

10. Survey businesses in the community to find out extent of metric measures used. What problems are involved in changing from one system to another?

11. Compute gross pay, using your own or simulated pay rate and work hours.

13 SAFETY AND SANITATION SKILLS

After studying Chapter 13 you should be able to:

1. Recognize conditions which cause accidents.
2. Identify fire hazards and explain what to do in case of a fire.
3. Demonstrate work habits which help prevent fire, accidents, and spread of disease.
4. Demonstrate how to report an emergency.
5. Demonstrate how to take emergency action for shock, severe bleeding, suffocation, poisoning, burns, and fractures.
6. Willingly follow rules and regulations for safety and sanitation.

Home economics occupations are people occupations. In most jobs, you are responsible for the safety and well-being of others. A child care worker is responsible for the safety of children, a home health aide for people who are ill or aged. A building service aide is responsible for safe conditions where people live, work, and shop. A short-order cook is responsible for preparing food which does not cause food poisoning or spread disease.

Another person to protect from harm is you, the worker. If your job is in the maintenance cluster you may work with electric motors and machines, strong chemicals, sharp tools, steam and pressure, and heavy loads. Food service workers face the same hazards at work. Drycleaners and launderers work with steam, heat, and chemicals. Many people in the interior design cluster work with sharp tools and toxic adhesives, and they lift heavy loads.

Laws have been passed to protect workers on the job. One unit of the Department of Labor is the Occupational Safety and Health Administration (OSHA). OSHA is responsible for preventing illness and injury in the work place.

There are also local laws, to protect both the worker and the consumer. These deal with sanitation in food service, inspection for fire hazards, and other safety conditions. But success on the job depends on you, and in home economics occupations, safety and sanitation skills are part of success.

Workers in the service group have one of the highest accident rates in the American work force. Operators and craftworkers also report many acci-

SAFETY ON THE JOB

dents each year. But accidents in the home, the work place for many of you, occur almost three times as often as industrial accidents.

Accidents do not just happen. They are caused. What causes accidents?

· Tension from time pressures, fear, or emotional upset
· Illness
· Fatigue
· Lack of skill in doing a task
· Overconfidence
· Showing off
· Breaking regulations

FIRE

Fire is one of the greatest accidental killers, and it strikes hardest at children and the elderly. Many injuries and deaths have occurred because the victims did not know what to do. Recognizing hazards, knowing what to do in case of fire, and working in a way that will reduce the chance of fire are all safety skills.

Three things are needed for a fire: fuel to burn, heat, and air. When you strike a match, for example, the tip flares for a moment. It ignites the matchstick, which is the fuel. The oxygen in the air then keeps the match burning.

Take away any of these—fuel, air, or heat—and the fire will not burn. A pan of burning fat can be smothered by putting a tight lid on it to remove air. Water puts out burning paper or wood by cooling it.

Fires and fire extinguishers are sometimes classified as:

· Class A. Fires in wood, paper, grass, and clothing, which can be put out with water (a cooling agent.)
· Class B. Fires in gas, oils, and greases which must be smothered with foam, dry powder, or carbon dioxide. (Water will scatter droplets of burning fat and spread the fire.)
· Class C. Fires in electric equipment, which are safely put out with dry powder or carbon dioxide. (Water cannot be used on electric fires because of the danger of electrocution.)

You will be taught on the job how to use the proper fire extinguisher.

Preventing Fires. Chief causes of fires are careless smoking, faulty electrical wiring, flammable liquids, misuse of heating and cooking equipment, and spontaneous combustion. Children playing with matches, lighting, and faulty chimneys are other common causes.

Fire fighters have a saying: "A clean building seldom burns." Many fires start in trash piles, rubbish, or stored odds and ends, all of which provide the fuel for a fire. When heat is supplied by cigarette ashes, electric sparks, a child's match, or a stove burner, the result is big trouble.

Figure 13-1. Many factors can cause accidents on the job. For example, rushing around under time pressure or recklessly showing off can cause workers to trip or fall.

Work Habits. Work habits that help prevent fires are:

· Throwing trash and paper in approved containers
· Not allowing flammable matter to collect near ranges or motors
· Being sure curtains do not blow over open flames or burners when the window is open
· Keeping oven and exhaust screens over ranges free of grease
· Wiping up spilled grease and flammable liquids at once
· Airing out a gas oven before lighting it, to let any gas which may have collected there escape
· Reporting frayed wires, loose sockets and plugs, or faulty appliances
· Storing oily rags, containers of wax, paint, and other flammables only in approved storage areas
· Never using gasoline or similar fluids indoors, where their vapors can be ignited by the spark of a light switch or an electric fan
· Cooperating with the building management and local fire department during fire drills and routine fire inspections.

If you work with the ill, the elderly, or children, there are special work habits to help prevent fires. The ill or elderly may be careless when smokivg and require constant watching to be sure they use ashtrays, do not smoke in bed, and are careful when discarding matches. Elderly people may turn on a stove, iron, or other heating appliance and forget it.

Never leave matches or cigarette lighters where young children can find them. Teach children the danger of fire and also teach them that alarm boxes are not toys. False alarms tie up fire fighters and equipment which may be needed to respond to a real emergency.

What to Do. Every family should have a fire plan and regular fire drills so that each member knows what to do. This includes planning *two* ways, if possible, to escape from a fire in case one way is blocked. It includes planning for a fire at night and having flashlights handy. Part of the plan is deciding on a place for all to meet once they are safely out.

In case of fire, the general rules are:

· Don't waste time getting dressed or hunting for valuables.
· *First*, warn everyone and get everyone out of the building. *Then*, call the fire department, if you safely can without being trapped. A neighbor or passerby can give the alarm.
· Go to the meeting place so lives are not lost trying to rescue someone who is already safe.
· Worry about people (who cannot be replaced) and not about things (which can be replaced).

At work there may be supervisors and highly trained people to help in case of a fire. But sometimes you must act alone. Such was the case for Joanne, and here is her story.

Joanne

Joanne was caring for three children overnight in a house far from any neighbors. The children were 5, 3, and 6 months old. Early in the morning a fire started, and Joanne and the children were trapped on the second floor.

First Joanne braced the doorway shut against the strong drafts of very hot air rising up the stairs. Then she helped the two older children out the window onto the little stoop built over the front door entrance. She gave the baby to the 5-year old to hold. The children loved and trusted Joanne and did exactly as she said.

Meanwhile she tied sheets tightly together, fastened them to a radiator by the window, and lowered herself to the ground. She found a ladder and was climbing up to bring the children down when a neighbor saw her and came to help.

When the fire fighters arrived they asked Joanne how she had known what to do to save herself and the children. She said she had learned what to do in an eighth-grade home economics class on child care.

The fire department held a special program in honor of Joanne, and she received letters of praise from her senators and even a letter from the governor.

Another true story has a sad ending.

Juan

Juan was caring for his sister, Alicia. It was a chilly morning and Alicia was wearing her bathrobe. She stood too close to a gas heater and her robe caught on fire.

Juan knew that Alicia should roll on the floor to put out the flames (remove the air). But Alicia was so frightened she ran, fanning the flames. Juan had to catch her and smother the flames with a rug. Alicia was badly burned, and spent many months in a hospital.

FALLS

More serious injuries are caused by falls than by any other accident. People younger than 6 and older than 65 are the chief victims of falls. Situations that often cause falls include:

· Clutter on stairs and traffic paths
· Climbing on makeshift ladders, or using ladders improperly
· Slippery or uneven floors and sidewalks
· Poor lighting on stairs and at entryways
· Unsafe or absent railing on stairs.

Work Habits. Safety skills you can practice at home and at work are:

· Wipe up spilled or splashed water, food, and grease immediately.
· Keep traffic ways clear.
· When you carry anything large or bulky, make sure you can see where you are stepping.
· Watch out for open drawers, cupboard doors, and swinging doors.
· Use stepstools and ladders for climbing
· Turn on the lights or use a flashlight when stairs or hallways are dark.

Protecting Children from Falls. There are special precautions to take to protect children from falls. At home, they include keeping babies and toddlers away from stairs, open windows, balconies, and porches. If any of these places have screens or guards, check to see that they are in good condition and securely closed. On the playground, children should be taught to use equipment safely.

Child care workers, such as nurses, can use the "football carry" when carrying infants. By cradling the baby's head on your wrist, resting the baby's body on your hip, and holding the baby close, you can safely carry an infant with one arm. Your other hand is free to hold onto a railing when going up and down stairs or to protect the baby if you should slip.

Once the baby can open doors keep them locked, especially car doors. Above all, watch children carefully and never leave them alone.

Protecting Aged People from Falling. To protect the aged, know how to lock the wheels on a wheelchair so it cannot roll when you are moving the person in or out of the chair. Bathtubs and showers should have strong bars for the people to hold onto and nonskid mats to prevent slipping. Make sure that ill or elderly people can turn on the lights without getting out of bed and can light their way ahead of them when they move about at night.

Injury from Tools and Equipment

Much equipment used in home economics occupations requires close attention in order to prevent accidents. Tools and equipment can cause cuts, burns, and electric shock. Consider, for example, the grinders, slicers, and mixers found in a commerical kitchen.

Some typical safety habits are listed here. As you become more safety conscious you will be able to add many more.

· Be sure you know the correct way to operate machines and use tools which are part of your job.
· If you must clean any electric equipment, turn off the master switch or pull the plug before touching the machine. Keep electric appliances away from sinks or tubs of water. Water and electricity are a dangerous com-

Figure 13-2. Turn off the master switch before you clean any electrical equipment. (Kenneth Karp)

bination, since electricity goes through water as easily as it goes through wires.

· When working around machines which have belts, gears, drives, or shafts, make sure these parts are covered by a guard. Do not wear loose clothing or jewelry which might get caught in the machine. Pull long hair back or wear a hairnet or cap.

· Keep knives and other cutting tools well sharpened so they will cut easily without a lot of extra pressure, which increases their chances of slipping. Handle and store them with extra care.

· Sweep up broken glass carefully.

· Make sure electric cords on irons and other appliances are placed where small children cannot reach them, and where no one can trip over them.

· Sharp tools should not be left lying around the house or in the yard. Have a safe place for tools and keep them there.

· Never touch electric switches while you are wet or standing on a wet floor.

· Children should not carry knives, scissors, or glass items which can break and cut them should they fall.

POISONS

Small children will put almost anything in their mouths. They must be protected against accidental poisoning. Materials which can poison children are found in almost every home. They include:

· Medicines, especially aspirin

· Pest killers

· Laundry bleach

· Furniture polish

· Kerosene

· Rubbing alcohol

· Cosmetics, such as fingernail polish remover

· Turpentine

· Ammonia

All of these products must be kept out of the reach of small children. And there are many others.

People who are ill or elderly must also be protected from poisoning. They may forget that they have already taken their medicine and take an overdose unless you are watchful.

IN CASE OF EMERGENCY

In case of emergency, you are expected to know how to report an accident and you may have to take action. Just as in the case of Joanne and the fire, there may be no one else around. It will be up to you. On the job you can expect some instruction in reporting accidents and taking emergency action. Better yet, you can take a first aid course. They are given in many schools and by community agencies such as the American Red Cross. The courses are free and available to any young person or adult. (If you take a course, be sure to list it on your resume under "Education and Training.")

REPORTING ACCIDENTS

Workers in home economics occupations should be able to give information calmly over the phone so that fire fighters, an ambulance team, or the police can quickly respond to an emergency. Carry with you, or tape to the phone where you work, emergency numbers for local fire fighters, police, family doctor, rescue team, emergency room, and poison control center. If you are faced with an emergency situation and cannot find the numbers, call the operator.

When you phone, tell where you are and what the situation is. It is crucial to give enough information so that emergency workers can find you, can understand the nature of the emergency, and can come prepared to help.

There is a *universal call for help*, should you have an emergency away from a telephone or get lost while hiking or camping. The universal call for help is three rapid signals repeated at regular intervals. They can be three blasts on a whistle, three flashes from a flashlight or lantern, three puffs of smoke from a campfire, or three shots. Honking a car horn three times would also give the signal.

TAKING EMERGENCY ACTION

Always call a doctor when faced with a health emergency. If a doctor or rescue team is not available, you may have to take action in order to save a life or prevent further injury.

In case of an accident, the general rules are:

· Keep the injured person lying down.
· *Don't move* an injured person unless absolutely necessary.
· Examine the injured person to see whether emergency action is needed.
· Do not give an unconscious or semiconscious person anything to drink.

In general, it is better for an untrained person to leave the injured person alone. But you may need to take action in case of severe bleeding, burns, suffocation, poisoning, or broken bones.

These severe injuries cause *shock*. This is not electric shock, but a kind of shock where the *vital signs* (pulse, respiration, and blood pressure) slow down enormously. Shock can cause death. Badly injured people must always be treated for shock, even when they seem to feel all right. There are two basic steps:

1. Have the injured person lie down.
2. Keep the injured person comfortably warm.

If the person can breathe well, the feet should be slightly raised. If the person has trouble breathing, or has a head or chest injury, the head and shoulders should be raised. Unless it is very hot, cover the injured person.

Bleeding. To stop severe bleeding, apply pressure to the wound. Use a first aid dressing or clean cloth if you can. If there is nothing else, use your hand. When bleeding has been controlled, add extra layers of cloth and bandage firmly. If the wound is in an arm or leg, raise it to help stop the bleeding.

There are *pressure points* you can learn about. Pressure points are places where you can press large blood vessels to help stop bleeding of arms and legs.

Doctors might use a *tourniquet*, a tight band that cuts off all blood going to an arm or leg. Other people do not use tourniquets because of the danger of severe injury if they are not tied right or are used when they are not needed.

What would you do if a bad accident happened? Consider the true story of Mike.

Mike

Two friends, 17 and 18 years old, were injured in an auto accident. Mike was badly hurt. He had a chest injury and a cut on his arm which was bleeding badly. Dave was not as severely hurt as Mike. He managed to hold his hand on Mike's wound and control the bleeding, but he felt faint.

A woman passed by. Dave asked her to help him stop the bleeding, but she said she couldn't do it. She did nothing to help. She just stood there until the police arrived.

How do you see yourself? As Dave, who saved his friend's life? As the woman, who did not help?

What is the first aid for small cuts you might get on the job? Wash with soap and water, and bandage to keep clean. For nosebleeds? Sit down and pinch your nose shut.

Suffocation. When someone stops breathing you have only a few minutes to act. You must give artificial respiration *(rescue breathing)* at once.

First:
· Clean the mouth (of gum, food, dentures).
· Tip the head far enough back to open the air passage.
· Pinch the nose shut.

Then:
· Blow in, once every 5 seconds.
· Listen, to be sure the air is getting through.

If you don't hear air rushing out of the victim's lungs, repeat the steps. Clean the mouth again; tip the head further back. Listen. If you still do not hear air, pat the victim's back to dislodge whatever is blocking the air. If, for some reason, you cannot give rescue breathing by mouth, you can hold the mouth closed and blow in the nose.

Rescue breathing for babies is slightly different.

· Cover the nose *and* mouth
· Tip the head back only slightly.
· Blow *gently,* once every 3 seconds.

If you do not hear air, hold the infant by the ankles. Open the baby's mouth to let any fluids or solids fall out.

Figure 13-3. By learning and practicing first aid techniques you can be sure you'll know what to do in an emergency. (Jane Hamilton-Merritt)

Always start rescue breathing *at once*. After only 2 or 3 minutes the victim can have brain damage; after 4 to 6 minutes the victim may die.

Don't waste time bringing drowning victims to shore. Start rescue breathing as soon as you safely can. Don't stop rescue breathing until the victim can breathe alone, or until help arrives.

Poisoning. If there is a poisoning accident, there is no time to spare. The Red Cross advises:[1]

· *First*, give the victim one-half a glass of water or milk.
· *Next*, decide whether or not to make the victim vomit.
· *Then*, call the doctor, police, or poison control center.

Giving water or milk dilutes the poison and gives you more time to act. Deciding whether or not to make the victim vomit is harder.

Do make the victim vomit if he or she has swallowed

1. Medicines
2. Pest killers

Don't make the victim vomit if he or she has swallowed

1. Gasoline, or products that smell like gas
2. Products that have already burned the mouth or throat

Gasoline–type products can hurt the victim's lungs, if made to vomit. More burns can cause the throat to swell shut.

[1]American National Red Cross, *Basic First Aid*, Doubleday, Garden City, 1971.

To make the victim vomit, stick your fingers in his or her mouth and tickle the back of the throat. Or give syrup of ipecac, a product you can buy at the drugstore and keep in your medicine cabinet.

Poison control centers are ready to help 24 hours a day. They can identify the ingredients in a household product and advise what *antidote* to use. An antidote is a remedy to counteract the poison. The label on many containers also gives an antidote. You can help the doctor or hospital by taking the container to the hospital.

Burns. With burns, it is a matter of degree:

· First degree—the skin is red
· Second degree—there are blisters
· Third degree—the skin is destroyed and the tissue charred

Run cold water over a first-degree burn, or apply wet cloths. Cover a second- or third- degree burn with a thick, dry dressing to keep out the air and reduce pain. Don't use oil, ointment, or anything else the doctor may have to painfully remove.

The big danger of severe burns is infection. Sterile (germ-free) dressings should be used. In an emergency, use the cleanest possible dry dressing. For extensive burns, the victim can be wrapped in a clean sheet.

Fractures. When a bone is broken, the best thing to do is nothing at all. The injured person should not be moved but should wait for the doctor or rescue team. If a broken bone has punctured the skin (a *compound fracture*), cover the wound with a sterile dressing or clean cloth. Control bleeding, if necessary, by hand pressure.

If the person must be moved, apply a splint. Use a board, a thick bundle of newspapers, or a pillow. Tie the splint firmly in place above and below the break. Keep the broken bone ends and the joints on either side of the break still. For example, for a broken forearm, prepare the splint so the wrist and elbow cannot move.

Broken bones in the hand, arm, or shoulder should be supported by a sling after splinting. Use a triangular bandage or a substitute such as a scarf, towel, or torn sheet, and tie the ends around the victim's neck. Or place the forearm across the person's chest and pin the sleeve to the coat or shirt.

The greatest risk is taken when moving a person who may have a broken neck or back or a severe head injury. If the victim must be moved from a danger that could take his or her life, move the victim on a wide board, such as an ironing board or a door. Slide the victim carefully onto the board, keeping the body level.

Practice. How can you be sure you will do what has to be done in an emergency? Know what to do and practice it. By practicing, sports figures are able to make a basket, or get a base hit, or catch a pass under pressure. If you practice fire drills and first aid, you, too, will be able to act under pressure. You will do the right thing.

Following good sanitary practices is part of your job. You are expected to **SANITATION** protect yourself and others from disease.

Many people are careless about sanitation because they do not understand something they cannot see. Bacteria and other organisms that cause disease can be seen only under a microscope. But they are present in the air and in and on the body. Bacteria are on clothing and on objects like plates, towels, food, tools, and equipment. Therefore, the best way to prevent disease or its spread is to keep yourself and everything you use as clean as possible.

The Food and Drug Administration estimates that there are more than 40 million cases of food poisoning each year in the United States. Most of them are caused by salmonella and staphylococcus bacteria. Bacteria thrive best under conditions of warmth and moisture. They particularly like protein foods like meat, fish, poultry, eggs, and milk. The food service worker, child care aide, and home health aide must take special care with these foods.

Bacteria grow slowly at temperatures below 40°F and over 140°F. They are killed rapidly at 170°F and over. Keeping food either very cold or very hot helps prevent rapid growth of bacteria and food poisoning. Washing dishes in hot (170°F) water kills most bacteria.

Botulism is a rare but deadly kind of food poisoning which is caused when foods are not properly canned. For this reason, cans with bulged ends or other signs of spoilage should not be used. Be especially wary of home canned products. The acid in fruits and tomatoes helps prevent botulism. Other vegetables and meats must be canned in a pressure cooker to be safe.

Some good sanitation habits are:

· Wash your hands *before* working with food, infants and children, the elderly, and patients.
· Wash your hands *after* caring for someone who is ill or removing old carpet, tiles, or upholstery.
· Follow rules for personal sanitation, such as using your own cup and comb, washing hands after trips to the bathroom, and keeping hands away from your mouth, nose, and hair.
· Use only clean towels to dry dishes or hands.
· Place food and clean dishes only on clean surfaces.
· Keep equipment, toys, and work areas clean.
· Keep food either very cold or very hot.
· Keep food and beverages covered and protected from dust, debris, and pests.
· Never work with food when you have boils or wounds on your hands, or when you have a cold or the flu. In other jobs, let your supervisor decide whether you should go to work when you have illnesses like these.
· Wear a hair net or cap when working with food.
· Keep fingers out of clean cups and glasses and away from eating surfaces of all utensils.

· Follow instructions in disposing of waste materials to prevent fires, accidents, and spread of disease.

· Help keep storerooms free of trash and stored supplies clean.

How many of these sanitary practices are already habits for you? Which ones do you need to work on?

**CHAPTER
SUMMARY**

1. Home economics occupations are people occupations. In most jobs you are responsible for the safety of others and also for your own safety and good health.

2. Accidents do not just happen. They are caused by *tension, illness, fatigue, lack of skill in doing a task, overconfidence, showing off,* and *breaking regulations.*

3. Fire is one of the greatest accidental killers, and it strikes hardest at children and the elderly. Three things are needed for a fire: *fuel, heat,* and *air.*

4. Chief causes of fires are *careless smoking, faulty electrical wiring, flammable liquids, misuse of heating and cooking equipment,* and *spontaneous combustion.* Children playing with *matches, lightning,* and *faulty chimneys* are other causes. You can develop work habits to help prevent fires.

5. In case of fire the *first* thing to do is *warn everyone* and get everyone out of the building. Then call the fire department, if you safely can without being trapped.

6. More serious injuries are caused by *falls* than any other single accident. Tools and equipment can cause *cuts, burns,* and *electric shock.* Small children are easily *poisoned* by common household products.

7. When you phone *to report an emergency,* give enough information so emergency workers can find you, know what the emergency is, and come prepared to help. In case of an accident, keep the injured person *lying down. Don't move* anyone who has been injured unless absolutely necessary, and *examine* to see if emergency action must be taken.

8. Injuries like severe bleeding, burns, broken bones, poisoning, or suffocation cause a special kind of *shock.* Always treat for shock after you have given the other necessary first aid.

9. To stop severe bleeding, apply pressure to the wound. When someone stops breathing you have only a few minutes to act. Everyone should know how to give *rescue breathing.* There is also no time to spare in cases of poisoning.

10. Severe burns should be covered with *thick, dry* cloths to keep out air and reduce the pain. Only clean dressings should be used because of the danger of infection.

11. If a person with a broken bone must be moved, *splint* the broken bone to keep it still. There is *great risk* in moving someone with a broken neck or back or a severe head injury.

12. Knowing what to do in an emergency, and *practicing* it, enables you to do the right thing should your help be needed.

13. Following sanitary practices is *part of your job*. You are expected to protect yourself and others from disease.

• FOLLOW-UP PROJECTS

1. Prepare a checklist of fire and safety hazards at home, at school, and on the job. What action can be taken to reduce the chance of accident?

2. Plan two escape routes for each room at home and on the job, in case of fire. Choose a meeting place for your family and conduct a fire drill at home.

3. Invite a member of your local fire department to class to demonstrate the use of fire extinguishers and answer questions like: What are safe procedures for leaving a burning building? What are the most common fire hazards in the workplace? The home? What should you do in case of fire if you are responsible for a patient who cannot be easily moved? How can you escape a fire in a highrise building?

4. Prepare a list of emergency phone numbers for use at home and on the job. Check your local phone directory to see whether there is a poison control center in your city. If not, ask your doctor or health department for the phone number of the nearest center.

5. Take turns dipping your fingers in fingerpaints and demonstrating how to set the table, using sanitary practices. The class should vote for the table setter most likely to succeed.

6. Invite a school custodian to class to discuss and demonstrate:
   a. Safe use of ladders
   b. Sanitary storage of food and other supplies
   c. Safe use of electrical equipment
   d. Safe storage of oily rags and paints
   e. How to lift heavy loads without injuring your back
   f. How to protect yourself from chemical burns and toxic fumes

7. Contact your local civil defense units for information on procedures to follow in case of emergencies such as a flood, tornado, hurricane, earthquake, or winter storm.

8. Role-play how to report a fire, how to report an accident, what to do when clothes catch on fire.

9. Practice taking emergency action for shock, severe bleeding, suffocation, broken bones, and burns. Discuss other first aid measures that

interest the class. Divide into small groups and research other first aid techniques. Demonstrate these techniques for the class, or invite the school nurse, a member of a rescue team, or another expert to do so.

10. Invite to class a panel of experts to discuss accident prevention and ways to handle emergencies. The panel could include an industrial arts teacher, a nurse, the school custodian, the cafeteria manager, the driver education teacher, a fire inspector, an ambulance driver, or a civil defense director.

11. Conduct a survey of students in your school. How many know basic first aid? What is their safety consciousness when driving a car, baby-sitting, mowing a lawn? Do they know what to do in case of a fire in their home? At work?

12. Develop a program for your school on accident prevention, CPR, fire safety, first aid, survival techniques, or a similar topic. Use closed circuit television, a showcase, bulletin boards, an assembly program or a short course to reach your audience.

14 EVALUATING YOUR JOB

After studying Chapter 14 you will be able to:

1. Explain what young workers like and dislike about their jobs.
2. Compare rights and responsibilities of workers and employers.
3. List opportunities to be found on your first job.
4. Rate your own job satisfaction in a paid or volunteer job.

How do you measure success at work? What is a good job? What is fair treatment on the job? When is treatment clearly unfair? How do you know when you should look for another job? These are common questions for the beginning worker.

When young people working in home economics occupations are asked what they like about their jobs they mention:

JOB SATIS-FACTION

· Training
· Gaining experience
· Meeting people
· Making friends
· Earning money
· Cooperating with a group of coworkers
· Knowing they are helping someone
· Learning about community problems
· Working conditions

You will recall reading in Chapter 1 about the basic human needs which work fills for many people. Perhaps you interviewed people about what work means to them and they mentioned the income, the challenge, the sense of belonging.

Now you see the same responses repeated in the satisfaction beginning workers get from their jobs. No matter that their first jobs are not quite perfect. They like the challenge of new experiences and new opportunities. They like being good enough at their jobs to be paid, to get a raise. They like working with others, belonging to a group. They like the self-esteem that comes from work.

223

As workers become more experienced, their satisfaction with their jobs continues to depend on working conditions. They must believe that the work they do is useful. They want a chance to use their abilities and skills, to have a voice when decisions are made which affect them and their jobs. They value a chance to advance and the sense of security that comes from a steady job and fringe benefits like a pension plan and insurance.

People who like their jobs most often mention the following points:

· A chance to use your skills and abilities
· A feeling that your work is useful
· Fair pay and fringe benefits
· A chance for advancement
· A reasonable workload
· Safe and pleasant working conditions
· A voice in decisions which affect you and freedom to express ideas for better ways to do things
· A sense of security
· Cooperative coworkers
· Helpful supervision

Job satisfaction is important to employers. When workers are unhappy, absenteeism rises and production goes down. But job satisfaction matters most to the worker, whose health and relationships with family and neighbors can be affected. People who like their jobs usually live longer!

Figure 14-1. When asked what they like best about their jobs, people in home economics occupations often say "helping people." (Mini Forsyth, Monkmeyer Press)

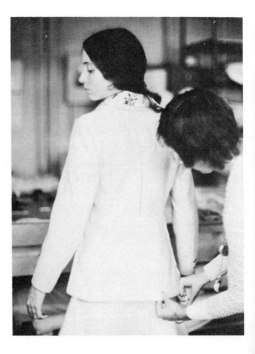

PROBLEMS ON THE JOB

When beginning workers in home economics are asked what they do *not* like about their jobs, some mention the weekend and evening hours, which interfere with their social life. Others report low pay, having too many bosses, and coworkers who do not cooperate or do not seem to know how to do their jobs. Securing transportation to work is often a problem. Some want to work more hours than are available to them. Sometimes new workers feel they are given more than their share of the work; sometimes they feel rushed. Occasionally workers find their jobs boring and say they do not yet have the kind of job they want.

Many problems of young workers are quickly solved as they move from part-time to full-time jobs and get more experience. Most find better-paying jobs within a short time. Even workers who are not able to hold their first jobs usually do well on their second jobs.

Some problems can be expected because of the nature of home economics occupations. Working to help others takes talent. "Others" may be noisy children. Or intoxicated customers. Or irritable patients. Or members of a culture you do not understand.

Probably most of your customers and clients are friendly people who appreciate what you do for them. But you can *expect* some people to be difficult, and some tasks tedious.

Knowledge of child guidance techniques (a home economics competence) helps the home health aide or salesperson in a children's clothing department or a waiter/waitress to work more easily with children. Older people have certain special characteristics that need understanding. They are often lonely, and lonely people tend to talk a lot. You may be the only person who has time or takes time to listen.

Intoxicated people should be treated like any other sick person. People from other cultures are just like everybody else you know, except for one thing. They are more interesting because they are new to you.

Consider how dull the world would be if people all looked alike and acted alike! Our very differences are what make life worthwhile.

A knowledge of human development helps workers in home economics understand the behavior of their supervisors, coworkers, customers, patients, and children in their care. A sense of humor and an optimistic outlook ease tensions where behavior is not understood. People may be having a bad day because they are tired, sick, ill at ease, or just "down." As a rule, they do not intend to be as ill-mannered or inconsiderate as they seem.

WHAT TO DO

If the problem is with customers or clients, your *coworkers* may be able to give you help and advice. If the problem is with coworkers, your *supervisor* may be the one to consult. If the problem is your supervisor, the wisest course is to turn to your teacher or to an *employment counselor*.

Figure 14-2. A sense of humor and empathy help you over those times when people treat you in an ill-mannered or unkind way.

Most crucial is your relationship with your supervisor. With good supervision, trouble spots with coworkers or clients can probably be eased. But unfair treatment by a supervisor places the beginning worker in a difficult position, and the only answer to the problem may be to seek another job.

If you cannot find pleasure in helping others, take another look at home economics occupations. Consider a job in the operator group, where you work more with products than with people. Or maybe home economics occupations are not for you at all. That in itself is good to know. In the search for an occupation that is right for you, it is useful to know what you do *not* want to do, as well as what you *do* want to do.

RIGHTS AND RESPONSI-BILITIES Workers have certain rights, just as they have responsibilities. You have the right to :

· Fair pay

· Safe working conditions
· Helpful supervision
· Recognition for work well done
· Be proud of the service or product you produce

Worker rights are employer responsibilities. Employers have a responsibility to observe labor laws, provide safe and sanitary working conditions, protect workers from humiliation by supervisors, and reward work well done with praise, advancement, and better pay. They have a responsibility to allow workers to voice their opinions when decisions are being made which affect them and their jobs. And to follow ethical business practices, so workers can be proud of where they work.

In return you, the worker, must meet *your* responsibilities. They include:

· Businesslike appearance
· Cooperation
· Acceptance of supervision
· Honesty
· Dependability
· Production of a reasonable amount and quality

There is much to be gained from your first job. You have a chance to show that you *can* meet your responsibilities as a worker. You establish a work record and secure a reference which can be used to get other, better jobs. You have a chance to learn both *how* and *how not* to perform tasks. You have a chance to practice your skills in human relationships, communication, computing, and safety. You have a chance to try out an occupation, to see what it is like, and to learn about the jobs of others with whom you work.

MAKING THE MOST OF YOUR FIRST JOB

You will almost surely make some new friends at work. You will become more realistic about what work is like. You will gain some judgment regarding when you should change jobs.

You will have a chance to develop confidence in yourself. The confidence spreads to your other *roles* in life, as a consumer, homemaker, and community member.

Table 14-1 is an evaluation chart. Making up a chart like this can help you consider the pros and cons of a job. The chart can help you decide if you are gaining all the benefits you deserve from your job. To complete the chart, you should read the descriptions within the chart. For example, if your employer is understanding, sympathetic, and considerate, then he or she deserves a score of (5), or "very good." If your employer is harsh and inconsiderate, then mark a score of (1) or "not acceptable."

TABLE 14-1 RATING MY JOB

	1*	2	3	4	5	Rating
My employer	Is mean and harsh; doesn't care about the employees as long as they get the work done.		Is rather stand-offish but is generally thoughtful of the employees.		Is understanding and sympathetic; always considerate of employees.	_____
		Has obvious favorites among the employees.		Seems to have favorites, but everyone is treated pretty much alike.	Is fair in treating all employees alike.	_____
		Never lets me know whether or not I am doing a good job.		Lets me know if I do something wrong, but not if I do something right.	Keeps me informed as to how well I am doing.	_____
		Someone always tells me what to do; I never get to make any decisions.		I make little decisions in my job but don't have any voice in really important things.	I have the opportunity to use my initiative and to help decide what is going on.	_____
Work load	Job is very tiring physically *or* too much concentration is involved.		Job is occasionally overtiring physically or mentally.		Workload and pressure are reasonable for this type of job.	_____
		Work pace is fast with too much to do.		Workload is sometimes too heavy or too rushed.	There is time enough to do the job well.	_____
Coworkers and public	I don't like the clients/customers.		The clients/customers are OK.		I really enjoy the clients/customers.	_____
		I have no friends at work.		I get along pretty well with everyone but have no close friends.	I have some real, lasting friends at work.	_____
		The workers disagree about who is supposed to do which job; there is a lot of rivalry.		Most of the workers do their share of the work with little friction among us.	We work together well as a team.	_____
Working conditions	The work area is dirty and/or too noisy.		The work area is clean but not very attractive or quiet.		The work area is attractive, clean, and fairly quiet.	_____

228

TABLE 14-1 RATING MY JOB (CONTINUED)

	1*	2	3	4	5	Rating
	The building is too hot or too cold to be comfortable.		The temperature of the building is usually comfortable.	The temperature is pleasant for the type of work being done.		_____
	Work hours are too late or too early.		The work hours are all right.	The work hours are good.		_____
	No one cares much about safety.		Some attention has been given to safety, but certain parts of the job are hazardous.	The employer continually stresses safety and uses many safety devices.		_____
	The work is boring.		The work is about average—sometimes interesting and sometimes boring.	The work is interesting and gives me a lot of personal satisfaction.		_____
Salary and benefits	The pay for this job isn't large enough to live on.		My pay is large enough for anything I really need.	My pay is large enough to buy what I need plus some extras.		_____
	The pay is the same for every worker.		The pay depends on how long a worker has been here.	The pay depends on how long the worker has been here, how hard the job is, and how well the job is done.		_____
	There are no benefits (sick leave pay, insurance, etc.) connected with this job.		The benefits are all right.	Benefits with this job are so good that they make me want to keep working here.		_____
Chance to advance	I am not sure I am able to do a good job in this kind of work.		I do pretty good work but still need to improve a great deal.	I feel that I am able to handle this job well.		_____
	I am ashamed to tell people what I do and where I work.		This job and company are as good as those for which my friends are working.	I am proud to say what my job is and where I work.		_____

229

TABLE 14-1 RATING MY JOB (CONTINUED)

	1*	2	3	4	5	Rating
Chance to advance	My job is fixed; I don't think I will ever get a promotion.		There are some opportunities for promotion here.		There is a good possibility of promotion if I work hard.	_____
	For all I know I may get fired tomorrow.		If I do a good job, I don't have to worry about getting fired.		I feel so sure of this job that I don't have to worry about losing it.	_____
	I am sorry that I took this job.		This job is fine, but I might like some other type of work better.		This job has convinced me that I would like to remain in this type of work permanently.	_____
					TOTAL SCORE	_____

*Not acceptable (1)   Poor (2)   Acceptable (3)   Good (4)   Very good (5)

Adapted from H.Y. Nelson and G.P. Jacoby, *Evaluation of Secondary School Programs to Prepare Students for Wage Earning in Occupations Related to Home Economics,* Department of Health, Education, and Welfare, Washington, 1967.

CHAPTER SUMMARY

1. When young people working in home economics occupations are asked what they like about their jobs they mention *training, experience, meeting people* and *making friends, earning money,* and *working with others.* Job satisfaction for more experienced workers depends on *working conditions,* sense of *security,* and having a chance to use their *abilities and skills.* They value a chance to *advance* and having a voice in *decisions.*

2. For beginning workers, *hours, pay, transportation,* and finding *enough work* are sometimes problems. Many problems of young workers are quickly solved as they move from part-time to full-time jobs and get more experience.

3. Some problems can be *expected* in the people occupations. Some people can be difficult and some tasks tedious. If the problem is with a customer or client, your *coworkers* may be able to help you. If the problem is with coworkers, your *supervisor* is the one to consult. If the problem is your supervisor, turn to an *employment counselor* for advice.

4. Workers have a *right* to fair pay, safe working conditions, helpful supervision, recognition for work well done, and pride in their work. Worker rights are employer responsibilities. Employers have a *respon-*

sibility to observe labor laws, provide safe working conditions, protect workers from humiliation by supervisors, reward work well done, and follow ethical business practices.

5. Worker responsibilities include businesslike appearance, cooperation, honesty, dependability, and productivity.

6. On your first job you have a chance to show that you can meet your responsibilities as a worker. You establish a *work record* and have a chance to practice your skills in human relationships, communication, computing, and safety. You have a chance to develop *confidence* in yourself in your *roles* as worker, consumer, homemaker, and community member.

• FOLLOW-UP PROJECTS

1. Survey three or more workers in home economics occupations, asking the question, "What is a good job?" Compare responses.

2. Interview each other regarding satisfaction with paid and volunteer jobs you now hold. Discuss problems which have arisen on the job. To whom did workers turn for help? Was that the right thing to do? Could the problem have been solved in a better way? (*Note*: Interview schedule will be included in the student workbook.)

3. Role-play a variety of job titles in home economics. Identify sources of difficulty (such as with supervisors, coworkers, the public) and sources of job satisfaction as portrayed by the actors.

4. Prepare a bulletin board or showcase display on rights and responsibilities of workers and employers.

5. Discuss the opportunities to be found on your first job.

6. Rate your own job.

PART FOUR

YOUR JOB AND YOUR LIFESTYLE

Just as you fill several roles as wage earner, you have multiple roles in your home life. How do these roles overlap? Do they use some of the same skills?

The overlap of these roles is the concern of this section. Because you are a worker you have money to spend, which makes you a consumer. What are other comparisons? Organizing your various roles, "getting it all together," takes skill. Skill in getting along with others at home as well as on the job. Skill in managing resources. Skill in making decisions.

Just as there are attitudes, knowledge, and skills that help you on the job, there are attitudes, knowledge, and skills that help you in your personal life. Both men and women are wage earners as well as homemakers.

Homemaking today is not the responsibility of one family member, but of all family members. This change evolved naturally as more women began working outside of the home. Men are now expected to assume their fair share of homemaking duties. They also share in the care of their children, arranging work schedules to allow them to become a true partner in child rearing.

Today young people more frequently leave home at an early age to set up their own homes. With this independence comes responsibility. They are free from the supervision of their parents, but they must assume the responsibility to feed, clothe, and care for themselves. They must also take responsibility as a community member.

A fortunate result of these present trends is that homemaking is coming to be viewed as neither a masculine nor a feminine activity, but as a *human* activity. This is a democratic ideal that fits right in with our American culture.

15 MAXIMIZING TIME, MONEY, SPACE, AND ENERGY

After studying Chapter 15 you will be able to:

1. Identify human, material, and community resources.
2. Explain trade-offs in use of resources.
3. Plan a time schedule.
4. Describe and use body mechanics, storage principles, work simplification.
5. Demonstrate good work habits.
6. Use the systems approach to management.

Good management is the key to "getting it all together." Any one task—or even several tasks—are no real problem. It is all of the decisions and all of the tasks together that most of us need help with.

For instance, most of us can manage a meal or two for ourselves. We can buy and take care of a shirt and pants outfit for work. Or bathe and feed a baby. Or clean the apartment. It is preparing meals for a group day after day, plus washing clothes for the entire family, plus giving attention to children, that causes problems. How does one person—or two people—get it all together?

Don't skip this step! It is your guide to successful management of time. What are your present goals? What is it that you want? To make friends? Enjoy leisure time? Learn worthwhile skills? Improve your appearance?

SET YOUR GOALS

What are your future goals? Success in a job? A happy marriage? A college degree?

Are your goals the same as your family's? Are your values and standards the same as theirs? Your family's *goal* for you may be a good education, but you may not *value* education and may have low *standards* of work at school.

Or you may value education and want to study, but the rest of the family is noisy and you are constantly interrupted. School may not be important to them. They may not value knowledge and education. Their goal may be for you to help more with housekeeping or to earn more money.

The values of one generation differ from those of the next generation as society changes. Values are different because experiences are different. Your parents, for example, have had very different experiences from those

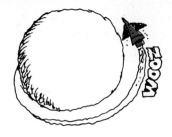

Figure 15-1. What are your goals? Are you doing what you want to do? Are you where you want to be?

of your own generation. Resources are different. A free community college may be around the corner from you, but your parents may not have had this chance.

How are you doing in terms of your own values, goals, and standards? Are you what and where you want to be? If not, maybe management basics can help you.

MANAGEMENT BASICS

Good management means making use of what you have (your *resources*) to obtain a satisfying lifestyle, to reach the goals you have for yourself and others. Who is a good manager? *On the job,* it is someone who can get the work done according to set standards at the least cost of time, supplies, and effort. *At home* a good manager does much the same.

On the job, employers and supervisors provide many of the resources and set most of the standards and goals. In homemaking *you* and your family provide the resources and make the decisions. *You* can plan a system of management that helps you meet your goals.

What are the management basics that help get work done at home and on the job? For one, there is the matter of recognizing the resources available to you. The good manager makes the most of them.

RECOGNIZING RESOURCES

What are the resources which can help you reach your goals? There are three basic kinds of resources.

Human resources are time, energy, knowledge, and skills, plus work habits and attitudes toward work. In home economics occupations, many skills can be used both on the job away from home and by the unpaid homemaker. Knowledge of nutrition and design applies at work and in your personal life. So does planning and a desire to find a better way of doing things.

Material resources are the supplies, tools, and equipment you use at work and the work space itself. Another material resource is money.

Community resources are schools and hospitals, day care and shopping centers, buslines and parks, and health clinics and consumer agencies.

Do you see how these resources can help you reach your goal? Suppose your goal is improved appearance. Do you plan *time* for rest? Use *energy* for shopping for attractive clothing? Do you know about weight control? Use your *skill* in sewing and mending? Have good grooming *habits*? What about material resources like grooming *supplies? Money* to buy them? *Space* to store them? Are there community resources like a good drycleaner? Hair stylist? A charm school or courses in home economics?

MAKING THE MOST OF YOUR RESOURCES

We don't all have the same resources. Some people have time and energy but little money. Some have more money than time. Some people have space but few tools. Some communities have more services than others.

Trade-offs which help you meet your goals can be made. A young mother chooses to stay home. She cares for her children, cans and freezes food, and sews her family's clothing. The children's father cares for the lawn, makes household repairs, and keeps the family car running. Together they paint, garden, and restore furniture. They add to the family's *real income* by providing the services themselves. They trade time and effort for money.

Another young couple both work outside the home. They trade off money for time and effort. They don't have much time to paint their home, although they do some painting. They pay someone else to help with painting, lawn care, and furniture finishing.

Many young parents have *neither* time *nor* money. They have to trade off some luxuries they enjoyed before their child was born. Caring for young children takes so much time and effort that a perfectly clean house at all times and dinner by candlelight may have to be given up. A home can be sanitary and safe, but it need not be perfect. Dinner can be simple and still be a time of family caring and sharing.

Saving Time. Some people need more time than others to get things done. Those who take *more* time may have the time to spend, may set very high standards for themselves, or may have many interruptions in their work.

On the other hand, those people who get things done quickly tend to have:

· Good health
· A deadline to meet
· Good equipment
· Experience and skill

They have more relaxed standards of work and a desire to get jobs they dislike out of the way in a hurry. They plan, and they simplify their work.

To *plan,* list the tasks to be done, estimate the time each will take, and develop a schedule. When working for someone else, plan only as much time as needed to do the job well enough to meet the standards set by your employer. At home, set your own standards.

Plan the best *sequence* for performing the tasks. What shall be done first? What tasks *must* be done? Then consider what tasks *should* be done? Last, sort out tasks that would be *nice to do.* A home health aide will schedule meals, the bath routine, and medication for the patient as "must do's" on the work schedule for the day. A "should do" is cleaning the patient's room. A "nice to do" is arranging flowers for the patient's tray.

When sequencing tasks, alternate heavy work with lighter tasks, and make the most of rest breaks. Are there peak hours in your workday, like mealtimes? Plan to do routine tasks (called *sidework* in food service) around the busy times, to try to steady your work pace. Are there tasks that require close concentration? If possible, schedule them when you can expect to have the fewest interruptions (during children's naptime, perhaps).

A schedule means deadlines, and deadlines help you get the work done on time. But in a good schedule, time to catch up is allowed. Your schedule must fit in with the others with whom you work. Most jobs, especially homemaking, are team efforts.

Once your plan is made, carry it out. Then look at the results. Was the plan you followed the best plan possible? Should another plan be followed the next time?

Making Your Effort Count. Your work will be easier if you *simplify tasks,* use *body mechanics, organize* your work space, and practice useful work *habits*.

To *simplify tasks*:

· Choose the right tool or equipment.
· Use aids like trays, carts, and tote bags.
· Team up with another person for tasks like setting tables and making beds.
· Combine or dovetail tasks (while waiting for a pan of water to boil, wipe up the counter).

Other ways to simplify work are to change your standards as discussed earlier or change the product. Buy a wash-and-wear uniform rather then one which requires ironing.

Still better, look at the task itself. Is it really necessary? Maybe the task does not need to be done at all.

Body mechanics means using your body to make work easier.

· Practice keeping a good posture when you sit or stand. If you must maintain one position for a long period (standing over a counter, bending over a sewing machine), relax or stretch frequently.

· Wear comfortable clothes, especially shoes.

· If your work involves much lifting (stock clerk, food server, homemaker), learn ways to lighten the loads. Put the weight on a rolling cart, if possible. Or make two trips instead of one.

· When lifting a heavy load, let your strong leg muscles carry most of the weight by bending at your knees instead of at your waist. Place one foot slightly in front of the other, and carry the load close to your body. Figure 15-2 shows how to lift a heavy load to save your back from strain.

Figure 15-2. Make your work easier by lifting and bending correctly. When lifting a heavy load, bend at the knees (left) instead of at the waist (right). (Jane Hamilton-Merritt)

Planning *storage* helps you organize your work space:

· Keep tools and materials you use often where you can reach them easily.
· Arrange utensils, equipment, and supplies so you do not have to move one item to get to another item.
· Place items at the point of first use; for example, store towels near a sink, pan lids at the range.
· Use every inch of space. Make or buy shelves and install them in closets and cupboards. Lazy susans (revolving shelves) can be used in deep corners, pegboards in odd-shaped spots. Files and dividers make good use of deep drawers.

Among the greatest resources the worker brings to the job are good *work habits*. Most jobs are made up of many routine tasks and, luckily, routines are habit forming. When routines become habits, you do not have to stop to think what to do next.

Think about your work habits. Do you:

· Think ahead, to save time and steps?
· Assemble supplies and tools before beginning a task?
· Use aids like trays and carts?
· Combine or dovetail duties?
· Use calm periods to prepare for rush times?
· Use body mechanics?
· Keep your work space organized?
· Concentrate on the job at hand, but keep alert to other responsibilities?
· Work as quietly as possible?
· Work carefully, to avoid waste, breakage, and accidents?
· Help the morale of others with your cheerful attitude?
· Put tools and supplies back where they belong after use?

THE SYSTEMS APPROACH TO MANAGEMENT

Businesses and governments use computers to plan the best use of their resources to reach their goals. This is called the *systems approach*.

Families can use the systems approach too, but they don't need computers to do it. However, many of the terms used by computer programmers are also helpful to families using the systems approach. Some of these terms are:

· *Inputs.* Inputs are everything that goes into a management system. They include all the available resources, such as people's skills and abilities, and the goods and services they can produce or buy. They include the standards, values, and goals we've just discussed. Inputs also include people's motivations, their desire to get things done.
· *Feedback.* We discussed feedback in Chapter 11 (Communicating with Others). You learned that feedback is the message "fed back" to you

Figure 15-3. You could use the systems approach (inputs, feedback, decision-making, and outputs) to achieve your lifetime goals.

about how well your own message is being received. In systems, feedback means checking the results you get in order to see how your system is working. If you are getting *good results* from your system, then you have *positive feedback. If not,* you have *negative feedback.*

· *Decision-making.* This includes choosing your standards, making plans, and taking steps to carry out the plans. It also includes deciding whether your feedback is positive or negative and choosing different actions to improve feedback when necessary.

· *Outputs.* These are your *results,* what your system has produced. If the results meet your goals, then your system is working well. If the results do not meet your goals, you must change your system in some way.

To see how the systems approach to management works, let's take an example of a young couple whose primary goal is that each one have a satisfactory job. Using the systems approach, they first consider all the inputs. They already know their primary goal, but they consider other goals as well. They consider their standards and values for a stable home life, for their health, for the amount of time they have for recreation, and for their economic security. They also consider their resources. What skills or knowledge can each contribute? What material and community resources can they call on?

Having considered the inputs, they see what the possibilities are and decide what steps they can take. They agree on which one of them will be responsible for which homemaking tasks, how they will arrange their transportation, and how they will budget their time and money. Then each person seeks a job which has a career ladder to the job that is his or her goal.

As time goes on, constant feedback helps them to check on their progress and to adjust or change as needed. For example, negative feedback may show that their expenses are too high, and they must cut back some place. They choose to cut back on recreational expenses. Or negative feedback may show that one of them is in a job with little or no chance for advancement, and that partner needs to move sideways on a career lattice to a job with more future.

Positive feedback may show that one partner is receiving good experience and training in the present job, and so they decide to concentrate on advancement there. Or positive feedback may show that their joint homemaking skills are very effective, and they have more time left to cook at home than they expected, so expenses can be cut in that area.

Their output will be their progress toward their goal—the results of how they used their inputs, made decisions, and checked their feedback to guide them in further decisions. Figure 15-4 shows the systems approach in a chart form.

The systems approach can be used for plans to reach short-term goals as well as for long-range goals. Some examples of short-term goals which could be approached by using systems are: finding the best means of transportation to work; finding a suitable place to live; sharing homemaking duties.

THE FAMILY COUNCIL

It should be clear by now that good communication among members of the family *is* a most important part of good management. Families need to share their various goals, standards, and values. They must share their resources. They must plan together and make decisions. A very helpful way to do this

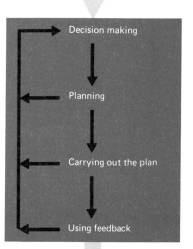

INPUT

Values

Goals

Standards

Resources

Personal or family factors

RELATED QUESTIONS

What's important to you?

What are you trying to do?

How good is "good enough"?

Who or what is available to help?

What's special about you?

Decision making

Planning

Carrying out the plan

Using feedback

What will you do?

How will you do it?

How are you doing?
Are you on target?

Off the track? Need to change course?

OUTPUT

Progress toward goal

Results

RELATED QUESTIONS

Did you reach your goal?

What resources did you use? How did the results affect others? Was it worth it?

Figure 15-4. You can use the systems approach to management to accomplish your personal short-term or long-term goals. Thinking things through in this manner is a big help in keeping focused on what you're trying to do.

is the *family council*. This is simply a meeting of all the members of the family for consultation. At the council each member should be able to say what he or she thinks about the family's plans and systems and to consider ways to improve them. Together they can look at various possibilities, make various decisions, and get and give feedback as the plans unfold.

The quality of life differs greatly from family to family, even where many human, material, and community resources are basically the same. What makes the difference? Good management is often the key factor. That is, good management enables you to make the most of all your resources in order to be both a successful wage earner and a successful homemaker.

CHAPTER SUMMARY

1. Any one task is no problem for most of us. It is all of the decisions and all of the tasks together that require *good management*. First, make the big *decisions*. Set your *goals*.

2. A good manager, whether on the job or at home, is someone who can get a job done on *time*, according to set *standards*, at least *cost*, and as *pleasantly* as possible. The good manager recognizes *resources* and makes the most of them.

3. *Human resources* are time, energy, knowledge, skills, habits, and attitudes. *Material resources* are supplies, tools, equipment, work space, and money. Schools and hospitals, buslines and parks, and shopping centers and health clinics are all *community resources*.

4. We don't all have the same resources, so we make *trade-offs* of time for money, standards for time. Trade-offs can be decided at *family councils*, where everyone takes part in the decision.

5. To make good use of time, *plan* time limits and *sequence* tasks. To make your effort count, *simplify* tasks, use *body mechanics, organize* your work space, and *practice* good work habits.

6. To simplify tasks, *choose* the right tool or equipment, *use* carts and trays, *team up* with another worker, and *combine* tasks. Body mechanics means using good posture, dividing a heavy load, and lifting weights properly to save your back.

7. Planning *storage* helps organize work space. Good *work habits* help you keep it organized. They make routine tasks easier.

8. Businesses and governments use the *systems approach* to management. Families can do the same to reach short-term as well as long-term goals.

• FOLLOW-UP PROJECTS

1. Work in small groups to compile names, addresses, phone numbers, and purposes of local community resources.

2. Describe how community resources can be used by workers in each of the six job clusters.

3. Record how you use your time for a week. Analyze the results and answer these questions: Does the way you use your time fit in with your priorities? Can you see where you are wasting time? Can some tasks be simplified? Eliminated? Try developing and using an improved time schedule, then see if you are getting more work and/or more leisure from the new schedule.

4. Visit a chef on the job to see how food preparation tasks are simplified.

5. Invite a maintenance manager to class to demonstrate ways to simplify maintenance tasks.

6. Invite a coach or physical education teacher to class to demonstrate proper use of the body in sitting, standing, climbing, and lifting. Practice what has been demonstrated.

7. Analyze how the work load is divided in your family. Record (on chart in the student workbook) who performs household tasks such as buying groceries, preparing meals, and washing dishes and how much time it takes each worker. Is the distribution of work fair? Is each member of the family contributing?

8. Analyze storage problems at home, school, and on the job. Plan solutions.

9. Meal management is a common challenge in home management, whether you are living alone or as a member of a family. Use the systems approach to reach the goal of better meal management. To do so, decide on personal and family factors: single, working couple, family with young children, family with teenage children, or whatever. Identify the values, goals, standards, and resources that—along with family characteristics—make up the inputs in this problem. Carry through the problem, using the systems approach.

16 TAXES, CREDIT, SAVINGS, INSURANCE

After studying Chapter 16 you should be able to:

1. Explain how stages in the family life cycle influence money management.
2. Develop a personal spending plan and an annual balance sheet.
3. Contrast methods of handling income in families.
4. Describe paycheck deductions.
5. Compare services of financial institutions.
6. Open a bank account and reconcile a bank statement.
7. Write and endorse a check.
8. File an income tax return.
9. Weigh advantages and disadvantages of using credit.
10. Describe kinds of credit and compare costs.
11. List points to consider when signing a contract.
12. Compare term, whole life, endowment, and homeowner's insurance.
13. Explain why people need a will.

You can't have everything. Your income just won't stretch that far. Especially those first paychecks. But it is possible to plan and use consumer skills so that you can have *some of the things* you want. Maybe what you want most is an attractive apartment or a car. Maybe clothes are what you want most. Or a vacation or college. Perhaps the security of a savings account. It all depends on you and your values. Think through your values and priorities (what you want most), and then plan how to spend your income. What is important? What is worth saving (waiting) for?

Values and priorities change as your place in the *family life cycle* changes. Young singles have different priorities and goals from young couples or young families. Interest in clothes and travel may give way to saving for the baby's education. Or a young couple may desire saving for a home of their own rather than spending Saturday nights out.

Families with teenage children represent another stage in the life cycle. They have different priorities from singles, couples, and families with young children. Retired people have still different priorities.

Getting something you want by cutting costs does not have to be unpleasant. The couple saving for a home of their own can find a satisfactory lifestyle in the meantime by decorating a less expensive apartment, restoring old furniture rather than buying new, entertaining friends at home rather than going out, and taking advantage of museums and art galleries, parks, and beaches.

SPEND SOME, SAVE SOME

Once you have your values in mind and your priorities sorted out, you are ready to make a money plan. The basics are to add up income, estimate expenses, keep records of spending, and adjust your income and outgo as you go along.

To *estimate expenses,* keep records for a month or two. Then look at your spending patterns. Are you satisfied with your money management? Most people get some surprises when they record and examine their spending habits. They see spending patterns which do not fit their value systems. Maybe they value good clothing, but are spending their money on junk food instead. Maybe they value a good credit rating but are slipping into debt.

YOUR MONEY PLAN

Many expenses, such as rent and mortgage payments, are *fixed.* They must be paid each month and you know ahead of time exactly what they will cost. But some spending is *flexible.* You have more choice. You may spend more money one month than the next. Examples are the sums you spend on food and clothing or toll calls.

Which of *your* expenses are fixed? Which ones are flexible? Experts usually divide expenses like this:

Fixed
Mortgage or rent
Taxes not withheld
Installment payments
Insurance premiums
  Life
  Car
  Household
  Health
Savings and
  Investments
  Emergency Fund
  Short-Range
  Long-Range

Flexible
Food
Fuel and utilities
  Gas or oil
  Electricity
  Telephone
Household
  Maintenance
  Furnishings
Transportation
  Trains, Buses
  Private Car
    Operation
    Maintenance
Clothing
Personal Care
  Haircuts
  Cosmetics/Grooming
    Aids
Recreation and
  Education

Flexible
Medical/Dental
Gifts and Contributions
Miscellaneous

Some people like to add a personal allowance to the list, to act as a pressure valve. An allowance gives freedom to spend more money which "doesn't count." Sometimes contributions are considered a fixed expense, when monthly pledges have been made to a united fund or religious institution, for example. For the college student, fixed expenses may be tuition and fees, and room and board.

Are you surprised to see savings in the column of *fixed* expenses? Experts advise that savings be taken out of income first, not last, especially savings to cover emergencies like a layoff or sudden illness. A short-range savings fund might be established to plan for a new winter coat. A long-range fund could be designed to save for college, furniture, a new house, or a new car.

Once you have decided on your fixed and flexible expenses you will need to organize your personal money plan. Figure 16-1 shows an example of a spending plan.

How far ahead you plan is up to you. Some people like to plan a year ahead, in order to be prepared for Christmas, a vacation, and the like. Others plan for a month or six months. Every planner has *some* way to get from payday to payday.

What if your income and your expenses don't balance? You have two choices. Increase your income or cut back spending. For most people, the adjustment is not that bad. Their record of expenses shows some wasteful spending. They can wait a little longer for purchases that are not absolutely necessary. Their shopping skills will improve if they look more carefully *before* buying.

Young families with many expenses can feel they are getting nowhere. However, if they look closely at their financial picture each year, they may see gains which do not show up as cash, but which are economic security just the same. Some examples are the cash value of life insurance policies, interest on savings bonds, contributions to pension systems, and their investment in their home. An *annual balance sheet* can show how these items are building up.

Business managers prepare quarterly reports to show how they are doing. Individuals and families can do the same. A format for this is shown in Figure 16-2.

Poor money management causes much unhappiness in families since it has such a heavy impact on lifestyle. Falling into heavy debt can make family life very grim. But debt is not the only cause of strained family relations. The manner in which money decisions are made can be the root of the trouble.

There are different methods of handling income in families. Sometimes one member controls the income and doles out money to the others. Children and teenagers sometimes think they are given more money this way

SPENDING PLAN FOR AUGUST

	AMOUNT PLANNED	AMOUNT SPENT
TAKE-HOME PAY	$500	
FIXED EXPENSES:		
PROPERTY TAXES	—	—
MORTGAGE OR RENT	200	200
INSURANCE	20	20
DEBT PAYMENTS	—	—
SAVINGS	30	30
LONG-TERM	10	10
SHORT-TERM		
FLEXIBLE EXPENSES		
FOOD	80	100
FUEL AND UTILITIES		
GAS	10	10
ELECTRICITY	10	12
WATER	5	5
TELEPHONE	10	20
OTHER (CABLE TV, ETC.)	5	5
FURNISHINGS	10	35
TRANSPORTATION		
TRAINS/BUSES	40	40
PRIVATE CAR	—	—
CLOTHING	20	25
PERSONAL CARE	20	20
RECREATION AND EDUCATION	20	40
MEDICAL/DENTAL	10	10
GIFTS/CONTRIBUTIONS	—	—
MISCELLANEOUS	—	—
TOTAL EXPENDITURES	$500	582

Figure 16-1. A spending plan helps you keep track of how you spend your money. At the beginning of the month, you list all your upcoming expenses. At the end of the month, you list all the amounts of money spent. By comparing the two totals, you can tell if you've overspent and where.

Balance Sheet

	1977	1978
Assets:		
House	35,000	37,500
Car	4,800	4,000
Life Insurance (cash value)	300	450
Pension fund	—	—
Stock	2,000	2,500
Cash (savings in bank)	1,000	1,500
Other	—	—
TOTAL ASSETS	$43,100	$45,950
Liabilities		
Mortgage	26,000	25,800
Loan (car)	4,000	3,000
Other	—	—
TOTAL LIABILITIES	$30,000	$28,800
NET WORTH	$13,100	$17,150

Figure 16-2. On an annual balance sheet, you add up all your assets and subtract all your liabilities. The final total tells you your net worth.

than when they have a set allowance. The drawback, however, is that the doler is subtly passing judgment on every purchase—deciding whether to approve or disapprove each request. An allowance lets children and teenagers make their own decisions and plans about using their money. They learn management in the process through trial and error.

Many spouses find both the dole and the allowance methods demeaning. Some couples use the fifty-fifty system, with each person assuming responsibility for half of the family expenses. Others throw their income into a common fund, pay expenses, and divide what is left. But the system proven by time and experience to be fair and satisfactory to nearly everyone is family finance planned at a family council. In this system the needs and wants of all family members are considered, and no one demands or accepts an unfair share.

UNDERSTANDING YOUR PAYCHECK

Figure 16-3 shows a typical paycheck stub. *Gross pay* includes all the money earned for the time period, which may be weekly, bi weekly, or monthly. By law, gross pay includes overtime and tips as well as regular pay.

Income tax will be automatically withheld unless the worker has filed a W-4E form, as we learned in Chapter 6. Deductions are also made automatically for social security, which may be shown on your paycheck stub under FICA (Federal Insurance Contributions Act). Other deductions shown in the example are for fringe benefits like insurance and pension plan. A paycheck stub also shows union dues and savings invested in the company credit union and in government bonds. *Net pay* is the final amount, the take-home pay after deductions have been made.

Keep your paycheck stubs for reference when you file your income tax and for proof of social security contributions. If you receive cash instead of a paycheck, ask your employer which deductions are being made and keep a record of them.

CHOOSING A BANK

Once you start work you will want to establish both a checking and a savings account to handle your money. Better yet, your community may have a bank that combines these two functions so that you can receive interest at all times on the money you have banked. Choosing the right banking services is a challenge. Many changes are occurring in the operation of savings and checking accounts. They often help to increase your earnings. The workers who keep all pay in cash run the risk of losing their money or having it stolen. The wise course is to take advantage of the banking services available to you.

There are several types of financial institutions: commercial banks, mutual savings banks, and savings and loan associations. *Commercial banks* are owned by stockholders and are operated to earn a profit for them. They

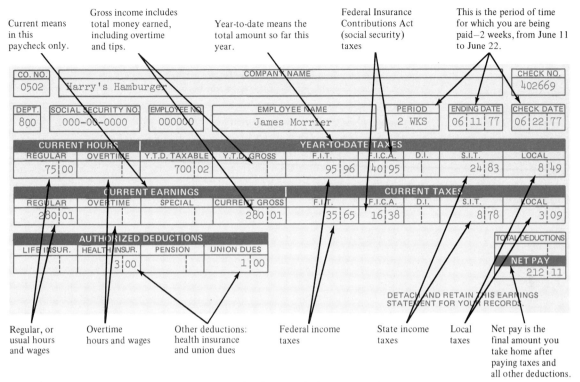

Current means in this paycheck only.

Gross income includes total money earned, including overtime and tips.

Year-to-date means the total amount so far this year.

Federal Insurance Contributions Act (social security) taxes

This is the period of time for which you are being paid—2 weeks, from June 11 to June 22.

CO. NO.	COMPANY NAME	CHECK NO.
0502	Harry's Hamburger	402669

DEPT.	SOCIAL SECURITY NO.	EMPLOYEE NO.	EMPLOYEE NAME	PERIOD	ENDING DATE	CHECK DATE
800	000-00-0000	000000	James Morrier	2 WKS	06 11 77	06 22 77

CURRENT HOURS		YEAR-TO-DATE TAXES						
REGULAR	OVERTIME	Y.T.D. TAXABLE	Y.T.D. GROSS	F.I.T.	F.I.C.A.	D.I.	S.I.T.	LOCAL
75 00		700 02		95 96	40 95		24 83	8 49

CURRENT EARNINGS				CURRENT TAXES				
REGULAR	OVERTIME	SPECIAL	CURRENT GROSS	F.I.T.	F.I.C.A.	D.I.	S.I.T.	LOCAL
280 01			280 01	35 65	16 38		8 78	3 09

AUTHORIZED DEDUCTIONS					TOTAL DEDUCTIONS
LIFE INSUR.	HEALTH INSUR.	PENSION	UNION DUES		
	3 00		1 00		NET PAY
					212 11

DETACH AND RETAIN THIS EARNINGS STATEMENT FOR YOUR RECORDS.

Regular, or usual hours and wages

Overtime hours and wages

Other deductions: health insurance and union dues

Federal income taxes

State income taxes

Local taxes

Net pay is the final amount you take home after paying taxes and all other deductions.

Figure 16-3. Your paycheck stub lists all the deductions made from your salary.

are established in all parts of the United States and make loans to businesses as well as to consumers (such as an auto loan). They also invest in mortgages.

Mutual savings banks are owned by their depositors. They are found mostly on the East and West coasts and were originally established as a place where "working people" or small investors could safely deposit savings and secure loans. Mutual savings banks specialize in mortgages and student loans but offer other services also.

Savings and loan associations, located in many cities and large towns, are mostly mutual associations owned by their members. They specialize in mortgage loans.

Individual savings accounts in most banks and savings and loan associations are insured up to $40,000, either by the Federal Deposit Insurance Corporation (FDIC) or the Federal Savings and Loan Insurance Corporation (FSLIC). Check to be sure your savings account has this protection.

Until recently checking accounts were available only in commercial banks. New banking laws make the services of the three main financial institutions more alike. Each offers a choice of savings accounts, including passbook accounts and investment certificates.

A *passbook account* is a good choice when you dip into your savings often. When you wish to save for a long-range goal, a *certificate of deposit* might be better.

With a certificate of deposit the saver agrees to leave money in the savings institution for a certain period of time. Because of this agreement, a higher rate of interest is paid. It is possible to withdraw money from a certificate of deposit ahead of time, but at reduced interest. Because most people have a combination of short- and long-range goals, a combination of savings accounts is usually desirable.

There are other places to invest savings: credit unions, for example, and stocks and bonds. For many families their largest investment is in real estate: their home. Others invest in a business or in life insurance.

Credit unions are groups of people with a common bond, such as belonging to the same union or working for the same company. Members pool their savings in a *cooperative* in order to have a place where they can easily secure loans and earn interest on their money from the proceeds. Cooperatives are controlled by their members. Sometimes they offer services other than savings accounts and consumer loans, perhaps group legal services and travel clubs. Technically, you do not deposit savings in a credit union; you buy shares, normally for as little as $5.00 each. Your account earns "dividends" rather than interest. One thing to check before joining is to see whether share accounts are federally insured. If so, the National Credit Union Administration protects individual accounts up to $40,000.

Opening an Account. Many changes are occurring in banking. The computer and electronic banking will simplify many operations for you. But for the present you will want to learn traditional banking practices.

Whatever your choice of bank, procedures for opening an account will be much the same. First, you will be asked for some identification. A driver's license is usually accepted. Take along your social security card. You will be asked to sign a signature card so that checks you write on your account can be inspected for forgery. Then you'll be given a check book with a set of stubs or a small notebook in which you will record every check you write.

Before you can write a check, you must deposit some money in the bank! The teller or bank officer at the "New Accounts" window or desk will probably fill out your first deposit slip. After that, it is up to you. Along with your book of blank checks you will receive a number of deposit slips. Fill one out each time you make a deposit.

When you deposit a check made out to you it must be properly endorsed. To *endorse* means to write your signature on the back of the check exactly as the check is written on the front. If the check is made out to John Doe, endorse the check "John Doe." If it is made out to J. Christopher Doe, endorse the check "J. Christopher Doe."

When you deposit or cash a check in person, wait until you are at the teller's window or at least in the bank before you endorse your check.

Figure 16-4. Before you can write a check, you must deposit some money in the bank!

When making a deposit by mail or in a night depository, endorse the check or checks as "Pay to the order of *(name of bank)*" or "For deposit only in *(name of bank)*." Cash can safely be put in a *night depository,* which is a slot on the outside of the bank that drops into a box inside the bank. Use it when the bank is closed. Never mail cash unless you send it *registered* mail, for which you pay a fee to insure that the money will be delivered only to your bank.

The reason for taking such care in endorsing checks is that an endorsed check can be used by anyone, just as cash can. If you should lose an endorsed check, the finder could probably cash it with little trouble.

Some employers will deposit your paycheck for you by *direct deposit.* Many people find this a real convenience and they are protected against the risk of losing their checks on the way to the bank.

A surprising number of mistakes can be made in the minute it takes to write a check. To reduce the risk that someone will change the amount on a check you have written or forge your signature, follow these few rules:

· Write in ink (checks written in pencil can be erased and changed).

· Do not cross out or change anything (bank will not honor your check).

· Never sign a blank check (if check should be lost or stolen, anyone could fill in an amount).

· Don't leave checkbooks, canceled checks, or other papers with your signature lying around (someone could copy and forge your signature).

· Keep records on your checkbook stubs.

· After you fill in your name and the amount, draw a line to the end of the space provided, so a name cannot be changed or the amount of money raised.

· Always sign your checks the same way.

Bank Statement. Once a month, or once every three months, your bank will send you a statement of your account, and will enclose all the checks it has cashed for you. Keep these "canceled" checks safe, for they are proofs of what you have paid.

As soon as you receive your statement, go back over your own check stubs and make sure that the bank's statement agrees with your records. This process is called *reconciling* (reck-un-SILE-ing). If there is a difference between your records and the bank statement, check your own arithmetic carefully. Banks do make mistakes, but very seldom. More than likely your own arithmetic is off, or possibly you haven't taken into account that some banks charge you a small amount for handling your money (called "service charges"), which has been deducted from your balance. If you can't reconcile the bank's statement with your records, take the statement to the bank. If they have made a mistake they will correct it. If the mistake is yours, the bank officer will help you find where you went wrong. Figures 16-5 and 16-6 show examples of a bank statement and a form to use for reconciliation.

YOUR TAXES By the last day in January of each year, every employer must send a statement of the total taxes withheld to every person employed during the previous year. This statement is called a W-2 form (see Figure 16-7).

WAGE AND TAX STATEMENT.

This form provides a record of the wages you were paid, the amount of federal income tax withheld, and the amount of social security (FICA) tax that was withheld from your pay. (If you filed a W-4E form when you started work, no taxes were withheld.)

You will also receive after the end of the year statements from banks, credit unions, insurance companies, and other savings institutions showing the taxable interest credited to your account. If you own stocks and bonds, dividends and interest from these investments are also taxable.

If you are required to file an income tax return, you will receive copies B and C of Form W-2. Your employer sends copy A to the Internal Revenue Service (IRS), gives you copy B to attach to your tax return and copy C for your records, and retains copy D. In most states, an additional copy is furnished to be filed with the state income tax return.

As an entry-level worker, it is quite likely that you will not have to pay any state or federal income tax. That is, any taxes you have paid may be

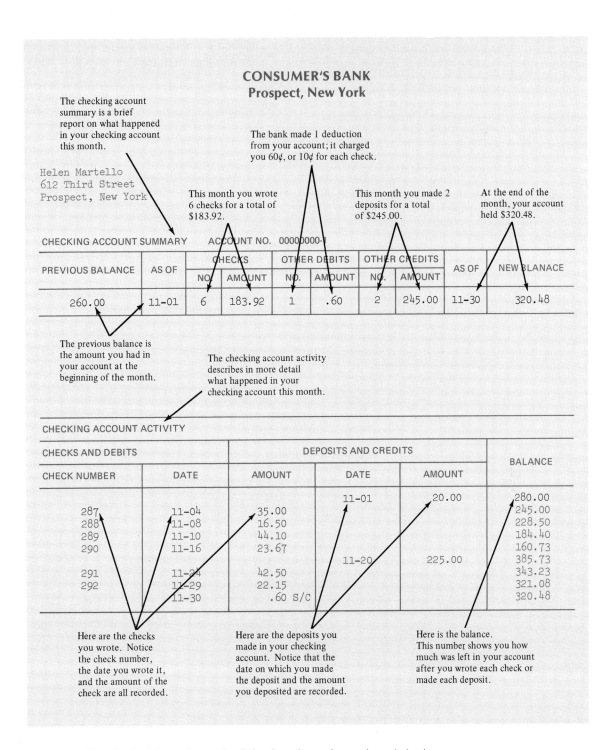

CONSUMER'S BANK
Prospect, New York

The checking account summary is a brief report on what happened in your checking account this month.

The bank made 1 deduction from your account; it charged you 60¢, or 10¢ for each check.

Helen Martello
612 Third Street
Prospect, New York

This month you wrote 6 checks for a total of $183.92.

This month you made 2 deposits for a total of $245.00.

At the end of the month, your account held $320.48.

CHECKING ACCOUNT SUMMARY   ACCOUNT NO. 00000000-

PREVIOUS BALANCE	AS OF	CHECKS		OTHER DEBITS		OTHER CREDITS		AS OF	NEW BLANACE
		NO.	AMOUNT	NO.	AMOUNT	NO.	AMOUNT		
260.00	11-01	6	183.92	1	.60	2	245.00	11-30	320.48

The previous balance is the amount you had in your account at the beginning of the month.

The checking account activity describes in more detail what happened in your checking account this month.

CHECKING ACCOUNT ACTIVITY

CHECKS AND DEBITS		DEPOSITS AND CREDITS			BALANCE
CHECK NUMBER	DATE	AMOUNT	DATE	AMOUNT	
			11-01	20.00	280.00
287	11-04	35.00			245.00
288	11-08	16.50			228.50
289	11-10	44.10			184.40
290	11-16	23.67			160.73
			11-20	225.00	385.73
291	11-24	42.50			343.23
292	11-29	22.15			321.08
	11-30	.60 S/C			320.48

Here are the checks you wrote. Notice the check number, the date you wrote it, and the amount of the check are all recorded.

Here are the deposits you made in your checking account. Notice that the date on which you made the deposit and the amount you deposited are recorded.

Here is the balance. This number shows you how much was left in your account after you wrote each check or made each deposit.

Figure 16-5. Your bank statement records all the deposits you've made and checks you've written during the previous month.

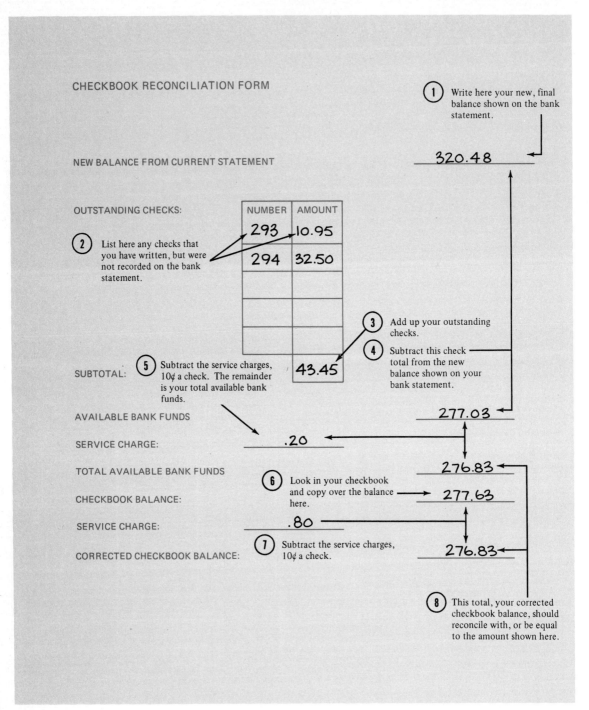

CHECKBOOK RECONCILIATION FORM

① Write here your new, final balance shown on the bank statement.

NEW BALANCE FROM CURRENT STATEMENT

320.48

OUTSTANDING CHECKS:

NUMBER	AMOUNT
293	10.95
294	32.50
	43.45

② List here any checks that you have written, but were not recorded on the bank statement.

③ Add up your outstanding checks.

④ Subtract this check total from the new balance shown on your bank statement.

SUBTOTAL:

⑤ Subtract the service charges, 10¢ a check. The remainder is your total available bank funds.

AVAILABLE BANK FUNDS

277.03

SERVICE CHARGE:

.20

TOTAL AVAILABLE BANK FUNDS

276.83

⑥ Look in your checkbook and copy over the balance here.

CHECKBOOK BALANCE:

277.63

SERVICE CHARGE:

.80

⑦ Subtract the service charges, 10¢ a check.

CORRECTED CHECKBOOK BALANCE:

276.83

⑧ This total, your corrected checkbook balance, should reconcile with, or be equal to the amount shown here.

Figure 16-6. By using a bank reconciliation form, you can figure out whether the bank statement is correct.

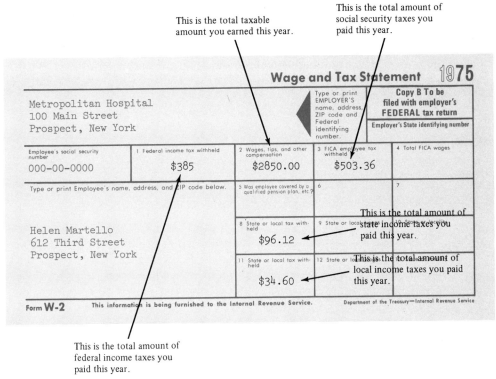

This is the total taxable amount you earned this year.

This is the total amount of social security taxes you paid this year.

This is the total amount of state income taxes you paid this year.

This is the total amount of local income taxes you paid this year.

This is the total amount of federal income taxes you paid this year.

Figure 16-7. The wage and tax statement provides a record of the wages you were paid and the amount of federal, state, and local taxes withheld.

returned to you. But they will not come back automatically. You must file—make an application—for them. You can pick up income tax forms, and written directions about filing them, at any post office. Once you have filed a return, you will receive forms in the mail every year.

FILING TAX RETURNS

Income tax laws are complicated, and both tax laws and forms are constantly changing. There are many regulations concerning who must pay taxes and how much, exemptions and deductions, tax credits, and many other questions. Therefore, the pamphlets that come with the forms may not answer all your questions. Your best course is to get the free help from a local branch of the IRS, or call the toll-free *800* number listed in your phone book under U.S. Government, Internal Revenue Service.

You must file your tax returns no later than April 15 of each year. The sooner you file, the sooner any taxes to be returned to you will be on their way.

YOUR RECORDS

In order to fill out tax forms, you will need to refer to your own records. You may be able to deduct child care and other business expenses, contributions to charities, interest on your mortgage, and other items from the tax you owe. Check the tax laws each year, and keep careful records to back up the expenses you claim.

USING CREDIT   Credit allows you to buy something now and pay for it in the future. Three major types of consumer credit are available:

· Charge accounts
· Installment plans
· Consumer loans

Department stores and other businesses extend credit through charge accounts and installment plans. Consumer loans are available from credit unions and banks. Buying with installment payments or consumer loans means paying finance charges. Many charge accounts also have a finance charge.

ADVANTAGES AND DISADVANTAGES

There are advantages and disadvantages to using credit. The most obvious advantage is that you can enjoy a product or service immediately. You do not have to wait to save up the money before buying it. Credit is, for some people, a kind of enforced savings. They cannot discipline themselves to save for a purchase, but they do make their payments on a loan or installment plan and keep their charge accounts paid up.

Some people do no like to take their savings out of the bank once they have started an account. They like to know they have some savings to rely on in an emergency. They prefer to borrow for short-term purchases and to leave their savings in the bank or credit union.

Some people argue that credit is a way to beat inflation. They think it is better to buy now, at a lower price, even though they have to add the cost of the interest to the price of the product or service.

Use of credit has obvious disadvantages. You can quickly get into more debt than can be easily handled. Monthly payments can sound low until they are all added up. Then many families find themselves in real financial trouble. The problem is so widespread that there is a home economics occupation to help individuals and families with money problems. Remember the family management counselor in the family and community services cluster?

Credit cuts future buying power and makes saving difficult, since much future income is already tied up. The cost of credit is perhaps its biggest drawback.

Two important federal laws relating to credit are the Truth-in-Lending Law and the Equal Credit Opportunity Act. The Truth-in-Lending Law requires lenders and other credit grantors (1) to state interest charges as an *annual percentage rate* (APR) so the consumer can compare costs of different kinds of credit, (2) to disclose all finance charges: the interest, credit investigation fee, service charge, or premium for credit life insurance if the lender requires you to purchase it.

The Equal Credit Opportunity Act makes it illegal to deny personal or commercial credit to anyone merely on the basis of sex or marital status. Prior to the act women were often discriminated against whey they tried to get credit.

KINDS OF CREDIT

Common kinds of credit are:

· *Regular charge accounts.* You buy an item or service when you need it and pay for it when you get the bill. There is no charge if you pay the entire balance due within the period allowed, usually one month.
· *Revolving charge accounts.* You may buy on credit up to a certain amount, usually $100. The seller must be repaid a certain amount each month, plus a finance charge. So long as the total amount you owe is under the limit, you can keep buying on credit and paying the monthly amount and charge.
· *Installment plans.* You buy high-cost items such as appliances, a car, or a television set. Usually you pay part in cash, called a *down payment,* at the time you buy. You also sign a contract agreeing to repay the balance in a series of regular payments, called *installments,* plus a finance charge.
· *Cash loans.* These are made by banks, finance companies, credit unions, or other lenders. Some are installment loans. Others you repay all at once, within a given time, plus the finance charge.
· *Credit cards*: These are made available by banks, retail stores, gasoline companies, and others. Some cards are used for purchases. Others make it possible to establish a *line of credit,* that is, make it possible to borrow cash.

COST OF CREDIT

The costs of credit vary all the way from nothing for a promptly paid regular checking account or credit card purchase to a possible 36 percent interest at a finance company. For illegal lenders (who are not a recommended source of credit!), interest rates are often incredibly high.

The cost of credit depends also on your credit rating, the security you can offer, the amount of the loan or purchase, and the length of time you take to pay. Security, called *collateral,* means such assets as your savings account, stocks and bonds, or a home.

In general, you pay the lowest interest charges for loans based on your own funds held in a savings account, in certificates of deposit, in life insurance policies, or in a pension account with your employer. You use one of these sources as security for the loan. In the middle range on the loan cost scale are personal loans from credit unions and commercial banks. Next on the loan cost scale come bank credit cards, then retail revolving credit. The most expensive legal source of credit is a finance company.

YOUR CREDIT RATING

What is a credit rating and how does a young person establish a good one? Before you open a charge account or borrow money, you must convince the store or lender that you are a good credit risk. They consider:

· *Stability*: how long you have worked for the same company or lived at the same address
· *Income*: how much you earn and how steady your income is
· *Possessions*: savings, a boat, or a car are examples
· *Credit history*: how promptly your bills have been paid in the past

All this information is put together into a *credit rating*. Some large operations use a credit scoring system where they assign certain points to each of the factors. Most businesses rely on a *credit bureau*, which serves as a clearinghouse of information on an individual's credit ratings. A merchant or lender wanting to investigate your credit rating can phone the local credit bureau for information. The local bureau, in turn, will check your file, which may be stored in a computer. The merchant or lender will be provided with the information in your file and will use that as a base for deciding whether or not to grant you credit.

You can check your credit rating also. Under the provisions of the Fair Credit Reporting Act, you have the right to review your file and challenge any information in it found to be untrue. The beginning worker can establish a credit rating by opening a savings account or joining a credit union, by managing a checking account, opening a charge account, or buying something on the installment plan and being sure to pay promptly.

If your family is known as one which pays its bills, and a parent is willing to *co-sign* for the loan, you may be able to get a loan with a lower annual percentage rate. A co-signer is a person who signs someone else's promise to pay. This gives the lender more security in making the loan. The co-signer is equally responsible for repayment of the loan if the borrower fails to pay.

SIGNING A CONTRACT

If you decide to use credit, sign a contract only after:

You have read it carefully

· You understand and are able to do what you promise
· You know what the creditor promises to do
· You know what will happen if you do not keep your promise
· All blank spaces are filled in on the contract

If you do not understand a contract, take it to someone you trust for help. In any case, consult an attorney or your legal aid society before you sign a contract for a large investment or substantial purchase.

· Don't forget to read the *disclosure statement* before you sign for a loan. It is a written statement a lender must give you before you sign a consumer contract for credit. It gives you information required by the Truth-in-Lending Law, such as amount borrowed, number of payments, size of each payment, and interest expressed in dollars as well as the APR.
· Always get a signed copy of the contract for your own records.
· Be careful with whom you deal. A contract is worthless if the other party disappears after you have paid but before the merchandise has been delivered or service rendered. The contract won't eliminate the expense involved if you have to sue someone for not fulfilling an obligation. In short, a contract is never a substitute for dealing with honest, reputable businesses.

Once you become a capitalist, a saver, and a worker, protecting what you have becomes a problem. Bank accounts protect your money. So does insurance. Life insurance may be a fringe benefit where you work. Most states require you to carry insurance on your car. You may have insurance on the new furniture you bought for your apartment. Everyone needs health insurance.

PROTECTING WHAT YOU HAVE

INSURANCE

Life insurance has two main purposes—protection and investment. Families are protected against loss of income should the head of the household die.

Some policies accent this protection feature. Others also serve as a way to invest savings for college, retirement, emergencies, or other purposes.

There are three basic types of life insurance. *Term* insurance offers protection for a certain period of time. *Premiums*, as payments for insurance are called, are cheapest for young policyholders and get increasingly more expensive as the insured get older. Term insurance gives the most protection for the money and is often used in families until children are grown.

Whole life policies, also called *straight life*, cover a person's entire life. Premiums remain the same throughout the life of the policy. Whole life policies have the advantage of building up cash values. *Cash value* is the sum you can borrow on your insurance. It is also the amount you receive if you must give up the insurance after paying for it for a while.

Figure 16-8. Liability insurance covers damage you may do to someone else's property.

Endowment insurance is life insurance that emphasizes savings. Should the policyholder die before the policy is paid up, and the savings program is complete, the face value of the policy will be paid to survivors. Endowment insurance is also protection, but it is more expensive than the other two kinds of insurance. Endowment policies are often used to help provide income for retirement.

Many families have both whole life and term insurance. Some have all three kinds of insurance, depending on their stage in the family lifecycle. In any case, insurance coverage should be planned to mesh with social security benefits for insured workers.

Another kind of insurance people buy to protect what they have is homeowners insurance. Homeowners insurance is a "package policy" which combines protection of real estate, fire insurance on personal property, and *personal liability* (responsibility). Homeowners should, of course, have fire insurance on their houses. Most also buy *extended coverage,* which means insurance against loss from windstorm, hail, explosion, and other hazards. People who rent apartments and houses can also buy homeowners policies for two of the kinds of insurance protection included: personal property (your clothes, furniture, and other belongings) and liability.

Ownership or occupancy of a home involves personal liability for injury to household help, delivery people, guests, or others who are on the property. Liability insurance may pay medical bills in such cases or pay the claim up to the amount of the policy. This kind of insurance also covers injury or property damage caused by your activities, such as accidentally hitting another player with a golf ball. Or by the activities of your family or pets. Liability insurance is not expensive and is a valuable kind of protection to have.

Fire insurance on real estate and personal property and liability insurance can be bought as separate insurance policies. Compare prices and coverage and decide on the best buy for you.

Be sure to buy any insurance from a reputable agent and, as in the case of all contracts, know what you are signing. The Federal Trade Commission gives the following hints for buying insurance by mail:

· If you buy insurance by mail, be sure it really protects you. Know:
  a. What it insures you against
  b. How much it will pay
  c. Under what conditions it will pay
  d. What the premium is
· If you don't understand the policy, ask your neighborhood legal service, an insurance agent, or a friend in business to explain it.
· Even though a mail order offer may look good, shop around until you find the best policy for you.

Two kinds of insurance are so important that state and federal governments have taken steps to be sure individuals and families are protected. They are auto and health insurance. Auto insurance will be discussed in Chapter 17.

The cost of health care has risen faster in recent years than most other costs of individuals and families. As a result many people do not receive adequate health care. Others are burdened with medical expenses they can scarcely pay. Government programs provide health insurance for some segments of the population. *Medicaid* assists low-income families. *Medicare* is a health insurance program for the elderly. The dilemma of providing health insurance for the rest of the population has been recognized by Congress and different plans for national health insurance are being debated.

YOUR WILL

One last consideration in money management is making a will. Once you have life insurance, a savings account, valuable possessions like a stereo and a car, you have an *estate*. Young parents in particular should have a will prepared to protect their children. Singles will want to be sure their estates are settled as they would wish also. If you don't have a will, the state will decide how to dispose of your property. What the state has in mind may be all right with you, but you better find out from a lawyer whether this is so. The charges for having a simple but sound will drawn up are low compared to the financial problems you could cause your family and close friends by not leaving a will.

CHAPTER SUMMARY

1. You can't have everything, but you can have some of the things that you want, if you plan carefully. Your values and priorities change as your place in the *family life cycle* changes. The basics for a money plan are to add up income, estimate expenses, keep records of spending, and adjust your income and outgo.

2. Many expenses are *fixed* and must be paid every month. Some spending is *flexible*. You have more choices to make. An *annual balance sheet* shows how your financial worth is building up in the cash value of your life insurance policies, interest on your savings bonds and savings account, your pension system, and investment in your home.

3. There are different methods of handling income in families: the *dole, allowance* system, *dividing* income and expenses fifty-fifty, using a *common fund,* and the *family council.*

4. Deductions may be shown on your paycheck stub for income tax, social security, pension funds, insurance, union dues, and savings in a credit union or government bonds. Banking services vary according to the kind of bank: *commercial* bank, *mutual savings* bank, or *savings and loan* association. Many changes are being made in banking practices, but you probably still need to know how to make out a *deposit slip*, write a *check, endorse* a check, and *reconcile* your bank balance.

5. By the end of January of each year, each one of your employers must send a statement of the money paid you and the taxes withheld. This is called the *W-2, Wage and Tax Statement.* It also shows the amount of social security tax that was withheld from your pay. (If you filed a W-4E form when you started work, no taxes were withheld.)

6. As an entry-level worker it is quite likely that you will not have to pay any state or federal income tax. But if taxes were withheld, you have to file a return in order to have your money returned to you. You can get *free help* from your local IRS office or by calling toll-free the *800* number listed in your phone book.

7. It is important to keep good *records* in order to fill out your income tax return. You may be able to deduct child care and other business expenses, contributions to charities, interest, and other items from the tax you owe. Tax laws are constantly *changing*.

8. *Credit* allows you to buy something now and pay for it in the future. Three types of consumer credit are *charge account, installment plans,* and *consumer loans* from credit unions, banks, finance companies, and insurance companies. *Costs* of credit vary from nothing for promptly paid regular charge accounts to a possible 36 percent interest at a finance company. Illegal sources of credit can go much higher. A *credit bureau* keeps on record the *credit ratings* of individuals.

9. To protect what you have, learn about kinds of *life insurance, home-owners* insurance, and *wills*.

● FOLLOW-UP PROJECTS

1. Invite a panel of guests to class to speak about their use of resources (time, energy, money, community services) during different stages in the family life cycle. Speakers might include a young couple, parents of small children, parents with children in high school or college, a retired couple, and an elderly single.

2. Discuss methods of handling family income. What are advantages and disadvantages of the different methods?

3. Compute your gross pay and your net pay for one month in your present job.

4. Keep records of spending for a month. Analyze spending habits. Do your habits agree with your values? Set up a personal spending plan. At the end of the period, take an anonymous poll of the class to identify the biggest problems: e.g., impulse spending, too little income, lack of planning, and record-keeping. Poll other students in the school and compare results.

5. Visit financial institutions in the community. Compare services, interest rates on savings, cost of credit, and ways to establish a credit rating through the institution.

6. Collect deposit and withdrawal slips and sample checkbooks from financial institutions. Practice filling in deposit and withdrawal slips, writing and endorsing checks, reconciling bank statement with checkbook.

7. Ask your IRS office for income tax forms and practice materials designed for student use. Practice filling out an income tax form.

8. Working individually or in small groups, decide on a large purchase you wish to make, the type of credit to use, costs of the credit, and kind of contract that may have to be signed. Explain in your own words what the contract is saying.

9. Visit a credit bureau or invite a credit bureau representative to class. Ask how credit bureaus operate. Ask the representative for samples of good and poor credit ratings. Ask how young workers can establish and protect their credit ratings.

10. Invite one or more insurance agents to class to discuss kinds of life insurance, laws in your state regarding homeowner's insurance and auto insurance. *Or,* visit various insurance agencies, interview the representatives, and report back to class. Ask the agents to relate life insurance to social security benefits.

11. Visit your legal aid society or invite a lawyer to class. Ask him or her to discuss contracts, wills, and other legal questions of interest.

17 CONSUMER SURVIVAL SKILLS

After studying Chapter 17 you will be able to:

1. Contrast rights and responsibilities of consumers.
2. Compare price and quality of products and services.
3. Analyze advertising.
4. Identify fraudulent selling practices.
5. Explain how to make a consumer complaint.
6. Demonstrate ability to choose an apartment, food, clothing, and transportation, using consumer skills.

Once you have a full-time job, a bank account, and a money plan you are ready to make some choices about:

· Your working wardrobe
· Your first apartment
· Your food
· Transportation to work

You are ready to test your skills as a consumer.

Consumer skills are often called survival skills. Can you survive in the marketplace? Use your income to obtain a satisfactory lifestyle?

In this chapter we'll consider some general rules about shopping. Then we'll see how they apply to your choice of housing, clothing, food, and transportation.

SKILLFUL SHOPPING

You can learn to shop skillfully. Learning your rights and responsibilities as a consumer; planning your shopping; reading advertisements; comparing one product with another; taking advantage of sales; avoiding fraudulent (cheating) sellers; and making a complaint if you are not satisfied with a product or service are all part of skillful shopping.

Let us look at each of these shopping skills in some detail so that you can become a better consumer.

RIGHTS AND RESPONSIBILITIES OF CONSUMERS

As a consumer you have four basic rights:

1. The right to *choose from a variety* of products and services.
2. The right to be *accurately informed* about what you are buying.
3. The right to *rely on the safety* of what you have bought.
4. The right to *"redress" (returned money or an exchange)* if a product is faulty or you have been cheated.

Each of your rights as a consumer is matched by a responsibility.

1. Your right to choose is matched by your responsibility to *choose as well as you can* and to treat merchants fairly.
2. Your right to be given accurate information is matched by your responsibility to *learn as much as you can* about products and services. Read advertisements, study labels, look out for fraud, and understand laws that affect consumers.
3. Your right to rely on the safety of a product is matched by your responsibility to *examine products for safety* before you buy them and to use them according to instructions.
4. Your right to redress is matched by your responsibility to *know how to make complaints* in a proper manner.

The information in this section will help you to protect your rights and carry out your responsibilities.

Figure 17-1. Be a careful consumer; compare prices, ingredients, and volume before you buy. (Kenneth Karp)

PLANNING YOUR SHOPPING

Good buying begins at home, where you can make buying decisions away from high-pressure salespersons and the temptation to buy on impulse things you do not need or may not even really want.

First, plan your buying priorities. (Remember that priority means what should come first.) Consider what you need or want most, what quality of product is suitable, and what price you can afford to pay.

Second, plan where you want to shop for various products. There are many places to buy: specialty shops, department stores, discount houses, manufacturer's outlets, consumer cooperatives, variety stores, and second-hand shops. There are also mail-order houses, and people who bring the store to you—door-to-door sellers. No matter where you shop, you should be able to do these things:

· Find prices clearly marked
· Look over merchandise carefully before you buy it
· Return an item if it is unsatisfactory

Door-to-door salespeople can provide a welcome service, but they can also be a danger spot for consumer fraud. Before you buy, ask to see the salesperson's identification, the card or license telling who the person is and what is sold. Stop and think. Do you really need what is being offered? Know the name and address of the salesperson's company, when you will get what you buy, whether you can return the product and get your money back, where you can get repairs if needed, how you pay for the product, and whether you have to sign a contract.

(Usually a contract signed by both parties cannot be cancelled. However, federal law gives you 3 days to cancel without penalty a contract for more than $25 which you signed *in your home*.)

ADVERTISING CAN INFORM

Advertising performs a service to the consumer trying to find out what products and services are available, where they can be purchased, and how much they cost. Advertising is commonly done through newspapers and magazines, radio and television, billboards and displays, and brochures and catalogues prepared by manufacturers and retail outlets.

Coupons are another advertising medium and are a popular way of introducing a new product or gaining new customers.

Advertisements, displays, and salespeople have the same purpose: to arouse your interest in a product or service and persuade you to buy. To do so they use appeals like newness, thrift, youth, adventure, independence, approval, and success.

The survival skill for the consumer is to separate information from promotion, since the major purpose of the advertisement is to make people want the product or service and buy it. To separate fact from fantasy, ask yourself questions like:

· Is this message helpful to me as a consumer? If not, is it useless? Misleading? In poor taste?
· Is this ad playing on my emotions? My need for status? Security?
· What does this ad promise?
· How can I check the truth of the information given?
· Do I need more information?
· Where can I get more information?
· Is the ad directed at a special group? Children? Teenagers? The aged? Is it fair to do this, e.g., create a demand for expensive toys at Christmas?

The Federal Trade Commission has the authority to regulate advertising. In recent years the consumer movement has demanded stricter enforcement of regulations. One result was the adoption by the FTC, in 1971, of a resolution requiring all advertisers to back up their claims about product safety, performance, effectiveness, quality, and comparative price.

Advertising is a major source of information for consumers about the wide variety of products and services available for sale. But consumers have a responsibility to question advertising claims, compare offers, and seek further information from cooperative extension bulletins, consumer reports, and the like.

COMPARE

Advertising helps you make some comparisons at home and decide which retail outlets to use. Also, when you are not sure about the price range of an item you can check prices in newspaper ads and catalogues. When you get to the outlet, continue to compare quality, design, and price.

Your greatest help is a good label. Labels tell you facts required by law, such as fiber content of fabrics and ingredients in canned foods. Some labels have special indicators of quality, like endorsement of the Underwriter's Laboratory for safety of electrical appliances and the American Dental Association for toothpaste. In general, a good label gives facts such as:

· What an item is made of
· Size, number, net weight, or volume
· Care needed
· How to use the product
· Name and address of manufacturer
· Safety precautions, if needed

In addition to comparing labels, examine the product. Look at the quality and check for a guarantee or warranty.

The Federal Trade Commission has set guidelines for guarantees, which require a company to explain the terms of the guarantee and be prepared to back it up. Read the guarantee or warranty carefully. What is covered? By whom? How long will it be in force? What must you do to make the

Figure 17-2. A good ad contains factual information and allows the consumer to make an educated decision.

guarantee good? A dated receipt will help you make a claim, so save your sales slip, cancelled check, or other receipt.

Before making your final decision when selecting a service, such as dry-cleaning or uniform rental, make the same comparison as when selecting a product. Find out who will do the service, when it will be ready, the cost, and what steps you can take if the service is not done on time or is not done properly.

TAKE ADVANTAGE OF SALES

Sales are held for many reasons, not all of them favorable for the consumer. Some "sales" are really below-standard items "on sale" without a genuine price cut. Regular merchandise may be marked down, however, to make room for new goods, get new customers, or introduce new products. Or stores may want to move a surplus of soiled stock, incomplete lines of goods, or close out outdated appliances, clothes, or cars.

The best sales are held by established firms at traditional sale times, such as end-of-season, preinventory, or holiday sales.

Regular, standard-quality goods are marked down at this time. Some sale goods may, however, be special purchases from manufacturers and whole-salers. Some special purchases are goods of standard quality. Others are "seconds," which do not pass inspection (quality control) at the factories. For good buys, inspect seconds carefully to be sure flaws are not too great for the product to be usable. A shopping calendar of traditional sales is shown in Table 17-1.

Not to be overlooked are garage sales and other sales held in private homes. Auctions are often the source of "good buys" and are a form of recreation for some people. Sales of this type are frequently announced in local newspapers.

WATCHING FOR FRAUD

Have you ever heard the term "caveat emptor"? If so, you know that it means "Let the buyer beware." It suggests that it is all right to sell anything someone is foolish enough to buy. The fact that the term is written in Latin, the language of the ancient Romans, tells you that the practice of cheating the consumer, if you can get away with it, has been going on for a long time.

There are several kinds of fraud to watch for:

Referral Selling. A salesperson (usually at your door) offers you a cash refund or a credit on the purchase of a product for every person you get to buy the same product. The catch is that you must buy the product and then get others to buy it too. The products are usually overpriced and you receive much less in credit or refunds than you were promised. You may receive nothing.

Table 17-1 SHOPPING CALENDAR OF TRADITIONAL SALES

January	February	March	April
"White sales" on linens and bedding Appliances Winter clothing Shoes Sports equipment	Furniture and home furnishings. Women's coats. Washington's Birthday sales.	Luggage	(After Easter clothing sales)

May	June	July	August
White sales	TV sets Fabrics	Appliances After 4th of July sales of summer clothing Sports equipment	White sales Home furnishings Tires Back-to-school supplies and clothing

September	October	November	December
Cars Housewares	Columbus Day coat sales Appliances	Coats and dresses	After-Christmas sales

Bait and Switch. A company or store will offer an item at an extremely low price as bait to lure you into the store. When you try to buy the advertised product, a salesperson will attempt to switch you to a higher-priced product. He or she may give you several reasons why you can't buy the advertised product—it is out of stock, or there is no guarantee with it, but there is with the higher-priced item, and so on.

Free Offer. You are offered a product free of charge, but you must buy something else in order to get the "free" item. For example, you may be offered a "free" food freezer. But you can have it only if you agree to buy the food to stock it from the same seller. The price of the food will be so high that it will actually cover the cost of the freezer as well. Another example might be a "free" sewing machine which requires a 10-year service contract that costs more than the machine.

Unordered Merchandise. Products are mailed to you that you did not order and then you are billed for them. The law is absolutely clear on this point. You do *not* have to pay for any merchandise you have not ordered. In fact, sellers are not allowed to send unordered merchandise, with two exceptions. First, a seller may send you a free sample to introduce you to a new product. Second, charitable organizations may send you some items. You do not have to pay for the items. But you may if you want to, consider it a gift to a charitable organization.

Figure 17-3. You do not have to pay for merchandise that is sent to you unordered.

Contest Winner. You are told you have won a contest. But in order to claim your prize you must buy some other product, usually one overpriced and of poor quality.

Deceptive Pricing. The price of an item is compared to a "former" or "regular" price, which is false. This is to make you think you are getting a bargain. Or you may be offered "two for the price of one," where the price of the single item has been raised.

Scare Selling. By telephone or at your door, a salesperson tells you that a dangerous condition exists in your home, for example, a roof needs repair or a furnace is defective. The salesperson advises you to take quick action and offers to repair it immediately. The truth is that the costly repairs are not needed.

HOW TO MAKE A COMPLAINT

If you have been the victim of any of these practices or if something you bought is defective, remember that you, as a consumer, have both the right and the responsibility to make a complaint. Your right is to protect yourself, and your responsibility is to help keep other consumers from being unfairly treated.

First, gather all the facts. These include the advertisements which you responded to, your receipt for the items you bought, and any labels, seals, or warranties that came with the item. Then, protest to the seller. If your purchase was made from a door-to-door salesperson you should have the name and address of the salesperson and the firm. If the purchase was made from a store, take your facts to the person who sold you the merchandise. If you are not helped, go to the store manager or customer service department. If you do not obtain satisfaction from the store, contact the manufacturer of the product, if appropriate, or a consumer protection organization like your local:

· Chamber of Commerce
· Better Business Bureau
· Legal Aid Society
· Consumer Affairs Department
· Cooperative Extension
· American Automobile Association or other trade associations
· District Attorney's office

You can also contact your newspaper and television station, your senator, representative, and state officials.

National offices which may be able to help with your consumer complaint include:

· National Bureau of Standards
  Washington, D.C. 20234
· Council of Better Business Bureaus
  1150 17th Street N.W.
  Washington, D.C. 20036
· Office of Consumer Affairs
  Executive Office Building
  Washington, D.C. 20506
· Food and Drug Administration
  5600 Fishers Lane
  Rockville, Md. 20852
· Major Appliance Consumer Action Panel (MACAP)
  20 North Wacker Drive
  Chicago, Ill. 60606

· Federal Trade Commission
6th Street and Pennsylvania Avenue N.W.
Washington, D.C. 20580

Field offices of the FTC are located in major cities. If you live in a big city, look under "Federal Trade Commission" in your telephone directory for address and telephone number.

CONSUMER DECISIONS

In Part One we saw that young people are leaving home earlier and marrying later. This trend means that many singles are making consumer decisions that once were family affairs. Young men are choosing their own clothing and furniture. Young women are buying cars on their own.

Every person has a stake in becoming an effective consumer. This section will suggest some ways to get started.

BUYING FOOD

Trade-offs are made in all consumer decisions. You may trade off money for time and energy and buy most of your meals away from home. But sooner or later you'll find yourself in a grocery store.

All the rules of sophisticated shopping apply to food buying. The skillful food shopper plans first, analyzes advertising, compares price and quality, and watches for fraud. You should:

· *Prepare a list before shopping.* Study the advertised specials and plan menus ahead for a week or two. Check your supplies and write on your list just what you'll need for your menus.
· *Shop alone.* The more people, the more impulse buying (buying things you had not planned on).
· *Compare prices.*
  a. Use *unit pricing,* where the cost per ounce, pound, liter, or other unit is shown.
  b. Try *store brands* rather than highly advertised products.
  c. Compare different *forms* of food: fresh, canned, frozen, dried, and already prepared convenience foods.
  d. For meats, compare *cost of serving* rather than *cost per pound.* (A market may offer both ground beef chuck and pork spareribs for 90c a pound. Because the spareribs contain bone and fat, a pound provides 1⅓ servings. In contrast, a pound of ground chuck provides 4 servings. What do the spareribs cost per serving? The chuck?)
  e. Save meat money by using *extenders* like rice and macaroni, and meat *substitutes* like eggs, cheese, poultry, fish, and beans.
· *Read labels.* By law, food labels must show the name of the product, the ingredients listed in order by weight, style of pack, and net weight, and the name and address of the manufacturer. New labeling practices helpful to the consumer are nutritional labeling, which shows amounts of nutrients in a product, and date labeling on perishables.

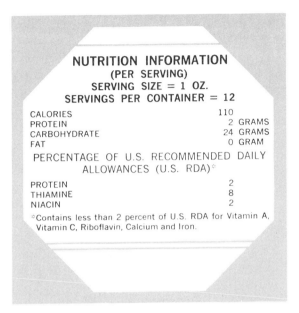

NUTRITION INFORMATION
(PER SERVING)
SERVING SIZE = 1 OZ.
SERVINGS PER CONTAINER = 12

CALORIES	110
PROTEIN	2 GRAMS
CARBOHYDRATE	24 GRAMS
FAT	0 GRAM

PERCENTAGE OF U.S. RECOMMENDED DAILY
ALLOWANCES (U.S. RDA)*

PROTEIN	2
THIAMINE	8
NIACIN	2

*Contains less than 2 percent of U.S. RDA for Vitamin A, Vitamin C, Riboflavin, Calcium and Iron.

Figure 17-4. Nutritional labels list amounts of nutrients in a product.

· *Stock up on staples* like flour and sugar during sales.
· *Watch the scale* when produce or other items are being weighed.
· *Watch the cashier* ring up your purchases.
· *Count your change*.

Don't be discouraged by small savings per item. So much money is spent every week for food that small savings add up to a surprisingly large amount over a year.

BUYING A USED CAR

Many young people buy used cars. Not only to they cost less than new cars, but insurance costs are much less also.

When buying a used car:

· Know the reputation of the dealer.
· Look the car over carefully. *Get advice* from an auto mechanic you trust. Ask for an estimate of repairs needed at once and those likely to be needed in the future.
· *Shop around* for the car, the car loan, and auto insurance to be sure you have the best buy on each of these.
· *Test drive* the car before you buy it. Drive it yourself or have someone you trust drive it. Try it out on hills and in traffic.
· *Don't be pressured* into buying before you have had time to think over the offer. High-pressure selling could mean the seller is trying to unload a car in poor condition.

Figure 17-5. Before you buy a used car, test drive it and have a trustworthy mechanic check it over very carefully.

· If, after purchase, you feel the dealer has broken your agreement, find out where consumer complaints can be made in your community. Do not delay, or it might be too late.
· Review the general rules for signing a contract given in Chapter 16. Do not depend on anything the dealer promises orally. Insist that all promises be written into the contract before you sign.

If you need to borrow money in order to buy your car, there are several places where you can obtain auto loans. Your credit union and banks make consumer loans. Finance companies and the auto dealers themselves are other sources. The annual percentage rate (APR) will be very different according to where you borrow the money. The lower the APR, the lower the payments.

Perhaps you already have a car. What does it cost you to drive to work? You will immediately think of the price of gasoline and oil. But there is more: maintenance and repair, parking, insurance, and depreciation. *Depreciation* is the difference between what you paid for your car and what you would get for it in a trade-in or sale. It will be less valuable because of use and age.

In 1977 the American Automobile Association reported that it cost 20.2

cents a mile to drive a new, intermediate-sized American car of eight cylinders 10,000 miles a year. About half of that cost was *fixed* and included depreciation (which is higher on new cars), insurance, and license fees. *Variable costs* include gasoline, oil, repairs, and maintenance.

Insurance costs are so high for young drivers that your cost per mile may be as high for a used car. Do you know how much it costs to drive to work? Have you tried a carpool?

RENTING AN APARTMENT

A common lifestyle is for several young people to share the expense of an apartment. Some kind of trade-off usually has to be made between housing costs and the time and money spent commuting to work. Housing in the area of your job may be very expensive, but commuting is expensive also. You may decide to pay higher rent and do without a car. Perhaps your job is in an industrial area and no desirable housing is nearby. You know you are going to commute. Where do you start looking for a place to live?

Using a compass pinpointed on the job location, draw a circle on a map. Make the circle diameter five miles, ten miles, or whatever distance you are willing to travel to and from work. If you must depend on public transportation, check out the bus or subway routes. What neighborhoods are served? Which neighborhoods are most desirable from the standpoint of personal safety, access to shopping, laundromat, recreation? What about traffic, ease of driving, and parking in the area?

Now, find out what is available. Ask your friends and relatives if they know of any apartments for rent. Next, try newspaper want ads. Studying these for a month or so can give you an idea of rents being charged in various locations.

Consider at least three apartments or rooms before making your decision, if possible. You may have to choose *between* a room and an apartment. Sometimes rooms with kitchen privileges are available, so you can do your own cooking. Otherwise, meals out can be costly.

Some rented rooms and apartments are furnished, others are not. The furnished ones cost more. Perhaps you can find enough furniture from secondhand sources to make your new home quite livable.

When choosing your apartment, some questions to ask are:

· Is the building well-maintained? Halls clean and lighted? Garbage collected? Steps repaired?

· Are there adequate locks on doors and windows? At least two ways out, in case of fire?

· How about heat, hot water, plumbing? Are the refrigerator and oven in working order?

· Are there screens and, where needed, storm windows? Is there ample ventilation?

· Are utilities (electricity and gas) included in the rent? What are typical costs for these if you have to pay?

· Is a security deposit required to cover any damage you might do? How much is it?

· Will you have to sign a lease?

Know what is in a lease before you sign it, and be sure you can (and want to) live up to the terms. A lease is designed to protect the landlord, but there are advantages for the renter. For one, as long as you meet the conditions, you are assured of a place to live for the period of the lease. Before signing a lease, ask yourself these questions:

· Does the lease spell out the exact rent each month and when it is due?

· Is there a "grace" period, usually 10 days, before the rent is overdue?

· To whom do you pay the rent?

· Can the landlord increase the rent before the lease runs out?

· Is there a security deposit and how will it be returned?

· What utilities are included in the rent?

· Who takes care of the garbage?

· Will painting be done and repairs made before you move in?

· Can you share the apartment with a roommate whose name is not on lease?

· Can you have a pet?

· Can you sublet (rent the apartment to someone else) if you want to move out before the lease is up?

· How long will the lease run?

· Do you have the right to renew the lease when it ends?

· Does the landlord have the right to enter your apartment?

· Can your landlord hold your furnishings and belongings until you pay any money you owe?

· Must you give notice that you intend to move when the lease expires? How much notice? Must the landlord give you notice? How much?

· What repairs will the landlord make?

The rights of tenants vary from state to state. Get out the phone book again and check to see if there is a local housing office or "authority." The services of this housing office are free. They can give you information about housing laws and also about rentals in your area. They have a special concern for helping low-income people find housing and are a place to turn to if you feel you are facing discrimination.

BUYING CLOTHING

Plan. Read advertisements. Compare quality. These shopping skills apply to clothing as well as to food, housing, or a car.

Machine Wash Warm
Tumble Dry Medium
No Chlorine Bleach
Iron at Low Setting
May Be Dry-Cleaned

Figure 17-6. Care labels, now required by law, tell you how to care for your clothing and help you avoid the expense of professional drycleaning and laundering.

Start wardrobe planning by taking inventory of the clothing you already have. The next step is to inventory your activities, and then match clothes with action. What clothing do you need to be well dressed for the activities in your life?

One way to stretch what you have and assure a coordinated look is to consider building your wardrobe around a basic color or two. In this way you can mix and match shirts, pants, skirts, sweaters, and jackets. You multiply your wardrobe without worrying about color clashes.

Another planning suggestion is to consider classic styles, which go more places, stay fashionable longer, and often cost less than high-fashion styles and fads.

Some classics are turtle-neck and V-neck sweaters, pleated skirts, loafers, and tailored slacks and shirts. Still another way to save money is to sew your own clothes or recycle what you have.

When you buy new clothing, try not to buy on impulse. Think through how well the clothing that catches your eye will fit into your wardrobe plan. Compare quality. Check for good fit and comfort.

Read the Label. *Care labels* are now required by law, so you can clearly see whether clothing (or fabric you buy to sew) can be machine washed and dried, or if it requires hand laundry or drycleaning. Drycleaning is expensive and somewhat inconvenient. With wash-and-wear clothing, you can easily care for your own wardrobe and not be dependent on others.

On-the-Job Clothes. On many home economics jobs you wear uniforms. Uniforms give you identity. They prove you are a member of the group whatever it may be—a football team, the police force, or a hotel staff. On most jobs, your uniforms will be furnished. But you may be expected to supply and care for your uniform.

When choosing uniforms, durability (strength) and comfort are of utmost importance. You may want to consider white cotton because this natural fiber feels cool and can be safely bleached to keep it snowy white. You may want nylon or polyester for their wrinkle-free and quick-drying qualities. Or you may choose blends which combine the best features of natural and synthetic fibers.

When selecting any clothing, check out fiber content, color fastness, the quality of construction, and special finishes such as whether the item is preshrunk. Be sure to read the care label and any hangtags before saying, "I'll take it."

CHAPTER SUMMARY

1. As a consumer you have four basic rights: to *choose,* to *be accurately informed,* to *rely on safety,* and to *redress* (compensation or exchange). Each right is matched by a responsibility: to choose as *well* as you can, to *learn* about products and services, to *examine* products for safety and follow instructions for use, and to make *complaints.*

2. *Plan* your buying priorities, *analyze* advertisements, and *compare* price and quality. Advertising can inform, but its purpose is to persuade consumers to buy.

3. Fraudulent selling practices include *referral selling, bait and switch* advertising, *"free" offers, unordered merchandise, contest winner, deceptive pricing,* and *scare selling.*

4. When buying food prepare a *list* before shopping, based on menus you have planned. *Read labels,* compare prices, and buy staples during sales. Watch the scale when food is weighed and the cash register when your purchases are rung up.

5. When buying a used car, know the *reputation* of the dealer, *get advice* from a mechanic you trust, and *test drive* the car. *Shop around* for the car, the car loan, and auto insurance, to be sure you have the *best buy* on each of these.

6. You can obtain car loans from *credit unions, banks, finance companies,* and *auto dealers.* The lower the *annual percentage rate* (APR), the less costly the loan.

7. *Depreciation* on your car is the difference between what you paid for your car and what you would get for it in a trade-in or sale. Depreciation is one cost of driving, along with maintenance and repair, parking, insurance, gasoline, and oil.

8. When renting an apartment, consider commuting distance, the neighborhood, and cost of furnishings. Inspect both the apartment and the lease.

9. Start *wardrobe planning* by matching up the clothes you have with your activities. Then decide what clothing is needed in order to be well dressed. Building a wardrobe around *basic colors,* buying *classics* instead of fads, and *sewing* new or *recycling* old clothes all stretch clothing dollars.

10. When buying new clothing, read the *labels* to find out the fiber content, color fastness, special finishes, and the method of care for the garment.

• FOLLOW-UP PROJECTS

1. Discuss how the following practices encourage impulse buying of food:
   a. Floor arrangement
   b. Shelf arrangement
   c. Grouping of items
   d. Special displays
   e. Emphasis on bargains
   f. Free samples

2. Select a total of one hour on television or radio.
   a. Count the number of advertisements.
   b. Total the time spent in advertising during the hour.
   c. List the products advertised.
   d. Note to whom the ad was directed (child, teen, elderly, etc.).
   e. Find out where you would buy each item.

3. Create your own ad for a new product such as Blue Cross/Blue Shield for Pets, Self-Destruct for carpet stains, a Robot Cleaning Service, or some other imaginary product or service.

4. Survey a small claims court judge, newspaper editors, Better Business Bureau, and consumer agencies in your community about the most common consumer complaints. Discuss how effective complaints can be made to secure redress in each case.

5. Divide class into two groups to role-play fraudulent advertising practices. Half should try to sell a product using one of the techniques. The other half of the class should demonstrate what to do for each kind of fraud.

6. Collect and analyze the following:
   a. Examples of informative and deceptive advertising
   b. Magazine articles and newspaper clippings on consumer concerns and new legislation and regulations.

7. Keep a log for a week of all purchases you made, including any you made for the family, such as buying groceries and using the laundromat. Analyze shopping skills. Did you plan ahead, read advertisements, compare products and services, watch for fraud? Should you make a consumer complaint based on the week's experiences? How would you do so?

8. Develop a list of addresses for sources of consumer information and assistance. Develop, also, phone numbers for a consumer hotline. Include local, state, and federal sources.

9. Select a clothing classic to add to your wardrobe.
   a. Analyze advertisements for this item.
   b. Check the price and quality in three different outlets.
   c. Inquire about the item in at least two or three outlets to see the types of sales techniques that are used.
   d. Describe your findings and tell the class your choice, giving your reasons.

10. Working in small groups,
    a. Investigate the best place to get an auto loan: credit union, bank, auto dealer, or finance company.
    b. If you already have a car, figure the cost of driving to school or work.
    c. Visit auto dealers and ask for sample copies of warranties for new and used cars.
    d. Check with the Bureau of Consumer Protection in your city or state to see how buyers of new and used cars are protected against fraud.
    e. If you do not have a driver's license, consult a driver training teacher or the state police about when and how to get this important document.

11. Find out what apartments or furnished rooms that beginning workers can afford are for rent in your area. Ask relatives and friends, read want ads, and consult real estate agents. Must you sign a lease? What are the terms? Is there a security deposit? What is the total monthly cost of rent and utilities?

12. Working in pairs, plan furnishings for an apartment two workers could share. Estimate costs. Consider what can be borrowed from home, purchased secondhand, and what must be bought new.

13. Plan a mini-wardrobe for your new job, choosing a basic color. Estimate costs. What items do you already have? Which can you sew or recycle?

18 | CHANGING ROLES AND VALUES

After studying Chapter 18 you will be better able to:

1. Explain why the family is important.
2. List factors to consider when choosing
   a. A mate.
   b. Child care.
3. Value responsible parenthood.
4. Give an example of positive child guidance.
5. Compare family roles in today's world.
6. Describe the status of women workers today.

The world is always changing. Every day, we see many examples of changes in families, in schools, in work, in standards, and in community values.

Nowhere is change more evident than in families. In general, families are smaller than they once were. More young singles and aged persons maintain their own homes, and couples have fewer children. There are more mothers working away from home including large numbers of women with young children. Families move from one community to another more frequently. They often live far away from their relatives.

People expect more from marriage and when they are not satisfied, they are more likely to end the marriage. One result is that more children live with parents who have been divorced.

These are some of the reasons that there are more variations in the kinds of family units today. In the future, there may be even more changes.

What kind of family you will have and what your home life will be like are perhaps the most important parts of your future. Why are families so important?

IMPORTANCE OF THE FAMILY

The family is important to its *members* because it protects and cares for them. The pregnant woman, the infant, and the growing child must all be protected and cared for. Other family members also need shelter and strength.

The family is important to *society* because it socializes its members, particularly its children. To *socialize* means to pass on knowledge and cultural

287

values from one generation to another, and to guide behavior so that the family members, particularly the children, can fit into the society they've been born into.

How does a family protect, care for, and socialize its members? Perhaps we can show this by describing a family which does these things well, that is, a "good family."

A GOOD FAMILY

First, a good family meets the basic physical needs of its members for food, clothing, and shelter. The family members have adequate and nutritious meals, which are properly prepared and agreeably served. Their clothes are clean, repaired, and safely stored. Their living spaces are clean, safe, and comfortable.

In a good family, members also receive the love and acceptance they need to become confident people who respect themselves and others. They can grow to make the most of their own capabilities.

Meeting these basic physical and emotional needs can be done in a variety of family structures in different patterns of living and at different income levels. Any family which meets these needs *is* a good family.

CHOOSING A MATE

Choosing a mate is a very personal matter, so no one else can give you much advice. However, looking at the experience of others can be helpful.

Age is an important factor in successful marriage. Between the teens and the middle twenties people change greatly. What you value at 15 may look very different to you when you are 17, or 19, or 22. During this period in your life you are finding out who and what you are. The first answers you give to the questions "Who am I?" and "What do I want?" will almost certainly not be the final answers or the best ones. Therefore, to make a commitment to marriage during the late teens or early twenties can carry great risks for both partners. Divorce statistics are absolutely clear on this point.

Income and education are also factors, closely related to each other. Marriage before either partner has finished enough education to earn an adequate income has a greater risk of failure.

Health is another important factor, especially because of the effects it can have on a couple's children. Religion and other cultural values also have a bearing on the success of a marriage. Where there are great differences between the partners, there is a larger possibility for future disagreement over many important issues.

In more personal areas, such as love and respect, it is even harder to find guidelines. One test of genuine love and mutual respect is to ask the following questions: Do you care more for the happiness and well-being of your partner than for your own? Are you sure your partner feels the same way about you? Have you let time and experience test the answers to these questions?

Personal Counseling. Another form of help available to you is personal counseling. Just as there are vocational counselors to help you with your job decisions and educational counselors to help you with your schooling decisions, there are personal counselors who can help you with choosing a mate.

Such counselors can be found among clergy members, teachers, social workers, and psychologists. These people all share a desire to help others with personal problems. They have also received professional training to give such help in the most effective ways.

Good counseling can also come from any person whose wisdom, maturity, and concern you trust. They may not be professionally trained, so they cannot substitute for a professional counselor. But if you feel they are wise and mature, if their own lives are good examples of what you would like to have or to be, then they can fill an important counseling role for you. They can listen to you and perhaps point out to you many things you might not be able to see for yourself.

Figure 18-1. It usually takes a while for people to relax and get to know each other's values, opinions, likes, and dislikes.

Marriage Contracts. Counselors have learned that couples considering marriage often have unrealistic expectations of each other. For example, a man may expect that his future wife will contribute to the family's income, but he does not expect to share the decisions regarding the management of their joint income with her. A woman may expect that her future husband will be willing to support her future educational plans. When these expectations are not met, then the marriage may be in serious trouble.

A way of avoiding such difficulties is for each couple to enter a "marriage contract" prior to marriage. They discuss what each expects of the other regarding the number and spacing of children, sharing of homemaking tasks and child rearing, career and education planning, and money management. They may even discuss conditions under which they may end the marriage contract and the marriage itself.

The chief value of the contract is that, in drawing it up, the couple must discuss their expectations of each other honestly and thoroughly. In these discussions they come to know each other better, to see where future problems may lie, and to consider ways of meeting the problems if and when they arise. Their marriage—if they decide to marry—has a far better chance of success because they know better what to expect of each other.

PARENTING: THE CARE AND GUIDANCE OF CHILDREN

No job in this world is more important than that of being a parent. Good parents are the single most important factor in any person's chances for health and happiness in life.

PLANNING PARENTHOOD

The job of parenting begins before the child is conceived. Obviously, both partners share responsibility for starting a new life in the first place. Therefore, the best gift parents can give their children is to plan for them, want them, and be able to care for them.

There are many agencies and organizations which can help young couples find information on planning their parenthood and on prenatal (before birth) care.

The American Home Economics Association, Planned Parenthood, The March of Dimes (a foundation devoted to the prevention of birth defects), and the American Medical Association are examples of organizations working for the emotional and physical health of parents and children. Your health department and public library are other sources of information. As usual, you can turn to doctors, nurses, teachers, counselors, and social workers for guidance.

Research done by the March of Dimes shows evidence that almost any kind of drugs—even aspirin, alcohol, and nicotine—can affect the devel-

Figure 18-2. The best gift parents can give their children is to plan for them, want them, and spend time with them. (Bruce A. Dart)

The nine months between conception and birth is the most important period in our development. Especially crucial is the first month and a half.... At any time, interference from outside—such as the mother's diet or her use of drugs—can affect the normal development of the fetus. Generally, the effect is greater earlier in pregnancy.[1]

oping infant. For example, "Stillbirths, early infant mortality, and low birthweight occur more frequently among the babies of women who smoke during pregnancy."[2]

Venereal disease and German measles (rubella) can cause birth defects, but these diseases can be prevented. New vaccines prevent rubella, and venereal disease can be treated.

Women should seek medical help as soon as they suspect they are pregnant, so they can be under the supervision of a doctor. The doctor will prescribe a diet and help make sure the environment of the fetus is the best possible for the mental and physical development of the child.

[1]*Birth Defects: The Tragedy and the Hope,* The National Foundation/March of Dimes, White Plains, N.Y., 1975, p. 6.
[2]Ibid., p. 9.

The father can help by encouraging the mother to get the medical care she needs to protect the unborn child. Remember, as we saw in Chapter 2, that good prenatal nutrition has been tied directly to the child's ability to learn. Only the mother can provide the nutrients, but the father can encourage her to do so.

MEETING THE NEEDS OF CHILDREN

Just as both parents accept responsibility for having the child and for proper prenatal care, they share in all aspects of meeting the child's needs. Needs include feeding and bathing, dressing, and giving love and supervision. Sharing responsibilities gives each parent confidence in the other's abilities, and also gives the child the love and care that he or she needs to grow up secure and confident.

Both parents are responsible for their child's education and health care. They must encourage their child to learn at school. At home, they provide good toys, the child's tools for learning. They take their child to parks, zoos, and museums. They talk and read to their child and visit the library together.

Figure 18-3. Children grow up feeling more secure when both their parents share in caring for them. (Kenneth Karp)

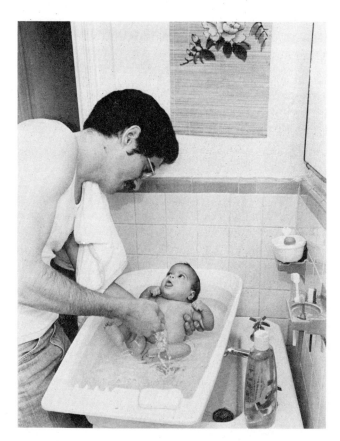

Regular trips must be made to health clinics and doctors. Children should receive the immunizations they need to protect them against disease. The usual immunization schedule is shown below:

When the Child Is:	Immunization
2, 4, and 6 months	1. DPT (diphtheria, pertussis, [whooping cough], tetanus) and polio
15 months	2. Measles, mumps, and rubella
18 months	3. DPT and polio
4-5 years	4. DPT and polio

When both parents are wage earners, a *surrogate* (substitute) caregiver must be found. The qualities of a good caregiver are listed below:[3]

Healthy
· Free from communicable disease
· Energetic
· Flexible
· Good-humored
· Patient
· Tolerant of individual differences
· Calm under pressure

Skillful
· Able to give simple first aid and to respond properly in an emergency
· Able to give positive child guidance
· Able to communicate with children and parents
· Able to manage routine duties in the home or center efficiently

Alert to
· Hazards
· Signs of illness
· Opportunities for learning

Cooperative and, willing to
· Follow directions of parents and/or supervisors
· Learn new techniques
· Support customs and language different from own
· Observe safety and sanitation rules

Well groomed
· Personally clean
· Appropriately dressed

[3]Adapted from Irene Rose and Mary E. White, *Child Care and Development Occupations,* Department of Health, Education, and Welfare, Washington 20402, 1974.

Caring and, able to

· Be warm and loving

· Encourage and praise children

· Listen to children and give them total attention

In Chapter 3 we learned about different kinds of child care. Perhaps you can care for your own child at the day care center where you work. You may become a day care parent and care for your child—and others—at home. Maybe there is day care for the children of employees where you work. Or you may decide to employ a relative to care for your child in your own home.

Your choice will depend on:

· Special needs of the child

· Quality of the care available

· Hours

· Cost

· Convenience

The child's early years are critical, because they are the best time to learn new things and how to get along with others. But while children are learning from new experiences, they need adult love and guidance.

Since a child's greatest development occurs in the first three years of life, some parents remain home with their children through these years. Where this is not possible, the surrogate caregiver can provide a loving and learning environment, and the child will thrive.

The amount of time you spend with your child is not as important as the *quality* of the time. Certainly the mother who is at home all day, but who is more concerned with cleaning or watching TV than reading to or talking with her child is not providing quality child care. A child allowed freedom to explore and learn in a day care center has a better chance for development that a child penned up in a crib all day at home.

If you work outside the home, get the best child care you can. Then, make the most of the time you do have with your child.

Good parents and surrogates know what to expect of children at different ages and how to give positive guidance. When they understand the patterns of child development, they can react properly to the child's behavior. They know when patience is called for and how to provide new experiences to help a child develop. They are alert when a child shows a significant departure from normal patterns, indicating that the child may have some problems which need professional attention. Table 18-1 shows typical behavior to expect at certain ages.

Simple rules of child guidance can be learned by all parents and surrogates. Professional child care specialists study child guidance in depth, especially in regard to working with groups of children. But parents can also become experts. Some basic rules of child guidance are given below. Study them carefully and think about ways to put them into practice with children

Figure 18-4. As a caregiver you should encourage children to dress and groom themselves. (Kenneth Karp)

Table 18-1 WHAT TO EXPECT AT DIFFERENT AGES

Age	Physical Development	Emotional/Social Skills
3 months	Turns from back to side Holds up head	Coos Laughs aloud
6 months	Sits with support	Smiles at familiar people and strangers
9 months	Sits alone Stands, holding furniture Picks up small objects from floor	Waves bye-bye Begins to tell those who are familiar from strangers
one year	Begins walking, holding on Holds cup Can finger-feed self Climbs and crawls to explore	Repeats performance laughed at Says two words Responds to positive and negative guidance
15 months	Walks alone	Says four words
18 months	Turns pages of a book Feeds self Ready for toilet training	Plays beside, rather than with, another child (called parallel play)
2 years	Can turn a doorknob or unscrew lid Strings beads Removes simple garments	Limits play to solitary play or parallel play Is negative, involved in "squabbles" Combines two or more words
3 years	Jumps Buttons and unbuttons large buttons Feeds self, rarely spills	Seeks friends and begins to play cooperatively Fears specific things, like dogs, dark, storms
4 years	Skips Dresses and undresses with little help	Shares more readily Makes up stories; cannot tell truth from fable
5 years	Brushes teeth Combs hair Draws a recognizable person	Participates in group play with children of same age Has short interest span Friendly
6 years	Cuts and pastes Swings Uses tools	Possessive of belongings Aggressive and stubborn

you already know—perhaps your own younger brothers and sisters, or children for whom you may care as part of a job.

· Focus on the *dos,* not the *don'ts*
Try to give positive guidance instead of always saying, "No."

Don't say this:	**Say this:**
Don't throw the ball.	Roll the ball on the floor.
No shouting.	Use quiet voices inside; you can
Don't squeeze the puppy.	shout outside.
	Hold the puppy gently.

· Build feelings of confidence.
Help children feel they are capable and worthwhile instead of belittling their efforts.

Don't say this:	**Say this:**
Can't you ever do anything right?	That's a hard job—next time
I told you it wouldn't work.	carry it this way and then it
	won't spill.
	Let's see why it didn't work.

· Give children choices.
Give children choices, where possible, but do not give a choice unless you are willing to accept the child's decision.

Don't say this:	**Say this:**
Do you want to eat lunch?	It's almost time for lunch.
(The child may say, "No.")	Do you want to wear your red
Do you want to put on your coat?	jacket or your blue coat?

· Show your affection
Affection for children gives them a sense of security based upon feelings of belonging to someone or some group.

Don't say this:	**Say this:**
You're a bad boy. I don't like	Sometimes little boys get tired;
you.	let's read a story and rest.

· Respect what the child can and cannot do.
Consider children's present stage of development and encourage them to try new undertakings and keep on trying. What others confidently expect of them they come to expect of themselves and they put forth their best efforts.

· Encourage independence and self-help in all activities.
Allow children to dress themselves, remove plates from the table, and so forth. However, do give them help when they really need it.

· Encourage self-expression in all forms.
Encourage the creativity in children by providing art supplies, building blocks, and new experiences. Praise their efforts.

· Redirect children's activity when needed.
Physical punishment is unnecessary when caregivers watch for signs of
fatigue and frustration and introduce new, acceptable activities.

· Remember that children have short attention spans.
Children cannot be expected to sit long or pay attention to any one thing
for a very long time. (Think of how short your own attention span is during
classes or lectures.)

FAMILY ROLES AND RELATIONSHIPS

A "role" means a part people play in their family. Your roles come partly
from your relationships to others in the family and you may have several
relationships within your own family. For example, if you are a young man,
you are a son to your parents and a brother to your parents' other children
(you may be older brother to some, younger brother to others). If other
people live in your home you have a relationship with them—for example,
you are a nephew to your father's brother or a grandson to your mother's
mother.

Your roles also come from the different jobs you do as a member of the
home. For example, you may be a housekeeper, cook, repairer, nurse,
student, message taker, and supervisor. You probably don't do all these
jobs all the time, but how many of them, or others like them, do you do at
least once in a while in your home?

Sometimes members of a family get confused about who is in what role
at any moment. They may not like the roles they find themselves in. This
is one of the things that makes family living a challenge. The fact that each
person can play several roles helps give the family strength. Each of its
members can have a wide variety of experiences and training.

WOMEN IN THE FAMILY

Today women play more roles in their families than they once did. Many
women are both wage earners and homemakers. Even women who are not
wage earners have much more to say in the decisions of the household than
they once did. They expect the man of the house to accept fully his responsibilities as a homemaker and a parent. Many women are the heads of
families; that is, they have no male partner with whom to share the homemaking, wage earning, and parenting responsibilities.

MEN IN THE FAMILY

Like women, many men today play more roles in their families than they
once did. They work for income to support the home and they share the
homemaking tasks. Some of them, too, are single heads of families. Some
are full-time homemakers while their partners are full-time wage earners.

MEN AND WOMEN IN THE FAMILY

In sum, both men and women today share and exchange roles within the family. This is a great change from the times when almost all married women were full-time homemakers, and men shared far fewer homemaking and parenting responsibilities.

For many men and women the change to the modern situation has been difficult. Important changes are always difficult. However, many young people today, who grow up expecting themselves and their partners to share roles, will have less trouble in working out the roles and relationships.

For many women, the chief difficulty is that society—and often their partners, and sometimes even they themselves—really expects women to be responsible for homemaking and parenting, even if they are also full-time wage earners. "A woman's place is in the home" is still a powerful notion, and even when a woman is out of the home for eight hours or more a day earning wages, many people still hold her chiefly responsible for keeping the home. This is unfair, and most women are aware of the injustice. Fortunately, many men are also aware of it, and many of them make determined and successful efforts to right the balance.

For many men, even those who sincerely want to play their roles fairly, the chief problem is with their own view of themselves. Washing dishes, changing diapers, cooking meals, sewing on buttons—they see these activities as "women's work." Whenever they do such tasks they feel they are less of a male. It may be a long while before the notion of what is women's work and what is men's work becomes a *person's* work, regardless of sex. As long as the old notions remain strong, the greatest challenge for both partners is to be as fair and considerate of each other's feelings as they possibly can.

If you are a woman, your challenge is to consider your partner's feelings about his homemaking and parenting responsibilities. If you are a man, your challenge is to consider how much can fairly be expected of the woman who is your partner. Both young men and women of today seem to show a greater sense of fairness and flexibility. Many women are quite willing not only to hold full-time jobs but also to mow the lawn, repair leaky faucets, and wash the car. Many men are finding more satisfaction than they thought possible in bathing children, ironing shirts, and vacuuming rugs.

CHILDREN IN THE FAMILY

The role of children in the "new family" is probably the most difficult of all. Sometimes the child is the caregiver, looking after him- or herself or younger children. Often the child is the household worker helping to maintain the home. Older children are students and wage earners as well as household workers and family members. Children may be given too much responsibility in the home.

In single-parent families the danger of overburdening children is especially grave. Where the father is the single parent, a daughter may try to do all the housework the mother would normally do. Where the mother is the single parent, the son may assume too much responsibility for wage earning too soon. The children do not have enough time, energy, or motivation to give to their school work, and they may even drop out before they've completed their education and training.

WOMEN AT WORK OUTSIDE THE HOME

Most women today either have worked, are working now, or expect to work in the future at some wage earning job outside their homes. Many young women of today hold some part-time job while they are still in school. Most will work full-time after they complete school whether they marry or not. Some may drop out of the labor force to have children and then return at some later time, perhaps in several weeks, perhaps in a few years.

In other words, today's woman is a working woman. What does she find in the work world?

PAY

Although federal law says that women should receive equal pay for equal work, the fact is that women overall earn less than men. Even when they are in the same occupations as men, they receive less pay. (See Table 18-2.)

TABLE 18-2 WOMEN'S PAY COMPARED TO MEN'S PAY

Major occupation group	Median wage or salary income		Women's median wage or salary income as percent of men's
	Women	Men	
Professional, technical workers	$9,095	$13,935	65.2
Managers, administrators	7,998	14,737	54.3
Salesworkers	4,674	12,031	38.8
Clerical workers	6,458	10,619	60.8
Craftworkers	6,315	11,308	55.8
Operators	5,420	9,481	57.2
Service workers	4,745	8,112	58.5
Laborers, nonfarm	5,286	8,037	65.8

Adapted from "The Earnings Gap," Women's Bureau, U.S. Department of Labor, March 1975.

Statistics show that more women than men are found in the lower-paid occupations. Several factors combine to create this situation. One is that men tend to have more advanced education than women, and higher-paying jobs go to the better-educated. Another is that when women become parents

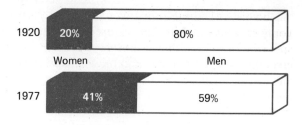

Figure 18-5. The percentage of women in the labor force changed dramatically between 1920 and 1977.

they tend to drop out of the labor market for some period of time. During those years they miss the experience which could lead to advancement. When they reenter the work force they are a number of years behind the men who did not drop out to become full-time parents. Or, when they return to work, it is often in part-time jobs which allow them more time for parenting.

There is a final reason that women are less well paid than men: discrimination. That is, many employers simply will not give their women workers the same opportunities as their men workers. They do not recognize the fact that most women work because of economic need.

Of the large proportion of women workers who are single, widowed, separated, or divorced, many are heads of families and work not only to support themselves but to support others also. Many other women workers are wives of men earning low incomes and their income is needed for basic living necessities like rent and food. In families where the husband's income is relatively high, many women work to help their families attain a higher standard of living, provide for their children's education, or support their parents. Some women work simply because they enjoy their jobs.

Whatever her pay, the working wife is making a big contribution to the family income. Working wives contributed one-fourth of the family income in the mid-seventies. When the wife was a full-time worker, her contribution was nearly two-fifths. About 12 percent of all wives who worked contributed half or more of the family income.

PROBLEMS OF REENTRY

Most men enter the work force as soon as they finish school and remain at work full-time until they retire. A common pattern for many women is to work until they become parents, drop out for a period of time, and then reenter the work force. Women have special problems in reentry.

For mothers of young children there is the problem of finding adequate care for their children. Older women face another set of problems. In the fifteen or more years that may have gone by since they were last employed, the work world may have changed a great deal. Her job skills may have grown rusty. She may need job training. Furthermore, having been her own supervisor and employer for many years, she must now adjust to meeting a fixed time schedule (her employer's, not her own), relating to other workers, and rearranging the accustomed patterns of her own household.

However, the mature woman has certain advantages not enjoyed by the younger woman. With her children grown, she has fewer homemaking responsibilities. Also, her years of experience as a full-time homemaker have given her a wisdom and perspective, a kind of stability that many employers value. She may be more reliable, more loyal, and more understanding of her employer's point of view.

A WOMAN'S FUTURE

In view of the fact that today's woman is a working woman and will be a working woman for much of her life, it is realistic for her to plan her working future. The Women's Bureau of the U.S. Department of Labor recommends that women plan and prepare for their careers just as men do. They, too, can make occupational decisions on the basis of job outlook, interests, and capabilities. They, too, can take advantage of all the counseling and job training available to them.

> In the past, too many women were forced to settle for second best in jobs. Others were willing to settle for the lesser jobs because they felt that their stay in the labor force would be temporary. However, the situation is changing as more and more women become aware of the probability of combining the roles of wife, mother, and homemaker with that of paid worker.[4]

EDUCATION, WORK, AND THE FAMILY

All young people should remember that their chief work, their most important job, is to complete their education. Education is the single most important factor in determining whether a family is poor. Another major factor is family stability. Many families slip into poverty when parents separate or divorce. Families can climb *above* the poverty level through marriage and the combining of incomes, changing occupations, or more education.

All family members, therefore, have a stake in the stability of the family for economic reasons. Quality of family life is something within the control of family members. If all members assume their responsibilities and help assure that the rights of each are protected, greater family stability will result.

What are the rights of each family member? Each member has a right to a healthful ecology: a safe and sanitary home; a sense of order and restfulness; space for family gatherings, for entertaining friends, for freedom and exercise, privacy and quiet; food that is nutritious and adequate; clothing that is clean and attractive and gives a sense of well-being. Children have a right to adequate care and freedom to grow; all family members have a

[4]USDOL. *Careers for Women in the 70's.* Employment Standards Administration. Women's Bureau, 1973.

Figure 18-6. The basis for having a happy,
secure satisfying life is to get training and a job
that interests you. (Kenneth Karp)

right to health care. Beyond the physical needs, all family members have a right to caring, acceptance, and love. All have a right to challenge and opportunity for achievement: through education, work outside the home, and creative homemaking. All have a right to the sense of security which a good home gives.

The responsibilities which young family members assume in order to protect the rights of all have been emphasized over and over. Complete as much education as you can, get job training and work experience, help with household work, learn to manage money and time and make the most of what you have, become skillful in human relationships and communication, and hold down a job. The job may be entry-level to begin with but it is a step on a career ladder which can lead to economic independence.

As you fulfill all these roles of family member, worker, consumer, student, manager, and friend, you are preparing for still another role: *voter*. Many references have been made to helpful laws and agencies, ecology and safe neighborhoods, job training and educational opportunities. These are all *community* concerns.

Individuals and families working as members of a community, keeping informed, and exercising their right to vote can preserve what is good in their quality of life, and work for change where it is needed.

1. The family is important to its *members* because it protects and cares for them. The family is important to society because it *socializes* its members, passing on from one generation to another knowledge, values, and guides to behavior. A *good family* meets the basic physical and emotional needs of its members.

2. According to the experiences of others, when choosing a mate, your age, income, education, health, and religious and cultural values are important. *Personal counseling* and thinking through a *marriage contract* can help with this decision.

3. There are many agencies and organizations which can *help* young couples find *information* on planning their parenthood and on prenatal (before birth) care. Doctors, nurses, counselors, and social workers can also give *guidance*. Normal development of the fetus (unborn child) can be affected by smoking, alcohol, poor diet, venereal disease, and rubella (German measles).

4. Both parents *share responsibility* for having the child, good prenatal care, and meeting the needs of children. This includes routine care, love, supervision, education, and health checkups.

5. When both parents are wage earners, a *surrogate* (substitute) *caregiver* must be found and quality child care provided. The amount of time you spend with your child is not as important as the *quality* of the time. Good parents and surrogates know *what to expect* of children at different ages, and how to give *positive* guidance.

6. Family *roles* come partly from your *relationships* to others in your family and also from the different *jobs* you do as a member of the home. Women, men, and children in the family today play *more* roles than they once did. Roles are shared and exchanged.

7. Today's woman is a *working woman*, and she will be a working woman for much of her life. It is realistic for her to *plan* her life as a worker outside the home. Today, she has special problems. Among them are overall lower *pay* than men and *reentering* the work force after a period when she has been a full-time parent.

8. The chief work of children and youth is to complete their education. *Education*, because of its relationship to employment, is the single most important factor in determining whether a family is poor. The next most important factor is *family stability*.

9. As you fulfill your roles as a student, worker, family member, and consumer you are preparing for another role, the *voter*. Individuals and families working as *members of a community*, keeping informed and exercising their right to vote, can preserve what is good in their *quality of life* and work for change where it is needed.

• FOLLOW-UP PROJECTS

1. Compile a collage expressing your personal idea of what a good home provides for family members. Using the collages as a base, develop a checklist answering: "What does a good home provide?" Who in your family can play a part in providing each item on the checklist?

2. Consider your own socialization as children. What manners, customs, values, skills, and knowledge did you acquire at home? At school? Through political and religious institutions?

3. Invite a panel of couples to class to discuss the relationship of age, education, health, income, religious and cultural differences, approval of family and friends, and common interests to successful marriage.

4. Compile a list of reliable marriage counselors, their addresses and phone numbers, and cost of services, if any.

5. Survey local clergy and agencies to determine serious social problems in local community: incidence of teenage pregnancy, drug abuse, vandalism, child abuse, and so on.

6. Invite at least one professional counselor to class for a question and answer period on common problems in personal relationships.

7. Investigate and report on local legal requirements related to marriage, separation, divorce, child custody, and adoption.

8. Working in pairs simulating a couple contemplating marriage, work out and discuss marriage contracts.

9. Invite a doctor or a public health nurse to class. Ask about prenatal care, prevention of rubella, immunization of children, treatment of venereal disease, and related questions of interest to the class.

10. Visit a day care center or conduct a nursery school in class to observe children and/or practice guidance techniques. Consider norms of expected behavior of children at various ages. Find out local licensing requirements for day care and kinds of child care available.

11. Discuss how ignorance of patterns of child development can lead to child abuse.

12. Suggest problems that might arise when family members do not carry out their roles as expected.

13. Develop a list of instructions that you as parents would give to a surrogate parent for their own children. Consider both care in the home and at a day care center.

14. Survey or invite to class a panel of working mothers. Ask them what their biggest problems have been and how they solved them. Also, ask what their greatest working opportunities have been.

15. Interview employers on their attitudes toward hiring women. *Or* analyze status of women in a local school or an industry.

16. Consider your personal aspirations. Discuss as a class or in individual conferences with teacher.

GLOSSARY

Administration The main department of a federal agency.

Aide A person who works as a helper to a professional.

Announcements Listings of job openings and descriptions of the education, experience, and testing required for each job and the location and pay.

Annual balance sheet A yearly financial picture.

Annual percentage rate Required method of stating interest charges so that consumers can tell what percentage of the amount borrowed will be the interest charge for one year.

Aptitude test A test designed to help a person discover their abilities and assets.

Assets Attitudes, skills, interests, training, and work experience which make a person employable and successful at work and at home.

Bait and switch A type of fraud where a company or store offers an item at an extremely low price and then attempts to switch the consumer to a higher-priced product.

Body-language The messages people send and receive through gestures, facial expressions, stances, and dress.

Body mechanics The use of the body to make work easier.

Bonus An extra sum of money given to a worker for a special reason.

Business references People who can testify to a person's performance and experience at work or to his or her qualifications.

Career ladder A path of advancement to higher positions.

Career lattice A branch going sideways between one career ladder and another.

Cash value The sum a person can borrow on his or her insurance.

Character references People who can testify to a person's honesty, reliability, and other character traits.

Civil service Employment by the federal, state, or local government.

Collateral Assets such as savings accounts, stocks and bonds, or a home.

Commercial banks Banks owned by stockholders and operated to earn a profit for them.

Commission A percentage of the price of an item sold, which is paid back to the salesperson.

Communication skills Listening and speaking, along with writing reports and reading directions.

Community resources Facilities and institutions such as schools, hospitals, day care and shopping centers, health clinics, consumer agencies, and so on.

Competency Knowledge, skill, or attitude which the student or worker can demonstrate at a specific level of performance.

Competitive positions Jobs like certain civil service positions for which workers compete on the basis of written tests.

Computation skills Skills involving mathematical processes such as taking measurements, keeping records, and estimating costs.

Compute To use arithmetic.

Connectors Teachers, employers, and counselors who can help a person move to various career ladders in an occupation.

Cooperative A place where members pool their savings so that they can easily secure loans and earn interest on their money.

Cosigner A person who signs someone else's promise to pay.

Cover letters Letters mailed with a resume. Either a letter of inquiry used to ask an employer about job vacancies, or a letter of application used when a vacancy has been advertised.

Coworkers Other workers who work with or near a person.

Credentials Certificates, diplomas, or similar documents proving a worker's qualifications for a certain job.

Credit An arrangement which allows a person to buy something now and pay for it in the future.

Credit bureau A clearing house of information on an individual's credit ratings.

Credit rating Information such as the duration of a person's employment with the same company, income, possessions, and the promptness of past bill payments.

Credits A measure of the amount of social security benefits a worker has earned.

Credit union A place where workers can save money and borrow at reasonable rates.

Custom production Produced by hand and designed for an individual customer.

Decision-making Choosing standards, making and carrying out plans, and analyzing and improving feedback.

Denseness In a family, the number of years between children.

Depreciation The difference between what was paid for an item and what one would get for it in a trade-in or sale.

Dictionary of Occupational Titles (D.O.T.) A book in which occupations are listed and coded according to special aptitudes needed for each job.

Direct deposit The deposit of a worker's paycheck by the employer into the worker's bank.

Disclosure statement A written statement given by a lender to a borrower and containing important information about the loan.

Down payment The initial cash payment toward the purchases of an item with the balance to be paid later.

Ecology A person's relationship with his or her environment.

Eligibles A list of persons who meet the requirements for job openings in civil service.

Empathy Putting oneself in another person's place.

Employment agencies Offices where workers look for jobs and where employers look for workers to fill jobs.

Employment counselor A person who give professional advice about finding employment and job related problems.

Endorse To write one's signature on the back of a check exactly as the check is written on the front.

Endowment insurance Life insurance which emphasizes savings.

Entry-level occupation A beginning job at the lower end of a career ladder.

Environment People's experiences and the surroundings in which they live.

Estate One's valuable possessions and assets.

Esthetic An appreciation for beauty and order.

Exemptions The people who are dependent on a worker's income for the purposes of calculating the amount of income withheld for taxes.

Exit interview An interview held between an employer and worker when the worker is about to leave a job.

Extended coverage Insurance against loss from windstorm, hail, explosion, and other hazards.

Family council A meeting of all the family members for consultation.

Fee Money paid by an employer to a private agency which finds workers for the employers.

Feedback The message "fed back" to a person indicating how well that person's own message is being received. In systems, checking the results received in order to see how a system is working.

Fixed costs Costs which are "set" and less flexible than others. In operating a car, costs such as depreciation, insurance, and license fees are fixed.

Fixed expenses Expenses paid regularly (such as each month) and the exact amounts of which are known in advance.

Flexible expenses Expenses whose amounts vary and change.

Follow-up letter A letter sent to an employer after a job interview thanking the employer and indicating continuing interest in the job.

Fringe benefits Benefits or services such as life insurance, paid vacations, or sick leave which are earned by employees in addition to regular wages or salaries.

Generalist A worker with skill or knowledge in all or many areas of an occupation.

Gross pay The pay a worker earns before any deductions are made.

Heredity Features passed from parent to child by the genes of the mother and father.

Home health aide A visiting homemaker. One of the newest occupations in household maintenance.

Human resources Time, energy, knowledge, skills, work habits, and attitudes toward work.

Incentive awards Cash prizes for suggestions that save the organization money.

Inputs Everything that goes into a management system.

Installment plan A type of credit whereby high cost items are paid for partly in cash and partly by a series of regular payments.

Interacting Giving messages and receiving immediate answers.
Invoice A bill.

Job banks Lists of jobs and workers for a large geographical area compiled through the use of computers.
Job cluster A group of jobs which are similar.
Job interview A face to face meeting between the person looking for the job and the employer or employer's representative.
Job orders Specifications which describe jobs and the required skills, wages, hours, and working conditions. They are submitted to employment agencies by employers who need workers.
Job specification A job description or summary of tasks which also includes information such as estimated training time and required skills.

Maintain To take care of something, to keep it in good condition.
Management Making use of resources to reach goals.
Markup An amount added to the basic cost of goods or services to determine the selling price.
Marriage contract An agreement developed prior to a marriage which outlines each partner's expectations of the other.
Material resources Supplies, tools, and equipment used at work and the work space itself. Also money.
Medicaid Government health insurance for low-income families.
Medicare Government health insurance for the elderly.
Merit System A system in the civil service by which people get jobs on the basis of their ability to do the work.
Metric Units The basic metric units are the gram, the meter, and the liter.
Money income Money which is earned and used to pay for such goods and services as food, clothing, or leisure activities.
Mutual savings banks Banks owned by depositors and specializing in mortgages and student loans.

Net pay (take-home pay) The final amount of a worker's pay after deductions have been made.
Notice of referral card A card given to a job applicant by an employment agency. It contains the employer's address, applicant's name and social security number, and other information related to a job interview.
Nutrition Eating the right kind of food in order to grow and keep healthy.

Occupational groups The nine major occupational groups are professional and technical workers, managers and administrators, clerical workers, farm workers, laborers, operators, service workers, craft workers, and salesworkers.
Occupational Outlook Handbook Publication prepared by the Bureau of Labor Statistics containing information on training and education requirements, advancement, earnings and working conditions in many occupations.
Occupational Safety and Health Administration (OSHA) A unit of the Department of Labor responsible for preventing illness.
On call A characteristic of some jobs which requires a person to be available for work 24 hours a day or on evenings and holidays.

Outputs Results that a system has produced.

Outreach workers Workers who contact people in neighborhoods to explain, discuss, and encourage the use of agency services.

Paraprofessionals Aides who work as members of a team with professionals like teachers or social workers.

Pension A sum of money paid regularly to a retired worker as a benefit.

People occupations Occupations in which workers help people and families.

Perpetual inventory A record showing the balance of supplies on hand at any one time.

Personal liability insurance Insurance to protect against injury to others who are on a person's property and against property damage caused by the person's own activities.

Personnel office A department within a major employer's company or business which specializes in hiring workers.

Physical inventory The actual count, taken periodically, of everything in the storeroom.

Pilot programs Certain family and community service jobs which are experimental and funded on a year-to-year basis.

Place in the family The position, by age, of a child within a family (first, second, third, or so on).

Placement service A department within a school which coordinates the working experience of the students.

Portfolio A collection of samples of a person's work.

Preference skills The abilities and job qualifications which are the most attractive and interesting to a worker.

Premiums Payments for insurance.

Pressure points Places on the body where large blood vessels can be pressed to help stop bleeding.

Preventive medicine The prevention of medical problems by such means as yearly physical examinations, immunizations, and regular dental care.

Productivity curve A person's pattern of efficiency and alertness during a day.

Purchase order A standard business form used to order supplies from the company which sells them.

Real income The combination of money income and home production.

Reconciling Making sure that a bank statement agrees with one's own records.

References Persons to whom employers can refer to find out more about you.

Referral selling Offering a consumer a refund or a credit on the purchase of a product if he or she buys it and gets others to do the same.

Regular charge account A type of credit that permits the purchase of an item when one needs it and payment when the bill is received.

Requisition A form used to request supplies from a storeroom.

Résumé A summary of a person's job qualifications presented clearly in one or two pages.

Revolving charge account A type of credit that permits buying up to a certain amount and requires monthly payments to the seller.

Salary schedule A schedule by which workers receive pay increases after certain periods of time.

Savings and loan associations Mutual associations owned by the members and specializing in mortgage loans.

Socialize To pass on knowledge and cultural values from one generation to another and to guide behavior so that family members can fit into society.

Social security benefits Payments to workers and their families who experience a loss of income due to retirement, disability, or death.

Specialist A worker with skill and knowledge in one or a few specific areas of an occupation.

Split shift The division or "splitting" of a worker's hours between one part of the day and another with time off in between.

Supervisor The person who oversees the performance of workers

Surrogate A substitute.

Systems approach A plan, often developed through computers, for the best use of resources to reach certain goals.

Take-home pay The amount a worker earns after deductions are made.

Task analysis Identifying the exact requirements of a job.

Term insurance Insurance offering protection for a certain period of time.

Tenure A job where a worker can work for a lifetime once he or she passes a trial period.

Test battery A group of tests.

Term appointment A civil service job which is temporary.

Time card A card which shows all the hours a worker has worked.

Total output of goods and services (the Gross National Product) The total value of every hour of work in a paid occupation.

Unemployment compensation A government insurance system which can provide income to workers during periods of unemployment.

Union protection The opportunity to join a union which, through collective bargaining, looks after worker interests.

Unit price The cost of each can, box, pound, or similar unit.

United States Department of Labor A department of the federal government created in 1913 which looks after the interests of workers.

Values Personal guides which people develop over time.

Variable costs Costs which can change or are flexible. In operating a car, costs such as gasoline, oil, and repairs are variable.

Wage and tax statement A record of wages paid to a worker, federal income tax withheld, and social security tax withheld.

Whole life policies (straight life) Insurance policies offering lifetime coverage.

Working papers Documents which young workers must have that verify age, physical fitness, type of work, and required hours.

Workmen's compensation An insurance for persons injured or killed at work.

INDEX